The Dead Microphones

Mark Oulton

Formatting by ebookpbook.com

Contents

Preface

This book is the sequel to my book, *The Lure of the Red Dragon*, published in 2019, which describes my induction as a British and American into a mainland Chinese life, into a Chinese family, and ultimately making China my home. That book could be thought of as a primer on coping as a foreigner in modern-day China. Within it was a love story, and that theme continues.

The Dead Microphones covers events from January 2019 to March 2021. Parts 1 and 2 were a logical extension of my first book, and by popular demand, in the two chapters called "Tips and Tricks", I have extended the advice I offered to those who want to visit China in *The Lure of the Red Dragon*. I have explored in more detail the differences between the different types of visitors, including the attitudes of some foreigners who have lived in China for several decades. In Part 2, there is a continuation of all the challenges, humour, and delights of living in this vast and fascinating country.

Just as in real life, the book then takes a sharp turn in Part 3 with the catastrophic events of December 2019 onwards and what it was like to live in China at a frightening time with the discovery of COVID-19 in Wuhan. There are also direct comparisons to China's initial fumbled and later creditable response compared to other countries and, in particular, the US. As many readers these days buy their books online and get a preview of the introduction and a couple of specimen chapters, I would like to make it clear that any diehard supporters of the 45th President of the United States and some of his allies will find this book uncomfortable reading. I describe how he let down ordinary.

Americans and damaged the image of the US abroad. Those with a more balanced view will find in *The Dead Microphones* both good and bad Democrats and Republicans.

Part 4 considers what a post-COVID-19 world might look like and its implications for China's future direction and interaction with the rest of the world. It has hope and warnings in equal quantities.

In Appendix 1, Language Updated, I have reproduced from *The Lure of the Red Dragon*, part of the previous section on the peculiarities and challenges of the Chinese language from an amateur perspective, and added some new thoughts. The writing is suitable for beginners, but more experienced speakers of Mandarin may well have memories, chuckle and wonder how they ever learned it.

In keeping with my previous book, I haven't weighed in much on the major geopolitical issues of the day, although they are mentioned. There are many other sources much more qualified than me to provide that type of analysis. I wanted something more concise and readable.

In Chapter 6, you will alight at the reason for the name *The Dead Microphones*. I will let you discover that for yourself.

In many cases, I have given both the Chinese script and the Pinyin equivalent and the meaning and use of these are shown in more detail in Appendix 1: "The Chinese Language and Getting a Name". Where I have done so it will look like this:

Crayfish (小龙虾 – xiao3long2xia1). – English, Modern Chinese and Pinyin in that order.

The Chinese Currency is called the RMB (人民币 – ren2min2bi4) which means "People's Currency" and it also often referred to as the Yuan with the international trading symbol CNY. The highest denomination note is 100 RMB (red in colour).

This book is written in UK English (rather than American English). That was a hard choice as my readership is split exactly 50/50.

This book is dedicated to Sallie Morgan (1938-2019), an important contributor to my first book, *The Lure of the Red Dragon* and to my wife Yan Yan, my inspiration and the love of my life. It is also dedicated to my friends Jill Zhu who helped me both with background information and also assisted me with the Chinese language, and Dave Lambert who helped me with compilation and has the eyes of an owl and a deep understanding of China. Finally, I would like to thank the many Chinese and foreigners living in China who helped me with the insights I needed.

Note: 1 pound sterling = 8.7 RMB and 1 USD$ = £1.4.

Introduction

I've lived in China for five years now, become competent in the main language, Mandarin, and it's become my home. I grow closer to my dear wife Yan Yan every day, though she still maintains her sometimes strict air with the cheeky smile and twinkling eye that usually goes with it. She speaks quite passable English now with a lovely accent and pronounces the word "colleague" perfectly, something that causes many Chinese learners difficulties.

Things have changed though. One weekend, I was sat on our balcony and had some music on. Yan Yan was in the kitchen next door, and I suddenly heard her mimicking extremely well the smoky voice of John Lee Hooker singing "One Whisky, One Bourbon, One Bill". This must be a first for a Chinese lady. She's moved a long way from reading and being enthralled by the 1982 Chinese geography school book, *Window on the World*, and has now travelled extensively outside China. I have also become better adapted. I've got used to eating a bowl of rice most days and now only crave potatoes and especially French fries once a month. I don't even know anymore who is leading the eastern division of the NFL, but I do get footage of my beloved Manchester United.

2019 was a life-changing experience for me as I became semi-retired at a relatively young age. I am no longer tied to phone and computer, sometimes working 14 hours a day because of the different time zones in a global management job. Yan Yan threw a fabulous retirement party for me, and some friends even flew in to take part. I received many gifts, but three are particularly memorable. The first was a Parker ink pen inscribed with the words "老马识途" (lao3ma3shi2tu2).

It's a clever triple play on words because "ma" is my Chinese surname, "lao ma" is my nickname and means old horse, and the complete phrase means "no need to teach you, you know your way home, old horse". The second gift was a set of chef's clothes and aprons, a nod to one of my hobbies. Now I have time to cook and even post some of my recipes online. My duck's legs in a wild mushroom and red wine sauce with potatoes gratin dauphinois has been the biggest hit so far, and duck is a cheap meat in China. When I go to the traditional vegetable and meat market, it's a treat and not a chore, and I grope and poke the vegetables like a native. The third and most memorable gift was the best of all: the time to be able to write.

Once adjusted, which took several difficult months, I began to enjoy the freedom to do some of the things I had always planned and never had time for. For a while, and currently temporarily lapsed, three times each week, I would get up at 5 am and cycle 15 km (9.3 miles) around our local and gorgeous lake. Sundays are the best because the racing cyclists are out timing themselves. The wheels on their bikes are so thin they look like they could cut paper and the bikes are surely lightweight, not like my Chinese Forever brand bike, which is made of seemingly mostly lead. These aficionados of the sport have beautiful racing shirts with team logos and snappy thigh-length shorts. Only my gloves and safety helmet looks the part. I am cycling at about 20km/hour (12 miles/hour) wearing a T-shirt flapping in the wind and an old pair of safari shorts and look shabby. As they come past me at I guess 35km/hour (20 miles/hour), they put out a hand with a thumbs up or shout encouragement, □□ (jia1you2), which means "give gas" to motivate the old man. We are all in it together.

Part 1: Tips and Tricks

Chapter 1: Spies in Hotels

Part 1 of this book is dedicated to three groups of people who come to China. I have called them "visitors", which include tourists and those on business trips, "short-termers", those coming to China to work on a short-term or renewable contract, and "stayers" who decided to try and make their life in China. Chapter 1 addresses some of the needs of the "visitors", and Chapter 2 relates to "short-termers" and "stayers". There is some overlap in areas such as medical treatment as this is relevant to all groups.

Modern-day visitors to China are sometimes startled by how accessible and safe the country is. They are sometimes surprised that they pretty much can wander around anywhere, even in the middle of the night if they so choose. So long as you avoid overt criticism on sensitive political issues, don't disparagingly use social media, or directly criticise the President and Communist Party, there is now little that can't be discussed. What you say in private is unlikely to cause any difficulties. Of course, it wasn't always like that. Improvements for foreigners come all the time. A good example is that there is no need to queue anymore to present a passport at the ticket office at the train station. Now it is possible to book online and a simple swipe of a passport will suffice.

In the early 1980s, at the dawn of my career working for the leading global grain merchant, an American company, I had the opportunity to talk to company delegates who had been to Beijing to try and sell soybeans and wheat. I was so jealous, but this wasn't the work of a trainee, although compensation came soon enough when I was sent as part of the company's first trade delegation to Lithuania and Communist USSR three years before the collapse in 1991. In China, our company delegates would be sat down in front of an interviewing committee and make their pitch. When it was over, the interviewers would file out, and from behind a curtain would be a second interviewing committee, who had secretly heard the first round. Then the process would be repeated just to make sure that the pitch was consistent. Just because China had "opened up" in 1978 under Deng Xiao Ping, this didn't mean old habits of suspicion and collective decisions had altered. Individual initiatives were frowned upon or could even be dangerous.

Whenever I visit Beijing, I like to stay in the Jianguo Hotel because of its history, surroundings, and convenience to the economic and political heart of the city. It's still a high-quality hotel, but nowadays the big international chains have classier places to stay. It still delights, and every evening for as long as anyone can remember, young musicians from the conservatoire come and play piano and violin while visitors drink cocktails overlooking the courtyard gardens and ponds. The Jianguo was opened in 1982 specifically to accommodate visiting foreigners and keep a close eye on them. One night, I talked to a senior politician who told me some of the hotel's early history. I am not sure it is true, but I find it believable. It's straight out of a Cold War spy thriller. There were two-way mirrors with hidden cine cameras to record indiscretions from "honey traps", although there is no Chinese equivalent of this saying. Phones and rooms were bugged, and there was always a minder for a step into the street. Even walking in the park, there were Chaoyang Da Ma (朝阳大妈) "Chinese Aunties", middle-aged volunteer spies, watching your every move. Chaoyang is the central part of Beijing hence the derivation. The Jianguo was also the first hotel to get a fax machine in China, and journalists and businessmen alike would cram the bar while waiting to communicate with their masters in the west.

There are two other hotels where you can feel the history. The first, The Diaoyutai State Guesthouse (钓鱼台国宾馆), Fucheng Road, Haidan District, is adjacent to one of the most photographed roads in Beijing, Diaoyutai Ginkgo Avenue. Although there are other places to view the autumn foliage, such as Fragrant Hills Park and the Tanzhe Temple, this avenue is tranquil and less crowded. When the ginkgo trees shed their leaves to produce a golden carpet, it is one of my favourite places to visit in Beijing. The guesthouse is set in beautiful gardens with an 800-year-old lake constructed for Jin Emperor Zhangzong (Diaoyoutai means fishing platform) and is the official guesthouse for visiting foreign dignitaries for both overnight stays and receptions. It sometimes has paid rooms available to the general public in the 16 villa complex and can be used as a venue for weddings and other banquets. Some villas always remain off-limits (Number 18 and number 12 – there are no villas numbered one or 13). Tourists may stumble across it or be taken there as a part of a tour in the autumn. It was the residence of Chairman Mao during the Cultural Revolution and has received over 1200 heads of state. Nixon stayed in number 18 villa in 1972, Thatcher in number 12 in 1982, and Kim Jong Un at number 18 in 2018. When Clinton stayed in 1998, he was warned by his team, "the walls have ears". Guests can expect elegantly plated delicacies from the ten executive chefs and 300 other chefs, such as braised whole abalone in oyster sauce, crisp fried quail roll with mango and tofu, and chrysanthemum in clear soup.

The second hotel definitely does not accept guests and is the one I would love to see inside and never will. It is the Jingxi Hotel (京西) at Number 1, Yanfangdian Road, also in Haidan District and built in 1964. This austere building with no hotel signs is under the control of the People's Liberation Army. There are a few clues to the purpose of the hotel. The security is extremely tight with both soldiers and wiry guards and others with dark suits and thin ties. They might not look like burly western security or bodyguards, but I have seen these guys at a couple of state visits and conferences where I was accidentally staying in the same hotel. They never smile, and I am sure they could karate chop you into little pieces before you had even opened your mouth. Even loitering outside this hotel, with or without intent, will probably get you moved on or worse. You are also likely to see a constant stream of black Audi A6's, the government's car of choice, with a white number plate and a red origin identifier and black numbers. These are important people coming and going, and the hotel's corridor's carpets are red. The Jingxi is the ultimate Chinese power brokers venue and serves distinguished guests at events like the National People's Congress. It was at the epicentre of the Cultural Revolution. On January 26, 1967, Marshal Ye Jianying announced, with the support of other senior commanders, that the army would not take part in the Cultural Revolution. He was pitted against Maoist radicals Lin Biao, Jiang Qing (Mao's fourth wife), and Zhang Chunqiao, the latter two of the later "Gang of Four". Apparently, Marshal Ye was so incensed his fist slammed the table so hard he broke several teacups. It didn't work out well for the Maoists. Lin Biao died in a mysterious 1971 plane crash, presumed fleeing for Russia. Jiang and Zhang were given the death sentence later commuted to life in 1981, with Jiang committing suicide in 1991.

So what can tourists and temporary visitors to a Chinese hotel expect today?

Back in the 1970s and 80s, there was little opportunity for tourism and virtually no chance of an extended stay. That has all changed.

I once met an American engineer who was making his 42nd trip to China. He was modest, highly skilled, and dedicated, and I hope well paid. Any company that employs such a loyal servant must have needed his skills rather than locate someone permanently in China. As he had enough Air Miles to fly to the moon and back, I hope when he retires or has more leisure time, he can use them to see the rest of the world.

The most common question I am asked for the visitors is about hotel accommodations, so I will try and address that. All the comments pre-date the COVID-19 pandemic, and it will be some considerable time before access to China becomes possible once again. Still, it might be time to do some research and planning.

Most visitors to China come as part of an assembled tour group with their compulsory visa arranged. Similarly, those coming for short business trips will have obtained a visa with letters of introduction from their company to obtain permission. It is theoretically possible to devise your own itinerary, arrange your visa with the Chinese consulate in your own country, as, say, a backpacker, and provide an intended itinerary in advance, but China does not accept an international driving licence. On arrival, you will be required to present your passport with a visa in most hotels and rental properties such as Airbnb, and the information is sent to the Department of Public Security. One newer possibility is to take advantage of a short 72-hour stopover in Beijing, Shanghai, Chengdu, Chongqing, or Guangzhou. A visa is issued on arrival, and you must be travelling to an onward third country destination. I have advised several people on this, and suitable sightseeing opportunities and they have all enjoyed it. It's a great way to break up an arduous journey from Europe and the US to South East Asia or the antipodean countries, and it's also a way to get a little look at China to assess it before considering a longer future sojourn. Some do it for bragging rights, for great duty-free shopping refundable at the airport, or to take in one or two of the most famous tourist attractions. Where hotel checkout times don't meet flight schedules, springing up have been short stay (by the hour) hotels and shower rooms at the airports, all clearly marked in English and often several other languages.

For the visitor coming for a typical two weeks, which really should be an absolute minimum for a tourist bearing in mind the often costly overseas travel element and the size of the country, it is worth checking out the reviews of the tour operator and the scheduled hotels. The former is more important than the latter. I have sat in the Jianguo Hotel bar listening to an initiation meeting for a group of tourists and felt compelled to interject; the advice was so bad. In general, though, the tour guides are helpful and knowledgeable and have good linguistic skills.

On my first visit to China, working for two weeks, books told me only to drink liquids using a straw, never to put ice in my drink, and only use bottled water to clean my teeth. I was given enough prophylactic medicine to be a walking pill box and several injections for a spectacularly wide range of diseases. None are actually required or needed, although there seems to be a consensus that a Hepatitis A injection is a worthwhile insurance policy. The books advised only to eat hotel food which is the opposite of the best advice as hotels don't care so much about their non-returning guests, and a crowded local restaurant with regulars is always your best place. One Chinese habit is worth observing, though, and one I use for every restaurant meal. Boiling hot tea is also a mild disinfectant and is always available. Chairman Mao even used it to clean his teeth instead of toothpaste. It is good practice to pour some into a bowl and wash the chopsticks, glasses, and bowls in it, and the waiter will be ready to take away the used liquid. Becoming increasingly common are pre-prepared sterilized and film-wrapped individual cutlery and bowl sets, although it is still worth washing these. In many more traditional Chinese hotels, if there is no cutlery on the table, such as at a buffet breakfast, it is because they are in a sterilizing cabinet in the corner. Water at any hotel level is safe to drink and will have been boiled and quite often filtered as well. Fruit is always washed in China both against bacteria but also potentially damaging pesticides. The exception is from fruit stalls in the market or from roadside vendors where you need to wash or at least peel your own. So relax: after a hard day's excursion, your evening G and T with ice cubes and lemon (with the skin on) are perfectly safe. Equally, although tap water is not potable, it is fine for rinsing your teeth and is not poisonous. Drinking several litres might give you an upset stomach though. For coffee or tea in a hotel room, cleaning the cup and using boiled water is safe enough. There is no substitute for common sense, so bread, fruit already cut, and candies left on open display in the street are probably best avoided, although I eat the bread.

China uses the same star rating as the west, from five stars for the best down to one star for something fairly Spartan. However, the star rating is not the same as in the west and will exceed, in some cases, surprise and disappoint. The five-star hotels are extravagant and often more sumptuous than in many western countries and, in many cases, a little less expensive. More often, visitors will be in a four-star or perhaps three stars in excursions to out-of-the-way places. English is widely spoken in the four and five-star establishments. Prices are for a room and not per occupant as in some other countries, although there may well be limits above a typical family-sized group. So what is to be expected?

All the likely hotels discussed will have complimentary bottles of water in the room, and some will offer extra, expensive premium bottles of with the price indicated. If you need more free water, just ask. One of the joys of travelling in China is being away from home without any need for an overstuffed toilet bag and related items. A typical four-star hotel will have disposable toothbrushes, toothpaste, soap, shampoo and often hair conditioner, body wash, tissues, a dual comb and hairbrush, razor and shaving foam, nail file, cotton wool buds, and slippers, all to hand. They will also have a compulsory full-face fire mask and breathing apparatus. Also likely will be an umbrella to borrow, a refrigerator (sometimes with drinks to purchase but not always), a safety deposit box, a phone, an iron and board (or one available), tea and kettle, snacks for purchase, central cooling and heating, hot and cold running water, and frequently the TV will have foreign channels. High-speed Wi-Fi is always available. Where necessary, rarely in city hotels, an electric mosquito-repelling device is also provided. There is always a work desk with an array of sockets meeting the requirements of most countries' electricity plugs, so no need to load up with more than one adaptor. In almost all cases, room service will be available. Religious books in the draw are rare, though I have seen an occasional bible or Buddhist enlightenment book. One word of warning: China is currently discussing the introduction of a ban on single-use plastics, and this could impact on the daily replacement of toiletries. The odd one out is coffee, only available in four-star and above and some three-star establishments, including at breakfast. Although becoming increasingly popular, coffee in China is the domain of Starbucks and its local rival Lukin Coffee and others. Carrying a few sachets of instant coffee in your suitcase is advisable for the needy.

At the five-star level, the enhancements are numerous. Typically there will be a CD player, video games, complimentary fruit or snacks, one zapper to control everything from the TV to the curtains, and exotic showers that squirt at you from all directions. A current fad is to have a glass partition between the bedroom and the shower cubicle so those who like watching their partner take a shower will be delighted, although a curtain for discretion is available. There should also be at least one swimming pool and a fully stocked gym, a massage service (in-room or the parlour), a convenience shop, tourist boutiques, and a wide range of restaurants and bars. Premium rooms may well also have a butler and expect complimentary drinks and canapés or wine tasting in a private VIP lounge.

The four and five-star establishments will also offer a concierge with baggage storage who should be able to arrange a taxi. There will also be tight security, especially in Beijing, and the lift will require a room key card to operate it. If you plan to bring a local back to your room, whether it be for a confidential business meeting or some rumpy-pumpy, they will have to sign in and present their ID card at reception. I would imagine the register is regularly checked for frequent visits from ladies of the night.

There are a few useful things to know that are less common or never found in western hotels. In the swimming pool, goggles and a rubberized cap are required for the sake of good hygiene. You can bring your own, or they are available for rent. Tips, including in restaurants, are rarely given, though a small remuneration for the porter if your baggage is taken to your room, is appreciated. In these higher-end establishments, smoking is an issue and is now banned in all Beijing hotels, although in other cities, it is possible to request a smoking room with non-smoking now considered the norm. If you lose your room key, which is frequent for careless foreigners and rare for the Chinese, you will have to pay a hefty fee for a new piece of plastic. A quick inspection of your room will be made, and a call made downstairs from housekeeping on check out. This is a useful check to make sure you haven't left anything behind, but if you have broken, damaged, or pilfered anything, you will have to pay for replacements. Beware in very high-end establishments because some of the rooms have genuine objet d'arts.

Numerous opportunities exist to save considerable sums of money in the high-end hotels, although a little bravery and pointing might be required for those with limited Mandarin. Around many of the larger hotels are clusters of similar practical services to those found inside the hotel. A massage or foot massage will cost you a tenth of the price, a bottle of wine a fifth, a bottle of whisky a thirtieth, a haircut a twentieth, and a bag of snacks a quarter of the hotel prices. I realize that many tourists will be on a package, including hotel food. The breakfast buffet is usually extensive and is delicious, catering to Chinese, Westerners and vegetarians, Japanese, Koreans, Indians, and others. If you are on half-board or a business person, go and escape for lunch or dinner, leave the hotel and discover authentic Chinese cuisine.

Three-star hotels are a little different. Most tourists won't encounter them, but a few on business in remote areas will. The furniture is likely to be heavy and clunky Chinese style, more worn, and the beds can sometimes be rock hard as preferred by the Chinese. Few staff will speak anything but Mandarin. The amenities will be much more basic but still fit for purpose, and a more basic toiletry kit is usually available. Baskets with items to purchase are common and usually filled with Chinese snacks and condoms. There is also likely to be an ashtray. Security is less tight, and one way to know this is that there are business-sized cards thrust under your door with a phone number and a picture of a scantily clad female. Hotel-associated restaurants for lunch and dinners tend to be franchised establishments adjoining the hotel, and breakfast in the hotel will be a Chinese affair. Although there are regional differences, typical fare would be bland rice porridge (congee) with pickled vegetables, hot chilli sauce, peanuts to provide some crunch, steamed buns, doughnut strips (油条 – you2tiao2), hardboiled egg, and a drink of soybean milk. Fish and meat are much less common. One issue with the lower-ranked hotels is smoking. It is possible to request a non-smoking room, but this often only means there is no ashtray, and a previous occupant can cause a lingering stale tobacco smell.

One and two-star hotels will be just functional with a bed and a shared bathroom, and you might get issued a bar of soap. There is un-likely to be complimentary bottled water. Some foreigners will encounter them as in this category are many youth hostels often sharing a room with several others and using bunk beds. A fair price should be around RMB 45-80 (£5-8) per night. These cheap hotels serve several other es-sential functions in China. They are often clustered around train and bus stations where aspiring workers from the countryside arriving with little money can get a bed for the night, and similarly for Chinese visitors who want to go to a city hospital or students visiting friends in a faraway city. You won't easily recognize another category unless you can read Chinese for "Forbidden Palace Hotel" or "Tunnel of Love Hotel", and these tend to be clustered around KTVs and bars. Because many Chinese families live together in multi-generational homes, young unmarried couples can't get a "try-out" easily at home and need a place to rent for a few hours. These love hotels don't have much of a social stigma anymore.

There are also much classier and expensive love hotels, all perfectly legal. The "Lots of Love Hotel" in Beijing will provide you with romantic circular beds, mirrors in all the right places, and foam-filled Jacuzzis. Another in Nanning, Guangxi, offers a red bed with straps, an adult chair, a gym ball, and a manual from a fully clothed employee showing how to use the equipment. If a TV is supplied, there are no pornographic films provided, so visitors will have to use their own fertile imaginations. This is China, after all.

Another frequently asked question is, "what if I get sick?" The simple answer is you go to the hospital, but there are actually two types of hospital in China: 25,000 private and 15,000 public, depending on definition, but over 80% of out-patients use the latter because they accept the country's public health insurance which covers 95% of the population, although some co-pays are required. I have met several Chinese who could easily afford a private hospital or clinic but choose not to, believing that the best doctors, especially in Tier 1 cities, are to be found in public institutions. It still remains the case that facilities may be basic and with inferior qualified staff in smaller towns and in the countryside, and with no private option available. This urban/rural imbalance is one of the challenges facing the government. Until recently, salaried government doctors could only earn the right to work in a private hospital with permission of the administration, who sometimes allowed their least experienced to participate. Nowadays, perhaps surprisingly for a socialist country, China is going full bore for private institutions, partly to alleviate pressure in the public sector and to provide specialist hospitals in fields such as ophthalmology and cosmetic surgery. Foreign investment in the private sector is actively encouraged. To supplement private hospitals, there are also a range of high-cost clinics and some VIP wards (高干病房 – gao1gan4 bing4fang2 – literally senior ward) in public hospitals. For dentistry, if you have a raging toothache in the middle of the night, you may not be able to find a private dentist, but all major hospitals retain a 24-hour dental department, often with scores of dentists on hand.

Most visitors will carry health insurance and will follow the private route and will probably avoid the sometimes rowdy public hospitals, but if the public route is taken or forced by emergency, there are a few things that are a little different in China. For a visitor, it is unlikely the public hospital will accept private medical insurance, payment may well be required upfront, and reimbursement from the insurer from accumulated receipts will be needed to discuss later. This is not as bad as it seems because foreigners are entitled to treatment at the same price as a local. An overnight stay is RMB 50 (£5.75) compared to RMB 4000 to 10,000 (£450 to £1150) in a private facility, and surgical costs should be around RMB 15,000 to 175,000 (£1725 to £20,000) compared to a western RMB 100,000 to 1 million (£11,500 to £115,000 or more). On arrival, for assessment, you go to the reception desk and are assigned a ticket which for a foreigner will typically be for a general practitioner, and then proceed to the pay station. After that, you will be sent to the waiting area and watch a large board for your name and number to come up (which will be in English) and the room number for the GP. I typically wait between a more normal ten minutes and one hour on a bad day. There isn't a queue on a Saturday night of stab and shooting wounds, drug overdoses, and other disorderly conduct, although there is frequently some shouts of frustration at the staff.

There is one notable and commendable exception to all this. If the services of a female gynaecologist are needed, women will be fast-tracked there, whether it is for period pains or something more sinister. It's a model that other countries should adopt. Increasingly, online appointments are possible. Don't expect privacy when with the GP who will be harassed by several noisy patients at one time. Most likely, you will need tests, so take the GP-issued papers for this to the pay station and then proceed with the tests at the relevant department. Do expect the tests to be on the latest gleaming and modern equipment, and do expect an orderly to escort you if you are old, infirm, or more likely have a broken arm or leg. On return to the GP, thrust the results on the GP's table along with everyone else doing the same and wait to catch his or her eye and expect a two-minute consultation. You will likely be picked soonest as the Chinese are often very polite (or nervous) of strangers although not amongst themselves. At this point, if needed, you will be directed to in-patient services or sent to the pay station and then onto the pharmacy for collection of any medicines, again waiting for your name to appear on a board.

One peculiarity of the Chinese medical system is the intravenous drip. Go to any public hospital, and you will find rooms with comfortable chairs and people of all ages on a drip. While this may be a suitable remedy for dehydration, it is baffling what all these people are doing there all day in various states of repose.

Whatever your chosen or forced route to medical attention, I think at least in major cities, it's really about whether you want to live (or hopefully not die) more comfortably and what is affordable. More challenging will be medical care in smaller (Tier 3) cities and in rural areas. Here, "qualified" doctors may have only spent two or three years at community college. In extreme cases in rural areas, if you are unfortunate enough to get sick, go and find the local schoolteacher who likely has a rudimentary training in emergency medicine and might even have a smattering of English. For more minor ailments, sunburn, coughs and colds, and minor

Buddha's revenge, China pharmacies are marked by a green cross. They are primarily geared to TCM, so a helpful word is for western medicine (西药 – xi1yao4).

A tour guide or company representative best handles more serious emergencies, but the procedures are currently changing for the independent traveller. The current system is similar to many countries: dial 110 for police, 119 for fire, 120 for an ambulance, 122 for traffic police, and an innovative 12110 text message number for the police to come and find you. If you text in English, it will, I am sure, be quickly translated. By the end of 2021, this system will be replaced by a single number to dial: 12345. This number will provide not only access to emergency services but to a range of social services and problem solvers in areas such as market regulation, public service, and ecological and environmental protection. There are prescribed limits and rules, and although hopefully not directly relevant to visitors, if you are lonely or suicidal, help will be on hand. If you are reporting that a neighbour is having an affair or that you are having a rent dispute with a landlord, you will be advised this is beyond the remit and spirit of the scheme. The former is excluded by personal privacy, and the latter should be covered by arbitration and court procedures. The best hotline operators, through voluntary feedback, will be rewarded and promoted.

Chapter 2: Here to Stay
(At Least For A While)

This chapter is dedicated to the other two groups previously described: "short-termers" and "stayers".

Typically those coming on short-term contracts will have their needs met by the company they work for, such as arranging sometimes tedious work, immigration and tax documentation, medical needs, suitable schools for any children, and even assisting in arranging accommodation. For some in business, it will be a pampered existence, and it's possible to see some of the executive types being picked up from their residential compound by a company chauffeur. There are limits though. The days of driving the visiting boss through grimy backstreets and taking him/her to an indescribably filthy restaurant and complaining about the food or relaying stories of death and destruction aren't going to work anymore. Nor are demands for all expenses paid home leave, and even free housing is now rare. The bosses can see with their own eyes what a pleasant life it is and travel to China more than is probably necessary. I have even met some bosses themselves who have offered to their most senior executives to take a short-term contract and tried complaining about the hardships involved. It won't work. If children are coming, though, it is worth asking for payment of school fees, with the most expensive schools charging RMB 260,000 (£30,000 per child per year). The demand for these schools is high both for foreign children and Chinese wishing their children to have a more western-style education. According to Relocate Magazine, the numbers of these schools will swell from 475,000 in 2017 to a projected 881,000 in 2022. Technically, the purely private overseas run (as opposed to Joint Venture schools) is the exclusive domain of foreign passport holders, but you will find Chinese children in them if their parents have acquired convenience passports from countries particularly in Africa and the Caribbean.

Another popular route for short-termers is teaching, and many of the private schools will offer accommodations as a supplement to salary. International students can find acceptable and inexpensive places to live, and the cost of living is agreeable. Although learning Mandarin remains popular for students, there are increasing numbers coming to study other subjects such as medicine, engineering, and even music. In one area, mining and mineral engineering, China has many of the best universities in the world and has invested heavily in this area. In such institutions, although not from the US and Europe, expect to find in particular students from Russia, Africa, and from other South-East Asia countries.

It used to be possible to come and work in China with skills and no formal certificates. Those days are gone. Having a skill in metalworking, printing, etc. and no degree won't work, and I have met several people who had to leave as their work permits were not renewed. Like many other countries, China has become a meritocracy based on its needs, and I understand that. It's unreasonable to expect foreigners with modest skills to take a position eminently suited to a Chinese person. Although the vetting process isn't transparent, a good degree, an international job, a desirable skill, and a good salary all seem to help. For language teachers, however much the need, these days, a TEFL or CITRA or equivalent will be required. It's not just English teachers anymore, and teaching skills in Arabic, Japanese, Korean and Spanish are sought after. Work permits are renewed annually at the Public Security Department. If you have a Ph.D. in a much-needed area such as biotechnology, quantum mechanics, biotechnology, and the like, expect the red carpet treatment from the Justice Ministry and National Immigration Administration which can include the much sought-after permanent residency after only one year or even less.

Others less well qualified will mostly manage with work or family permits, although a few will eventually get the elusive permanent residency permit.

Short-termers often fare well in China, especially in their personal lives, and much of the joy of discovering China can be found in this book. The friendly people, reasonable individual tax rates and cost of living, good holiday entitlement (not for the Chinese who are workaholics just as much as the Japanese) all spring to mind.

There are a few different procedures to learn and none more than concerning expenses, but these are only minor aggravations if you follow the strict procedures. This revolves around collecting receipts/invoices (发票 – fa1piao4, and although there are other words, this one is universally understood). You will not endear yourself if you collect and hand in infrequently a pile of credit card till receipts or worse, have an assistant sort through them. Every expense item such as a meal requires you to give your company's name (in my case 22 characters) and a Tax ID code. This is then typed into a grey machine, and it spits out the receipt that is then given a red stamp of approval (红印hong2yin4). This also applies to hotel accommodation receipts, easily forgotten at a hurried checkout. The easiest way to do this is to either have a business card to hand or have all the details in your notes section on your phone (as your card doesn't have the tax number) and give your phone to the server or get him/her to photograph it. Do this as soon as you have finished eating, as it can take up to 15 minutes. The good news is that some fapiao have a scratch card in the corner, and if you win, it could be a free meal or some little treat. An increasing trend in coffee shops and fashionable places is to just get a till receipt with a QR code on it, so you or someone else can scan it later to generate the receipt. Always keep your rail tickets as these also count as a receipt.

Where problems arise for short-termers and beyond often relate to doing business, and a great deal of guile and patience is needed. One of the dangers is to assume that with a captive market of 1.4 billion people, attaining even a tiny market share will lead to success. If only it were that simple. In business, the Chinese are ruthless negotiators and proud of it, and comments from the foreign party such as "they already took the shirt off my back, and now they want my blood" are not uncommon. It's all too easy to finish up with a negative margin in the hope things will improve, which they rarely do.

Supposing you have a product that is suitable for the Chinese market, or even sure of this if you have carried out the proper market research. Let's say it is a sophisticated machine part that requires a production facility in China. After a year or so, production is at full throttle, and the parent company in the west is more than satisfied with sales. One day, as the General Manager, you receive a friendly visit from the local government department responsible for encouraging R&D. They are behind on their quota of attracting new revenue for this area and in China government is a highly quota-driven one, including using five-year plans. You agree that you could help out and increase your R&D, something you had been thinking about any way to support improving sales. Shortly after, you start to get visits from other government officials. First, it's the tax authorities who explain that because of the increase in R&D (congratulations), this must be generating increased sales and, therefore, a need to check the taxes are accounted for. Next, it's a visit about increased emission controls from the factory, another area that is also highly quota driven. Next, it's health and safety. At the same time, you become aware that some customers' orders are mysteriously dropping and, upon detailed investigation, discover that your Key Accounts Manager is placing a few orders elsewhere with an alternative local supplier to supplement his income. As your product is patent protected, this is particularly aggravating because the local supplier is producing an inexpensive copy, a fake, if you like. And it's not just products that wander into this alternative pipeline. I had one case of a client who lost sales to a home-produced copy and at an alarming rate. It was becoming an emergency. The speed of decline was caused by one of the managers selling the customer lists to several local manufacturers.

The events described are all ones I have encountered. China does indeed have patent laws, and although it is impossible to know how many infringement cases are considered or dropped, those that make it to court have a 90% success rate and slightly more for foreign companies than Chinese ones. Sometimes the awards are substantial, though not the billions sued for in the US. In 2020, the Chinese company New Barlun was successfully sued for mimicking the signature slanting "N" in the logo of the famous sports brand New Balance. The award was RMB 10.8 million (£1.25 million) plus costs.

An alternative and increasingly popular route in China for more minor commercial disputes is to go to arbitration, and many of the panels are set up to look like a mock court. It's not without humour. In one reported and filmed case, a trader from Azerbaijan had bought several thousand pairs of gloves and went to arbitration with his Chinese supplier. The problem was that each perfect packet contained two left-handed gloves. The belligerent Chinese trader pointed out that the contract was to provide pairs of gloves with no specification for one right and one left in each packet. He only narrowly lost his case.

There are also new business practices to learn, and the foreigner's account and expenses paid team will run out of patience if you don't remember them.

The important point is to know which battles in business are winnable, worth fighting, and which worth considering a workaround. Take this hypothetical example.

Your company has developed a new fungicide for two debilitating coffee diseases (Berry Disease and Leaf Rust). It introduces it as a patented product into the major producing province of Yunnan. It brings substantial financial benefits to impoverished coffee farmers and to your company. Later, a cheaper Chinese-made generic product appears, breaching the patent, and your sales plummet. It should be a clear legal case. However, the Chinese government has made eliminating poverty a major national priority and is justifiably proud of its success, and the coffee farmers have become a little better off. Good luck in winning that case!

Sometimes foreign companies also have self-inflicted wounds. A few years ago, I purchased in the open market a range of agricultural machinery spare parts for a leading foreign manufacturer and shipped them back to the company's home country. It turned out that 70% of the products after testing and destruction testing were fakes, even down to the boxes with the correct colours and logos. It caused great indignation. The Chinese farmers were likely aware that they were buying fakes at a considerable discount to the genuine article and that the life expectancy of the part was going to be reduced. They actually would have preferred the genuine article, but it turned out the supply chain was so slow in delivering the authentic products, they felt they had little choice.

Even in the case of the errant Key Accounts Manager, common sense is better than outright indignation and immediate termination of employment. There is a difference between pocketing small sums on the side and major fraud. Chinese companies are a revolving door for experienced personnel, and it's a constant battle to keep employees. Even for the vast majority of hard-working, honest, and dedicated workers, improved job offers come frequently, and wage inflation has become a scourge in the last ten years or so. Contractual non-compete clauses and penalties in contracts do exist in Chinese law, but the system is complex and sometimes includes lengthy post-employment payments.

Many of the difficulties I have described are avoidable by constantly improving products and services to keep a competitive edge, hiring competent, loyal staff, and especially in key areas such as sales and HR, due diligence, and the law. The alternative pipelines, shadow banking, quota system, and other peculiarities aren't going to disappear. The good news is that there are plenty of companies that have navigated through this and tapped into that elusive 1.4 billion people market and made a lot of money in the process.

Stayers are those who came to China and liked it sufficiently that they either have remained in China for a protracted period or plan never to leave. I have only recently fallen into this category, but only just because I know several people who have been in the country for more than twenty years. I can only provide a broad catalogue of characteristics because there are so many stories to tell.

Several times a week, I meet with one of my best friends at our local "pub". He's Spanish, has a wife from Sichuan, and they have a six-year-old child. Their child is already tri-lingual and even making progress in the local Wu language, Sichuanese, Korean, and Japanese. He is handsome, a charming scallywag, and will be a lady magnet when he gets older. My friend has already achieved the twenty-year residency mark. The pub is actually a Sichuan restaurant, and sometimes both families get together for an evening meal as the food is delicious. We are definitely locals and have our favourite Table 7, help ourselves to the recent addition of cold Carlsberg on draft and the owner of this family business has got used to our strange habits of liking a snack with our drinks. We sometimes get free little dishes of salty garlic and cucumber or fried peas. In our own little way, we have shared the success and watched this hardworking family move from modest premises to a much larger one where for most of the year, tables spill outside onto the pavement as the inside is bursting and even then at peak time's people have to wait. A second sitting takes place in the early hours of the morning before closing at 6 am. The setting is noisy with barking sounds of "fuwuyuan" (waiter) or "laobanniang" (polite for the bosses wife but still shouted), no English spoken here, and the place is a little shabby and radically different from the nearby bierkeller frequented by short-termers where they pay three times the price for an inferior beer. Ours cost RMB 15 (£1.70) per half litre, although local and quaffable brands are much cheaper. We are no longer much interested in short-termers, but as an unsaid code would help any out in need. There have just been too many invitations to our homes, never returned, and too many transient friendships broken as they leave.

Sometimes, stayer families get together on weekends or for special occasions, which can be lengthy and enjoyable affairs. My favourite venues are a British man and his Chinese wife who own a substantial villa with a garden complete with, as best I know, has the only personal home-built pizza oven in Suzhou. Inside they have a baby grand piano and frequently invite friends to a musical evening which includes everything from classical music from members of the local (and accomplished) symphony orchestra to good 'ole American country classics. Another favourite is another Spaniard, with friends from many countries, who is an expert at producing barbequed food and side dishes and even sets up football posts in his garden for the kids and the wannabee kids to play. One common occurrence at this event and many similar is that the women and the men huddle in their own groups. The mostly Chinese women prefer their own company to gossip about their foreign men, and the men like to discuss incomprehensible and boring topics for the spouses. I used to find this a little embarrassing and would make a polite point of talking to the women until I realized my company was not really wanted. I don't have a garden yet; that rare luxury is coming on a new home under construction, so I have to rely on my home cooking skills to present elaborate food. If I have to cook confit of duck and clafoutis one more time, I'm going to weep, but it always returns to my menu by popular demand appeasing both foreign and Chinese taste buds.

Stayers are mostly confident. They often buy homes and almost always speak good Mandarin, sometimes even with a regional accent. They drive, Chinese style, with zeal, and the men can often even drink copious quantities of baiju without falling over, and both sexes can summon up a Didi taxi or takeaway with aplomb, in Mandarin of course. They are masters of the "sticks" and might even know how to play Mah Jong or even make money gambling at it. They often retain connections to the home country through family and property and visit, but many attributes of their former lives become hazy, although their Chinese wives will frequently acquire some level of naturalization to the home country, such as a green card in the US. Foreign citizenship for a Chinese spouse is extremely rare unless planning to leave eventually, as China does not accept dual nationality. Stayers know how to circumvent bureaucracy, know their rights, and rely on the Chinese government to look after them, which it does with generosity.

There are rules for stayers, and I hit some of these on my retirement date.

I can't stress enough to those who want to become a stayer how important it is to follow the rules. A week before I was about to retire, compulsory at age 60 in my jurisdiction, I went to the public security office to switch my work permit to a married visa as I hadn't been married quite long enough to get permanent residency (sometimes possible after five years of marriage but not a right). The procedure was simple enough, although the proof needed to prove financial capability and no need for state resources created half a rain forest of paper. After the paperwork inspection, Yan Yan and I were invited to a brief interview. This was carried out by the second most senior policeman I have ever met in China, only outranked by one I had met at a function who was the

Chief of Police for a large city. This officer asked me a few questions in Chinese, and we all laughed as he told me I must not, under any circumstances, work anymore. My job was to go home, wash the dishes, clean the house, etc. Then in a more sombre tone and half a smile, he told me if I disobeyed this, he would put me in jail and then deport me☐ I said in English, "you have got to be joking", and he replied in English, "I am not joking". Switching back to Chinese, I said one of my future ambitions was to help Chinese children in a poorer area learn English for no pay, to thank China for the way I had been treated. He explained, even this, and very sad to me, is forbidden. Then aside, he said something shocking. "You saw that young (Chinese) lady just before your turn. We already have her foreign husband in custody, and we will deport him as he was working illegally without documentation. They have a child together as well. I'll see you in six months. Go home and enjoy your retirement. Please follow the rules!" These rules are not much different from many other countries where without demonstrating financial support or working illegally is jeopardous, and it was a stark reminder.

To me, there are two defining characteristics of a true stayer. The first is when you hear "we don't do that here": "we", meaning China. The second is if you know where you are going to be interred. None of this Livingstonian heart in Africa and body returned to the home country, although I have to admit, 1 Saville Row for interment and the home of the Royal Geographical Society, is a top spot as befitted Livingstone. But at least I know family won't stuff me in an old people's home as an inconvenience to be managed or forgotten. When I finally pass, my ashes will be placed in a box and placed under a memorial stone in the graveyard of my adopted family. It's a windy flat place by a river, bitterly cold in winter, but all around in autumn are fields of golden wheat and rice at harvest. And I hope at Table 7 in the pub, they will somehow remember the crazy British writer who wrote about and loved China and their signature spicy Sichuan chicken dish.

Part 2: Pre-COVID-19

Chapter 3: The Year of the Rat

When my wife, Yan Yan, recalls childhood memories of Chinese New Year in the mid-1970s, it's a happy picture. Often unavailable meat and fish could be temporarily purchased with government vouchers for the celebration. Even given the austerity and egalitarianism of the time, she was from a relatively prosperous family. She was given two yuan (£0.20) as a present when most children in hometown only got a few mao (one yuan equals ten mao, a mao means a feather). Most of the year, children weren't allowed to go out and play in the evenings, but in the build-up period to New Year, Mama would kick her out of the house to concentrate on the preparation work. The children would hold hands and play games on the ancient bridges around town. It was also a time to get new clothes and a winter coat made of something colourful as a contrast to the conventional drab attire. Many were handmade, and these were the most prized. The children, however, were invited indoors to make the pastries in advance of the day (小圆子 – xiao3yuan2zi), but Yan Yan never mastered the art of rolling hers into a perfect symbolic round ball, and it looked more like a rugby ball, called "olive" ball in China (橄榄球 – gan3lan3qiu2). Happy times.

It's 2019, The Year of the Pig, and it's time to go back to my adopted hometown, Shengze (盛泽), which means something like "the place where water collects". Locally I am known as "the rain man",, and on more than three-quarters of the numerous times I have been there, it has been raining or starts as I arrive. There will never be a drought in Shengze while I am alive, but the Gods have not contrived to give me the gift of making it stop at will. It's a local joke now.

I tease Yan Yan that Shengze could win an award for the scruffiest town in China, but it has a permanent and indelible place in my heart, and now I see this scruffiness (邋遢 – la1ta4 and onomatopoeic in Chinese) as characterful. When we were dating, I would sneak away early from the office on a Friday afternoon and take the beaten-up public bus from Suzhou to Shengze, a journey of about one hour costing RMB14 (£1.35). The first few times, the regulars were wide-eyed in astonishment and just stared at me, and I may have been the first-ever foreigner to have made this journey. Eventually, they pushed forward an older man as my inquisitor as he was judged to have the best Mandarin skills, as at that time, I didn't know a single word of the local vernacular. Once they got used to the fact I was going to make this journey every weekend and my Chinese girlfriend, a Shengze lass no less, was going to pick me up in her car, a car no less, we became friends, and they would share their peanuts and sunflower seeds although I couldn't quite bring myself to spit the residues on the floor of the bus as is common in this situation. I'd check-in at a local hotel, always the same, getting a knowing nod and smile, and we would go out for dinner. On Saturday morning, I'd stay in the hotel and practice my Chinese writing, which at that time was about the standard of a four-year-old, before walking down the street to pick up Yan Yan at her offices at lunchtime. When he found out about our relationship, her enterprising boss asked if I could go to the thriving accountancy practice for a photographic session so that I could be featured in a new brochure as a foreigner would surely add credibility to the firm. I refused. The rest of the weekend was then ours.

Preparation for New Year takes place well in advance and definitely before the greedy-eyed vendors put up their meat and vegetable prices by 40% for latecomers. When I explained to Yan Yan that we call it "taking your eyes out", she told me the Chinese equivalent is to "rip your glasses off". Extra care when shopping is required at this time of year, partly to choose the freshest and best produce but also the pickpockets are out in force as they know that people's wallets are bulging from the holiday bonus. I did have one friend who, at this time of year, put her hand into her coat pocket to take out her purse, only to find another hand there at the same time.

As we hit town, true to form, it started to rain. Typically, we would have a meal at brother-in-law's home as he is an excellent cook, but this year it was chosen to have the celebration meal in a restaurant. The streets were deserted; even the dogs that played in the street had all gone home searching for a tasty pork knuckle. All the shops were shuttered except for the fruit shops, as fruit is frequently given as a last-minute gift. These open shops were so full of stock that boxes of strawberries and cherries were piled up outside on the pavement. Later, after dinner, some out-of-towners set up street stalls with little games just like an old-fashioned fairground. I am sure they had good takings from all the children desperate to spend their money from their red packets. But they had to stay open most of the night in the cold, and it's a hard way to make a living.

In the next-door private room, a party was underway, and wine and laughter were flowing. It wasn't long before that party group had entered our room to share shots of the strong stuff, and they proudly said: "cheers" in deference to me rather than the Chinese "dry glass" (干杯 – gan1bei1). It was a process to be repeated many times that night.

As is customary, during the meal, red packets (红包 – hong2bao1) with "anchor money for the year" (压岁钱 – ya1sui4qian2) inside were exchanged but that are never opened during dinner. It's essential to know the going rate for each red packet depending on how close the relative is, family circumstances, and geographical location. Nobody ever gives me one, perhaps because they think foreigners prefer real gifts rather than just cash, and in my case, it's true. For me, there was a carton of Chung Wa cigarettes, an exclusive brand, and one yellow box of even more exclusive Nanjing. The latter I knew cost over RMB100/£11.50 per pack: ten times my usual brand. There were also gifts of two bottles of high-quality baijiu and a half case of tasty Chateau Fasiman red wine from Yantai, Shandong Province. It was a generous collection of items of vice, and fortunately for me, the Chinese don't have New Year resolutions such as to abstain from alcohol or tobacco as I would have stood no chance.

The food was all auspicious, and each dish has a meaning. Fish with the head on and the cheeks being given first to the most senior person, beans sprouts, braised duck in a gloopy sauce, whole chicken soup, stir-fried steak and onions, hair cake (发糕 – fa1gao1), smoked salmon (for the foreigner), lake crab, bamboo root and wood ear mushrooms, eel, winter greens and soft-shelled turtle (not the endangered one) and one of my favourites, braised pork hock (体胖– ti3pan2). The name sounds like everything is up: stock market, a promotion, etc.

Eventually, and fuzzy-headed, and after one last toast, we all spilled onto the street together. Now I know why Chinese people shout even louder than usual at New Year. They are both badly drunk, and the insane strings of firecrackers have perforated their eardrums. All thoughts of safety had gone away at this point, and I watched people place firecrackers in the street right next to cars with no doubt full fuel tanks ready for the festivities and sparks flying underneath. Suicidal. Although fireworks are banned in many of the larger cities (because of air pollution), in hometown, there are no such restrictions.

Arriving back at our home, it was time for the traditional New Year Television Gala (春晚 – chun1wan3). For a foreigner, it's a mixture of the fascinating, dire, and incomprehensible. There are no concessions to pop stars and boy bands here. I think you need to be Chinese, a patriot,

28

and preferably a communist to get it. There were a couple of highlights, such as a famous magician (Liu Qian) from Taiwan who managed to produce red wine, white wine, beer, red tea, and dou jiang (a tofu drink) out of a teapot that had been thoroughly examined as empty with a torch by an audience member. Also, a troupe of acrobatic tumblers dazzled.

Six channels (five CCTV and BTV that I could find) air the show. It's undisputedly the most-watched TV show on earth with probably more than 700 million viewers, although it's hard to get to the numbers with some exotic claims of over 95% of households watching it. It's difficult to get national audience number ratings, and the 2016 ratings were not published at all. In line with the Chinese zodiac animal for that year, perhaps someone monkeyed around with the figures? Well, yes, the TV is on in the background with deaf grandpa in the corner keeping an eye on it, children playing games on their phones, younger adults shaking their phones to see if they have won the Alipay "Fu" good luck game, and that is indeed a household. Still, I suspect the younger viewers are unlikely to be very interested. The sometimes-elderly operatic stars of yore present songs praising the Communist Party and other patriotic songs with Chinese warplanes, tanks, space rockets, etc., scrolled on a massive screen behind, and the top brass in the military are on prominent display in the audience. Although it wasn't like this in its earlier years, the event is overtly political, and performers from the ethnic groups and Taiwan, Hong Kong, and Macau are all often seen. The program does have a smattering of foreigners speaking excellent Mandarin. The message is clear, "we are one China". It is beamed to some of the Diaspora (Malaysia, Indonesia, and Singapore). Other TV stations that offer mass audience programs and especially Hunan TV (nickname Mango TV because of the logo), famous for its "Singer" program, 11/11 Online Shopping Gala, and Happy Camp Variety Show", wisely schedule their New Year events on other days nearby.

In the morning, a bowl of pre-prepared soup was served for break-fast with round rice balls (equals harmony – family together). It is pre-prepared because no kitchen knife can be used on this day, and this is the one day you can't get a takeaway delivery at any price. There are other complicated rules such as no bathing allowed as this is water nymph day and you will wash away all your wealth, no house cleaning (I like that one), and no gruel to be served as this is a poor person's dish. As no afternoon nap is allowed as this will make you lazy for a year, I decided to settle down to read my Chinese astrological calendar of the future.

As you probably won't be surprised by now, there are auspicious and inauspicious days to do things, but the level of detail is incredible. There are auspicious days for a wedding or signing a contract, but my calendar told me that for 2021, July 10 and 23 are the auspicious days for getting a haircut (at 9.00-10.59 and several other times) so that I could plan well in advance. I'd better also remember that March 2020 is a lousy month for digging a well. There are even auspicious months to take a bath, although thankfully no inauspicious ones as the smell would be rather ripe. It's a lovely way to while away an afternoon.

As the New Year lasts a week or more, my Yan Yan wanted us to visit some friends the next day. Her friend and family (and extended fam-ily) were keen to have me there as the friend had recently been online dating a British businessman who regularly travelled to the Orient. As a precursor to meeting her, he had strangely started to ask for money, and as a favour to this friend, I had called him at his hotel in Malaysia and exposed him as a complete charlatan. During lunch, I heard my wife speaking in a mixture of Mandarin and the local Wu language about trac-tors and Lamborghinis, and she suddenly asked me to tell the story (in Mandarin Chinese). We were on holiday in France and staying on a farm, and in the barn was a vintage tractor made by Lamborghini. I took a photo and sent it to an Italian agricultural machinery client in Shanghai, asking how this was possible, and he emailed me back. It was a true story. Mr. Lamborghini did start out as a tractor maker, and only when his good friend, Mr. Maserati challenged him that he could never make a decent sports car did he try. Lamborghini tractors are still made to this day. I told the story in Mandarin Chinese, with a few stutters, and it was a defining moment to me as from that day forward, if I am asked, "do you speak Chinese?" I answer "yes".

Chapter 4: Mother in Law's Tongue

Last week, I was putting out the rubbish, and someone had left by the trash boxes an ornamental tangerine (橘子– ju2zi) tree. Actually, I am not sure if it is a Mandarin orange, regular orange, or a tangerine, as the Chinese word can be the same for all three. These are popular gifts for Chinese New Year as they symbolize abundance and good fortune, and I surmised that this tree had been one such and had been owned for about a month. It had never been watered, and the leaves were desiccated and crisp to the touch. If there were a Chinese Cruelty to Plants Society, the owners would have been named and shamed. I dragged it upstairs and stripped off all the dead leaves, leaving the very few live ones, and started cutting the branches into the shape for my eventual topiary. By the end of the summer, I was confident that I would have a magnificent specimen tree to accompany my already flourishing and summer fruiting lemon tree I bought last year. Now all I needed was a pot as presumably, the previous owners had kept this, as to them it was probably infinitely more valuable than the tree. Time to go to the plant market near the 1000-year-old Song Dynasty town of Lu Zhi (甪直镇), which I had discovered the previous year. We also had my mother-in-law, Mama, with us on this excursion.

The plant market was huge, with eight greenhouses each about the size of a football field, some cold for outdoor plants and some warm or even hot in the case of the orchid houses. Although it was a wholesale market, it was open to the public, although not well attended by them. Around the edges, on side roads were smaller tented stalls, no doubt hoping to cash in under the limelight of the main buildings. Early spring is the best time to go, even if some specimens haven't yet arrived. You exchange WeChat identities so the vendors can tell you when what you seek has arrived if not currently available. They were mystified by my request for decorative sweet peas and kept suggesting suitable edible snap pea varieties (called Dutch beans (荷兰豆 – he2lan2dou4). The traders were hungry for business after a long penniless winter, and it was quiet enough and worthwhile to talk to them as they are experts on floriculture. No quick pushy sales in this emporium. Here, knowledge and discussion of the insect pests of azaleas or the climatic zones of the Chinese Cobra Lily are going to earn respect and a better price, although hard bargaining is still expected. At one stall, selling plants that were mainstays of every western 1970s living room, there was much laughter as I explained that the spiky *Sanseviera trifasciata* was nicknamed in the west "mother in law's tongue". This allusion was not lost as a Chinese mother-in-law, mine not in earshot, are revered and feared and known for their razor-like tongues. The allusion of the Swiss Cheese Plant was lost, though, as the assembled listeners have never eaten cheese, and the substitute tofu doesn't have holes in it.

There were also stalls selling plant pots. It's a good idea to choose a single vendor who has an arena of them as you can negotiate a bulk discount. These pots were painted and fired ceramics which the Chinese have been making since the year dot. By luck, I managed an even more considerable discount. I told the vendor the story of the tangerine tree and the dimensions of the pot I needed. I selected a traditional blue and white one with rustic scenes as sold by reputable dealers in Europe as willow pattern from the 17th Century onwards. He told me all his adult life he had wanted to know what the foreign words (in several languages) meant on some of the pots, and I was happy to translate. "La Reigne", "Enjoy the Simple Life", "Welcome!", "Love Grows Best in Little Houses" etc. Done deal. One large pot (for the tangerine tree), two medium-sized pots, and one small pot (RMB150/£17 for all four). There was also a section for pet animals and birds, miniature dogs, rabbits, and birds. Although personally, I could never keep a bird in a cage, even an ornate bamboo one as is traditional in China, I was fascinated. My own experience had been tarnished by a large tropical parrot my aunt in Yorkshire owns, and it lives in sumptuous surroundings. It's a crazy bird and will have a loud squawking fit if the TV in the corner of the conservatory is turned off when it is watching a favourite cartoon. I couldn't teach this larger brained bird with advanced language skills (compared to a budgie) to say hello in Chinese (你好 – ni3hao3), and when I put my finger close, it took a painful slice out of it, though it immediately swooned at the sight of Yan Yan. Parrots are notoriously tricky to sex, but this one was for sure a male. It politely said "goodbye" as Yan Yan left the room, and I was waiting for a "fuck off" for me, but he had not mastered the finer points of Anglo-Saxon. The Chinese vendor told me that the budgerigars could live for more than eight years and learn one word or phrase every three months: a vocabulary of 32 in total. But could it become bilingual? Nobody seemed to know.

I wasn't looking for expensive specimen plants, just filler colours and forms for our apartment's three areas: interior, enclosed south balcony only suitable for desert and heavily watered tropical plants, and outdoor north balcony/terrace. This configuration, perfect for plants (and outdoor barbeques and cocktails), is almost unheard of in the middle of a Chinese city. Further haggling and purchasing continued.

One hanging basket with purple and white viola (RMB 50/£6), one sizeable ornamental foxglove (RMB25/£3), four African chrysanthemums (RMB 6/£0.70 each), one large mauve chrysanthemum (native to China and much loved) (RMB25/£3), one *Maranta* (RMB 20/£2) and one flowering bromeliad (free). The final purchase was a Calla Lily (the Chinese call it horse foot lily) RMB 55/£6. This was marked as coming from Holland and reminded me what an international business this is. It also reminded me of a long-ago pre-dawn trip to the globally renowned Amsterdam Aalsmeer flower auction, a full 50 football fields, and held the Chinese vendors in awe telling them about it. There is found an actual "Dutch" auction where prices start high and drop, with the winner being the lowest bidder. Trying to explain this to Chinese traders, they concluded I was making it up, or the Dutch are mad, or both.

Later, I went online and wanted to know how my total spend would compare with a British garden centre. I had spent RMB349/£41, a considerable sum in China. Choosing the cheapest UK options and using either own-collection or free delivery came to £145, and if I add in my free tangerine tree, £217. Lunch was going to my treat.

I knew of a family-run farm restaurant nearby where I had eaten once before. These countryside restaurants are well worth seeking out in China as they pride themselves on using fresh seasonal and locally sourced produce, some of which is usually on display. There is often a lake or fish pond, fields of vegetables and animals running around: chickens, geese, ducks, sheep, all fattening up for the pot. If found, the donkeys and horses are for children to pet, and although the meat of both is eaten in China, there is no need to stress out the young ones. The goose dish was memorable, and so were the chitterlings (pig's intestines) in spring onion sauce, although I only discovered what I had eaten afterwards, which is probably a good thing. I bought a 500ml bottle of baijiu, the ubiquitous firewater of China, to wash it down. Mama is a bit of a lush and likes this firewater, and this one was a modest 45% alcohol by volume, compared to a bottle of Gordon's Gin in the UK at 37.5% (some baijiu can be up to a throat-swelling and mind-numbing nearly 70%). Her face became redder and her voice louder and louder and remained so for the rest of the day. Nobody in the restaurant seemed to care. She was excited anyway because the next week, she was going out of China for the first time in her life, on holiday with my wife to Cambodia. She was 78 years old and the maximum age to get a tour group to accept her, so it was now or never.

Finally, we stopped at the ancient town of Lu Zhi in nearby Kunshan City. Signs proclaim it is the oldest town in China, which is not even close to the truth being wrong by at least 600 years but is within the bounds of normal modern Chinese artistic licence.

The locals have a different name for Lu Zhi, namely Pu Li (甫里), which was one of the pseudonyms of a famous Tang dynasty poet, Lu Guimeng (陆龟蒙), although the town was a haven for famous poets from several dynasties. Mama knew of this alternative name, and I think she was a little bit proud I knew it too. More about this eccentric poet later.

Lu Zhi is one of the best water towns in Jiangsu and is recognized by both UNESCO and the Chinese government. It's that compelling and timeless blend of narrow cobblestone streets, medieval canal bridges, and whispering willow trees.

Mama, who is very fit and healthy and belies her age, weaved not particularly elegantly through the ancient streets bursting with the Sunday hordes, buying maltose candy (麦芽糖– mai4ya2tang2) and plum candy rounds (梅饼 – mei2bing3), both of which tasted unpleasant to me. I could have just died at this time for a Cornish clotted cream ice cream or any ice cream at all, but there were none. She eventually arrived at a shop selling flavoured Chinese wines and baijiu in large vats. The shop owner offered her a small plastic cup to taste the local Osmanthus wine, but Mama insists on tasting from every vat, perhaps ten in all, as well as two cups of the much stronger baijiu. The owner didn't look happy but knew better than to protest to an elderly Chinese lady who no doubt possessed a "mother-in-law's tongue". By now, she was garrulous, but I did mollify the shop owner by buying a delicious plum wine which is both sweet and sour to the taste buds all at the same time.

In the car home, Mama wouldn't shut up. She was gibbering in her impenetrable (to me) local Wu language, and I started to get a headache. I was relieved to see the gateway to our home finally but nevertheless recognized it as a near-perfect Sunday.

Back to Lu Guimeng (Mr. Pu Li., birthdate unknown, died in 881 AD) and whose tomb is near the Baoshan Temple and his home close to two Gingko trees he planted (Gingko trees can live up to 2500 years) and amid his much-loved duck pond. Mr. Pu Li was from a well-known family, and his ancestors had been ministers to Empress Dowager Wu Zetian (武则天 – 690-705 AD as ruler). He succeeded in the highest imperial exam, the (進士 – jin4shi4), but it seems he found the civil service and work as a magistrate mundane. The reason I am so fascinated by him is that many of his interests and mine coincide: poetry, agriculture (and especially associated machinery), fishing, gastronomy, and wine. He was also a brilliant essayist, songwriter, avid book collector, medical doctor, practical joker and wit, and an expert tea grader.

His poetry writing is important for several reasons. At a chance encounter at a library, he met with Pi Rixiu (皮日休), originally from Xiang Yang, Hubei, an accomplished poet and well-known scholar. Mr. Pu Li (Lu) introduced him to his poetry which impressed Pi. Lu was at the library because he needed books to read on his travels as he had lost most of his in the rebel Pan Xun (龐勛) uprising of 868 and 869 AD, a bloody war that the emperor finally won. What followed was a lifelong friendship, and writing partnership often called Pi-Lu. These two men created the 9th century equivalent of something like postal chess. Each author wrote one matched rhyming verse in sequence and sent it to the other as both men, and especially Pi's, duties meant extensive travel. The complexities of these then-new styles and forms are sadly for me beyond more than a basic understanding. There was also a competitive element, similar to duelling pianos. They wrote over 600 duelling poems together, of which about half have survived. Pi-Lu were also important because the literati of the day were shifting from formal, elitist, and strictly classical to a more inclusive scholarly grouping, and "poetry societies" were forming, including in Lu Zhi, which had 12 good or excellent poets. The townsfolk seemingly got used to their revered eccentric hermit poet Mr. Pu Li, wandering around carrying books under his arm, lumping a tea stove, and meeting his great friend Pi at the Fair Wind Pavilion for a cup of wine or tea, although Lu eventually became teetotal.

The old elite was so formal as not to get their fingernails dirty with anything but ink, and this is what singles out Mr. Pu Li as a most unusual exception. Fingernail dirt from the land is the domain of the peasants. Even today, the Chinese word for a farmer is nong min (农民) which translates as a peasant, although this is not derogatory. Lu was a man who retired early from his civil service duties and then had a third age on steroids when most people should be putting their feet up. On retirement, he moved from his old home, and that later became in the 12th Century, the world-famous Humble Administrator's Garden (拙政园– zhuo1zheng4yuan2) in Suzhou. He settled into a life of seclusion. The eccentric and brilliant Mr. Pu Li farmed around 40 hectares (16 acres) as well as owning 30 worker's houses and ten cows along the Wusong River, (吴淞江), also known as Suzhou Creek (苏州河). The land in this area was not of great quality, and still isn't, with stagnant bitter water and frequent flooding but sufficient for him to grow a variety of crops. Unusually, he grafted on the land with his employees and used his spare time to take his boat to go fishing to the nearby Great Lake Tai (太湖 – tai4hu2) and raised ducks when not writing.

Uniquely for a poet of any dynasty, he wrote a short farming treatise on five agricultural tools and in detail on the subject of the curved-beam iron plough, in the book called "The Passage of the Plough" (耒耜经

– lei3si4jing1). This increased the efficiency of the old straight plough, invented by the Chinese in the second century BC. It now only required one driver and water buffalo or oxen compared to the old two buffalo and three driver configuration. The 11 interlocking parts are all correctly identified, such as the mouldboard (犁壁 – li2bi4) and harrows (犁底 – li2di3), still essential components today and technically described and modern replicas work well. In his introduction, Mr. Pu Li explains that whatever the status of a person, they can't do without farm equipment. I think, with some evidence from his satirical essays and swipes at feudal rulers, that he had a twinkle in his eye when he wrote this, and there is a possible hidden meaning of "you toffs can't tell a cabbage from a cauliflower in the field and need to understand less ethereal things better". He also wrote a treatise on fishing techniques and types of reels. There are no drawings or pictures in both treatises: it seems he failed in this one skill, although modern reconstructions based on the text work just as described.

Mr. Pu Li is also remembered for his gastronomy and practical jokes. Much inferior but still tasty variants of his best dishes such as Pu Li Duck (甫里鸭 – pu3li3ya1) and Pu Li Pigs Trotters (甫里蹄 – pu3li3ti2) can still be found today in Lu Zhi along with the Qing Dynasty favourite of the pickled Lu Zhi Radish Dish (甪直萝卜 – lu4zhi2luo2bo5). However, the original version of Pu Li duck was a spectacular (and humorous) affair, a little like stacking Russian dolls. It was created for eight guests at a Dragon Boat Festival. After several appetizers and three passes of wine, the waft of the entrée seduced the assembled. It was one of his ducks from the pond on a bed of lotus leaf and garnished with seasonal greens, garlic, and pink rose petals with a red pomegranate flower, and the duck's tilted backward, open beak. The duck skin was perfectly crisp, and the guests dived in as this was known as the tastiest part of the bird. As the chopsticks delved deeper, there was something more inside the carcass: a pigeon for each guest and inside the pigeon a sparrow, and inside the sparrow a pigeon egg.

Mr. Pu Li's duck pond was one of his joys and hobbies. There were fighting ducks, beautiful ducks, and of course, ducks suitable for the pot. There is an old story with several different versions about his ducks. Powerful eunuchs and intellectuals like Mr. Pu Li were often at odds in old China, and the powerful eunuchs were known to be spineless as well as ball-less. They had the ear of the ruling dynasty, not least because they weren't a threat to siring a new dynasty. One day a eunuch on horseback came to Lu Zhi, and to taunt Mr. Pu Li pulled out his catapult and shot dead his favourite drake. Mr. Pu Li came out of his house and, incensed, told the eunuch he had just killed a rare duck that could talk and spoke tributes to the emperor. The upset ducks, cackling in fright, could seemingly also speak and bear witness to the terrible deed. He then said he would add this incident to a book he was writing for the emperor. The eunuch, ashen-faced, screeched in falsetto and pleaded, "send the emperor the book but keep my name out of it. I will pay, I will pay". One variant of the story is that after being paid, Mr. Pu Li told the eunuch that the only thing that the ducks could say was their own name, and in another version, he returned the money to the humbled eunuch.

Even a gentle old hermit can get angry, although Mr. Pu Li allegedly never raised his voice during this altercation.

Chapter 5:   The White Rabbit

In 1973, I was sent away from Kenya to a boarding school in the UK. It started five years of misery. Britain was still coming to terms with decimalization, and shortly after, workers were reduced to a three-day working week. I was the youngest and shortest person in the school, and as we went to the housemaster's welcoming tea party, I was nervous and had never worn a suit before. As we stood on the lawn, my mother and father started to talk to another new incumbent's parents, Mr. and Mrs. Clarkson from Doncaster, who had proudly made their fortune from selling Paddington teddy bears. Little could I have guessed that their already gangling boy, Jeremy, was going to go on to be expelled from the school, become the future antihero of BBC Top Gear, also expelled from that, and was going to be the school bully with particular venom towards me but usually only directed through cronies: the mark of a true coward and bully. One time, I did try and hit him, but he was so tall I couldn't reach him and then took a severe beating from his mates. Within days, we had all gained nicknames. Mine was "mango" because of my peculiar African accent; Clarkson's was "Nessie" (Loch Ness monster) because of his less than attractive features and still apparent, fanged lip. There were also a couple of new boys from Hong Kong attending without parents. This gave me my first exposure to something close to Chinese cuisine and, in particular, pot noodles, White Rabbit Candy, and individually wrapped salty plums: the last one I found addictive.

On Sundays, we were allowed to cook our own food in a small kitchen area with a couple of gas rings. When the Hong Kong boys were cooking, there was this delicious chicken smell. It was pot noodles, not cooked in the actual pot but with the contents in a frying pan, just as Chinese people would do today. Adding hot water to the cup is generally reserved for inconvenient places like trains or hotels. Pot noodles were a new-fangled thing in 1973 and had only been invented two years earlier by Momofuku Ando (Japanese: 安藤百福 or Go Pek-Hok, Taiwanese:吳百福). However, Ando had invented packaged Ramen Noodles as early as 1958. The cup noodles were the foundation of the now Japanese giant Nissin Foods.

The White Rabbit Candy (大白兔 – da4bai2tu4), individually wrapped with an inner coating of clear edible rice paper, was delicious: creamy, tasty, and chewy, and I seek them out to this day. They are a little like the British Walkers' Nonsuch Toffee or the American Cow Tales. As most Chinese children know, the best way to eat them is to let the edible rice paper inner wrapper melt in the mouth before getting down to the chewing. Although they had been made since 1943 by the ABC factory in Shanghai when a Chinese merchant returned home and adapted an English recipe to local ingredients, they became well known in the west when Premier Zhou Enlai gave President Nixon a box of them to take home in 1972. Like Trump grazing on his late-night Lay's potato chips, Enlai was a midnight snacker, and White Rabbit Candy was his choice for solace. Nixon, by the way, was a healthy snacker.

Advertising exaggeration is not a new thing in China, and the early White Rabbit slogan was "seven white rabbit candies is the equivalent of a pint of milk" (七颗大白兔奶糖一杯牛奶 – qi1ke1da4bai2tu4nai3tang2yi1bei1niu2nai3) which is like trying to get nine pints into a pint pot. Advertising hyperbole has continued through to the present day, and no better example can be found than in the Chinese coconut water industry, of which the canned type can easily be found in the west. However, none of the described promotional initiatives ever made it there. Here's the problem: making the main product, canned coconut water, is a simple industrial process. The coconut fruit is washed, cracked, filtered, sterilized, and canned, although numerous by-products, flavours, and additives in the process also have hyperbole potential. So, it's hard to get a competitive edge. The Medaille D'Or of spin has to go to the Chinese Coconut Palm Group (CPG), which in 2018 produced an outrageous TV campaign extolling their coconut water product as improving breast size. It had young, well-endowed and beautiful female models posing in swimming costumes on the beach, claiming that "a can (of coconut water) each day will keep you white, soft and busty". It is doubly cynical because Chinese and Asian women generally consider a lighter skin shade as attractive and is the reason for the ever-popular parasol in summer. CPG was placed under investigation for this ad as there were multiple breaches of Chinese consumer law. The company's website also milks every possible angle with some misleading or outrageous claims. The spelling is exactly as found on the website.

"The Coconut Palm Brand Natural Coconut Juice.....are State Banquet Beverages designated by the Diaoyutai State Guess House of Beijing.....They have been served to heads of state and leaders of over 150 countries..... (they served it, doesn't mean all 150 actually drank the stuff)

"Zeng Qinghong, Vice-Chairman of the Country, after hearing the report of Director Wang Guangxing of Cocoanut Group, pointed out: "Now, our brands with the independent intellectual property right are few, and Haier, Changhong, TCL are our Chinese famous brands, and 'Cocoanut Palm 'is one too. Cocoanut Palm Group, as beverage enterprise, has lasted for more than ten years; that is not easy".' (There is no Vice-Chairman of the Country: the post was phased out in 1982).

"...it has helped 500 thousand Hainan farmers getting rid of the poor and becoming rich" (500,000 coconut farmers? Hainan farmers are still some of the poorest in China)".

I am pleased to report that the White Rabbit has kept multiplying, as rabbits quickly do, and there is now a wide range of flavours, including chocolate, mango, red bean lychee, and coffee.

My other exposure to China in my school years was when in 1975, one of the seniors asked me if I believed in the Chinese Nationalist or Communist cause. I had no clue what he was talking about, so I mumbled, "Communist". A month or so later, I was rewarded with a calendar sent from Beijing with Chinese scenes on it and pictures of a youthful Chairman Mao on it (Mao died the following year). It all seemed so exotic.

The next major Chinese food and beverage export coming to an outlet near you, actually it has already arrived on a small scale, is wine. China and wine? Surely, the Chinese are beer and strong liquor boozers? Try this question. Which country has had the most significant influence on Chinese domestic wine production? Answer later, but if you know it, you might consider giving up your day job and becoming a qualified sommelier or Master of Wine.

As always in China, things are changing quickly. China is now the world's largest consumer of red wines, and Chinese entrepreneurs own more than 100 top European, mostly French, vineyards. Domestic consumption from its 450 wineries might only equate to a thimble full per person, but collectively, that's still nearly one billion cases of 12 bottles each.

Over Chinese New Year, I turned on BBC Saturday Kitchen to see starring those stalwarts of Chinese cooking in the west, chefs Ken Hom and Ching He-Huang. The wine buff, pink-faced, flowery shirted, cross-hatched unmatched jackets, and ever-smiling, Olly Smith, paired one of the dishes with a bottle of Chinese wine, a peachy and delicious Chinese

Château Changyu Moser 2016 white cabernet sauvignon, more like a blush wine, £15.95 from slurp.co.uk. Please understand me; Olly is a true wine expert. It's just his, I think deliberate, sartorial pairings don't quite match his skill with wine pairings, but he does bring a ray of sunlight into our dusk as the team is working live early morning in the UK. Don't change a thing, Olly, we love you in China! You could become a new trendsetter for fashion here. The wine was a hit with the assembled foodies. Some UK friends wrote to me recently that they had found a Chinese "Cab" in the supermarket chain, Sainsbury's, and were sharing it discussing China stories.

The Chinese can easily recognize the mid-range priced locally-produced Changyu because it is packaged in a sumptuous box with a classy-looking foreigner with curly grey hair, perhaps an Italian or Spaniard, contentedly swirling the wine by a roaring open fire. The message is clear enough. If you want an overpriced and heavily taxed Vin de la Communauté Européenne, which may have been adulterated and is often only suitable for making vinegar, fine, otherwise buy me! Nobody would dare fake China's premier brand unless they wanted to spend a long stretch in jail making Christmas tree lights for the export market 14 hours each day. Changyu is a slick operation and contrasts with the delicious naivety of the White Rabbit Candy and the over-the-top marketing strategy of the Coconut Palm Group. Changyu has built a château and vineyard in China's Ningxia (Hui) Autonomous Province and, for 12 years, has very cleverly partnered with Moser, the famous Austrian viticulture family. There's your answer to the question posed earlier. The associated château looks like its European counterparts and cost £60 million to build. The barrels were originally made from imported French oak, but now Chinese oak has been substituted. This is just one of eight Changyu wineries, each with its own château, but the flagship site, in Ningxia, is in a land of arid mountains and deserts about half the size of England with a population of 8 million and has always been extremely poor. However, there are even poorer regions and provinces such as Gansu, Yunnan, and Guizhou. When the Chinese government has alleviated poverty in areas such as this, it won't just have won the battle but the war. Ningxia first came to my attention when I carried out a research project on the Chinese dairy industry. At the time, I went back for context to 1949 and discovered that in 1951, two years after China became communist, all of Ningxia had only two milk cows.

Two high-value products offer Ningxia a ray of hope: wolfberries and wine. The Helan Mountain Region has an area of 10,000 hectares (4000 acres) identified as suitable for viticulture. The dry mountain climate with valleys irrigated from the Yellow River and long daylight hours are excellent for wine production. The stony, free-draining soil and altitudes up to 1200 metres (4000 feet) make for a low-yielding but high-quality wine. The growing season is relatively short, though, and winters are severe, and the vines have to be buried under a mound of soil in the autumn to prevent winter kill.

Although Château Moser offers a range of wines, for its premier brand of red wine, expect to pay at least £50 for a good vintage. Suppose you wanted to be sneaky and put it into a blindfold wine tasting. In that case, you could upend a wine expert, who could easily be fooled into thinking it a Chilean, Argentinean, or possibly even a southern Italian offering. The best vintages have now won a tonne of top international prizes. It's not quite up to the best French reds, but it's only a spit or three away.

On the back of this flurry of development come some serious international wine heavyweights and an explosion in varietals from Pernod Ricard (Ningxia) Winemakers Company Limited and Moet Hennessey with their "Chandon Me" range. The latter is currently only for the domestic market because Chinese wine drinkers don't want "acidic" wines, and they don't enjoy their white wines (sparkling or not) or any other drink, even beer, served at anything but room temperature. My wife is constantly berating me for drinking cold liquids, which she assures me, will do everything from damage my sex life to my stomach and bowels. The "Me" in Chandon Me sounds like the Chinese word for sweet or honey (蜜 – mi4). It is marketed as "the first sparkling wine that can be enjoyed at room temperature". I like my champagne brut and chilled but launched in 2017, Chandon Me is hurtling towards a very impressive half a million bottles in sales.

China is the world's largest producer of wolfberries or goji berries (*Lyciumbarbarum* and related – 枸杞– gou3ji3). Ningxia produces nearly half of them, in particular in the Zhongning area of the Yellow River. It's been cultivated there for at least 1500 years. Every Chinese person knows this usually dried red fruit. It's one of the flavours of choice to top off your rice porridge, also used as a general culinary decoration, and it's a common ingredient of traditional Chinese medicine. More recently, it has become available in Western health shops as a healthy antioxidant. Its history is also marred by exaggeration, starting with Li Ching Yun (李清雲), the Sichuan herbalist and purveyor of wild herbs and martial arts expert who died at the ripe old age of either 197 years or 250 years, depending on the source. His diet consisted of wild herbs, including goji berries and rice wine. In 1927, the National Revolutionary Army General, Yang Sen (杨森) met with Li and after his death wrote a book, 一个250岁长寿老人的真实记载，A True Record of a Man with a Lifespan of 250 Years.

Chapter 6: Festivals, Remembrance, and Celebrations

In *The Lure of the Red Dragon*, I covered some of the most important festivals: Spring Festival and the Lantern Festival, Dragon Boat Festival, and the Ching Ming Grave Sweeping Festival. I saved back National Week for this book because of the significance of 2019.

National Week starts on October 1 and lasts for seven days, and is also called Golden Week. Its origins go back to a week of factory closures to give the workers a break. It celebrates the founding of the PRC in 1949. The Communist Party leaves nothing to chance, and the coordination and stage management is always slick. The streets are adorned with the national flag, and it's the only time I can guarantee that the numerous fountains in our apartment complex will all work. The well-scrubbed children run around dressed in their best clothes, playing with their flag and red balloons. If you are planning to China and are sensitive to a temporary loss of liberties, this is not the week to come. This is the Communist Party's big day, and they are bloody well going to make sure it is inch-perfect even if they have to put the country in virtual lockdown. It is the one time of year to really curb any unpatriotic displays (verbal or otherwise).

If you are planning to visit during this week, a modicum of forward preparation is needed. The internet is going to present the biggest problem for most. The censors go into overdrive, and even simple things you have been used to don't work. The traditional workaround for the rest of the year, a Virtual Private Network (VPN), will not work, however much the VPN suppliers implore you to upgrade your software and try different access locations and devices. Websites and search engines using normal Great Firewall of China approved (non-VPN) sites start doing strange things. I use Yahoo! search engine (Google is not available in China without a VPN), and during this week, I can frequently click on a news item, and it is a blind link. Some foreign internet banking, credit card, and brokerage services won't work either. For example, I can't get the fund prices for my UK personal pension from their site. I sometimes like to buy things in dollars from my US bank account, such as online airline tickets, but that option will likely not be available because the websites will automatically assume you are in China and want you to pay in RMB. For sport, the same applies. Typing "nba.com" will automatically take you to the Chinese NBA site, but "nfl.com" takes you to the American website. Equally, paying for music top-up or computer game tokens may also not work. It's a lottery. The best advice I can offer is to make sure you have the telephone numbers of critical financial and travel contacts with you and make sure your Fortnite account is topped up. Sometimes another workaround is to first go to a Chinese search engine (Baidu is the biggest) and gain access by this method, but its haphazard. For news, cable or satellite TV is best, and stations such as RAI Italia, BBC, CNN, TVE, France 24, TVBS, Bloomberg, Aljazeera, and many more are readily available but with some blackouts and time delays. Their corresponding website news services, however, are not all available. Similarly, many newspaper websites are unavailable, including The Guardian, The New York Times, the Washington Post, Le Monde, Spiegel Online, and The Wall Street Journal.

I suppose I should be grateful that I don't live in India. That country has easily the largest reported service cuts and an increasing number of total internet blackouts globally. It recently has deactivated mobile phones in some areas for months at a time. No filtering required; just hit the kill switch. I say reported because I doubt Iranians and North Koreans, for example, report their shutdowns. But this method is crude at best and dangerous at worst. If you are in rural Arunachal Pradesh or Assam and need help, it might not be forthcoming.

2019 was different. This was the year to celebrate 70 years of the PRC's foundation, making it the longest reigning communist bloc ever (the FSU lasted 69 years) with the biggest parade in world history held in Beijing. The censorship and other related security matters were Draconian. In Beijing, tourists found themselves locked in hotels for twelve hours each day for practice sessions along the parade route. Beijingers were also greatly inconvenienced by snarled traffic and blocked streets, and a week before the event, kite flying and pigeon racing were banned in Beijing. I think any unfortunate feral pigeon flying in the wrong airspace would have faced a fearsome flack battery.

VPNs were shut down on September 26 and only worked again on October 3. The Rugby World Cup was being played in Japan, and I couldn't find the fixtures and their timing anywhere (the obviously seditious BBC Sport website was blocked). Nothing worked, including Yahoo! or Baidu rugby searches, although I wasn't surprised in the latter's case. No self-respecting Chinese mother is going to let her precious little darling (妈宝 – ma1bao3, although the older generation will not know this phrase) get interested in, never mind play, this brutal heathen sport. There is a Chinese translation of the scrum-induced "cauliflower ears", but it relates solely to boxing. Because of this, I nearly missed the sensational win by The Brave Blossoms (Japan) and their captain Michael Geoffrey Leitch (リーチマイケル) beating Ireland 19-12 as I couldn't find the start time. Leitch really is Japanese (pronounced Leechee).

Internet and social media censorship were particularly severe, not just because of this event but also because of the simultaneous political turbulence in Hong Kong. Many Chinese people knew of the volatile situation in Hong Kong from regular mainland media, although the reporting, of course, had its own spin. I did accidentally find one serious temporary breach of censorship. At 11.49 am, China Standard Time (CST) on September 28, I found an article from a senior foreign journalist from a major international news network based in Hong Kong (I had no VPN). It would have been seen in China as incredibly incendiary and hostile by the Chinese government. It was not about Hong Kong but concerned his portrayal of President Xi. I found it deliberately offensive, scurrilous, and obviously timed to be so. Within the space of two hours, the article had disappeared from the website in mainland China, and it shows the difficulties of keeping a lid on every news article. I would imagine the censor who missed this one was in serious trouble. If I were a Chinese censor, I would have taken it down in less than one minute. The writer, a human rights student educated at the University of Liverpool, is also the author of The Great Firewall of China: *How to Build And Control An Alternative Version Of The Internet*, so perhaps he has a special knowledge of how to circumvent it? The same journalist, still based in Hong Kong, continued with provocative articles about the mainland during the Wuhan crisis and has clearly forgotten the words of Noah Shachtman, his former boss and Editor in Chief at the punchy Daily Beast, and his three main rules:

"So don't be an open partisan, avoiding hate speech and posts that could offend a group, and "don't get your fellow reporters in trouble".

The big day was spectacular and had been preceded the week before by the opening of the "starfish", the new mammoth Beijing Daxing International airport (Code PKX, rather than the older PEK, which is 65 kilometres (40 miles). On the day, there was a moderate haze of pollution. A pity that, as two months earlier, multiple western media sources announced that the capital was on target to drop off the list of the 200 worst polluted global cities. I hadn't wholly known what to expect, and there were many surprises for me. One peculiarity was that there were no throngs of the masses lining the parade route like you would see down the Champs Elysée on Bastille Day or like the more than quarter of a million soldiers and civilians who saw the 1949 Chairman Mao flag raising and declaration. There were large crowds, for sure, but these were all invitees.

The event started with a short speech by President Xi from the Heavenly Gate of Peace (Tiananmen) on the same spot as Mao delivered his 1949 speech. To me, Xi's slow and measured oratory was clear and concise, so unlike Mao in 1949 with his heavy Hunan accent, which was incomprehensible to many Beijingers and others, and lacked modern microphones. Xi's was an all-inclusive speech with multiple references to the Chinese nation, including all the ethnic groups: the Han majority plus the 55 ethnic groups (中华民族 – zhong1hua2ming2zu2). Xi then inspecting the 15,000 troops, 580 pieces of equipment, and 160 aircraft in an open-top limousine, with air force General Yi Xiaoguang, number plate VA02019 (a first for this branch of the forces) and accompanied by a third empty car, a Hong Qi number plate VA01949, along Chang'an Avenue. As is customary, the President's car only had the badge of China and no number plate and a flag flying. The display of militaria, especially the ballistics, drones, and aircraft were a clear message, with enough intentionally displayed firepower to say, "don't mess with us". This was the first time the world had seen the 200 tonne D-26 (A and B) mobile launched missiles which have a range of 2000 miles (3200 km) with a 1.8 tonne conventional or nuclear warhead and the "ship busting" variant able to hit a target within the radius of the centre circle of a football pitch (all figures approximate).

One poignant moment brought many to tears, not typically seen in public by the Chinese, communist believers or not: the third car with VA01949 on the number plate. It had the same four microphones as the other two leading cars, but apart from the driver, it was empty. There was no attempt by the commentator to explain it, and none needed. For the faithful, it perhaps meant the loss of comrades Mao Zedong and Zhou Enlai, or for all the fallen tens of millions of soldiers and civilian casualties of the Sino-Japanese War, World War II, and Civil War from 1937-1945. It is the rationale behind the title of this book, *The Dead Microphones*. The onlookers, all the former presidents still alive, the top brass, the distinguished veterans, probably reminisced. Not one showed a moment's breach of respect or discipline by sipping from the covered porcelain cups of tea in front of them.

Another pleasant surprise to me was the inclusion of many more women than previous parades in the marching groups with female Major Generals, Cheng and Tang, heading up a PLA and People's Armed Police marching unit; a first. But the highlight for me had to be the Women's Militia, marching in their cherry-red uniforms with on the knee skirts, toned legs, and "light" make-up as the Chinese military and police like to call it. They might be trained battlefield killers in another life, but on this day, they were dressed to look beautiful, and indeed several members of this militia are graduates of the Beijing Institute of Fashion Technology. I must include in this group of pleasant surprises a contingent of the light blue berets. These were the UN peacekeepers, a comparatively new and growing role for China. In every case, the marching was absolutely precise in the Chinese style, a modest goose step unlike the Prussian high kick or the cancan style beloved by North Korea and the former Soviet Union. Lastly came a parade of 100,000 civilians on a range of gaudy floats with patriotic themes such as flight and space exploration.

If anything, the evening event was even more spectacular. It consisted of three elements. The first was a massive firework display which the commentator on CCTV explained needed more than 2000 pyrotechnical experts to arrange. It included painting a "70" in the sky by launching the fireworks at differential heights. I have got to believe that is really difficult to achieve. The second element was mind-blowing. It consisted of a series of pastiches of humans each holding a rectangular reflective silver-coloured light board. By coordinating their movement and reflecting the light sources, it was possible to produce stunning moving images of different popular images of China, including some with Chinese characters. I can't imagine how many thousand or even tens of thousands of hours it took to make this work so seamlessly. The third element was a series of complex dance routines by all the ethnic groups and accompanied by a vast orchestra. If you put together all the Berlin, London, and New York Philharmonic violins and, for good measure, threw in some extras from the Concertgebouw, there probably still wouldn't have been enough violins to meet quota. It was entertaining for me to guess the origins of the ethnic minorities by their costumes. I got about a third right for regional origin (not ethnic name), correct primarily based on the costumes, but this is a diverse bunch, including the Chaoxian (originally from Korea), Kazaks, and Tartars. The masses, and any visiting tourists, might not have been able to see the events live, but I would think the firework display could have been seen from outer space.

The Communist Party got its wish: the event was flawless in both design and execution.

Internet disturbance and the general inconvenience to the public and tourists alike occur in varying degrees on all significant events, including G20 and G7 and other Asian summits, foreign heads of government visits, World War II remembrances, etc., so it is worth cross-checking your itinerary. A little like Spring Festival, Golden Week is also a period of travel with a little less emphasis on returning to hometown and more on the concept of holiday and nowadays also going abroad. At the front and back ends of the week, planning is required. I got caught out this time around as Yan Yan and I had to go to the Cyprus consular service in Nanjing on the last day of the festival: no choice. As we had no idea how long the interview would take, it was impossible to pre-book a return train ticket. On arrival at the railway station, the only tickets available were four hours hence on a K Class with a hard sleeper berth, and no seats at all for the day at the nearby coach station. "K" is for ☐ – kuia4 and means quick, which is a misnomer as these yellow and green trains run at a comparative snail's pace to the G and D (☐☐ – gao tie) trains which can go at 350 km/h (217 mph). Definitely check which ticket you are purchasing if using Chinese trains. K trains are frequently sleepers with hard and soft seat options available, neither available on this day. The sleeper portion also comes in several types: hard, soft, and deluxe. The only option available to us was a hard sleeper; six to a berth, bunk beds stacked three high with a top bunk not recommended for those who suffer from vertigo, and no enclosure, just an open corridor. If you want a low bunk, you have to go to the train station to reserve it in advance as this cannot be done online. K trains have a top speed of 75 mph (120 km/hr), but I don't think they often reach it and have frequent stops. Sleepers are useful as they run up and down the length and breadth of China. Z trains are "Express" class with a top speed of 160km/hr (99 mph). A journey from Guangzhou to Urumqi will take you 48 hours and 13 minutes on a Z class, but that was a journey that took one week when my wife was a teenager. The journey will cost you RMB 60.83 (£7) on a hard seat, less than a taxi trip around the corner in London or New York. They are perfect for sturdy backpackers on a budget or an impoverished urban migrant worker trying to cross China to get a bed and hot dinner from Mum in hometown.

I settled down on my bunk, and after three people had poked me incorrectly claiming I was in their bed, I took a nap dreaming the slow train was Thomas the Tank Engine trying to get to the top of a hill: "I think I can, I think I can, I think I can, I know I can". Thomas the Tank Engine, as in many other countries, is wildly popular with Chinese children. It also neatly fits into Marxist philosophy of the belligerent upper-crust capitalist, the Fat Controller (Sir Topham Hatt), oppressing the poor workers complete with their regional working-class accents: Thomas, James, Gordon, Henry et al. When I was reading about Thomas to my children in the '80s, I would never have believed that there would have been female engines, never mind foreign ones. Pandering to global commerce, later, Thomas, in the movies, went to China and there he met Red Plum (红梅 – hong2mei2), China Railways GJ 0-6-0T designed by Dalian Locomotive Works (1958-1961) for train spotters, with a logo describing her as Number One (一号 – yi1hao4) as she is important enough to pull the mail carriages. She also sometimes pulls regular carriages: An An (Annie) and Yin-Long (Silver Dragon) (安安 – an1an1 and 银龙 – yin2long2) and yes, they wear the yellow and green and yellow K train livery. Hong Mei is a self-confident, naughty, blue engine (same colour as Thomas) and loves racing, but when Thomas derailed in a race, she came to his rescue, and there are now two Number One engines in the stories: Thomas and Hong Mei. An outbound journey that took less than two hours door to door had been replaced by a homeward bound journey of seven and a half hours.

Festivals, remembrances, and celebrations are commonplace in China, and it's entirely possible to stumble on them by accident. One celebration, Fang Sheng (放生 – fang4sheng1 – animal release), I have twice discovered accidentally. The first time was on a day trip from our home in Suzhou to one corner of the Great Lake (太湖 – tai4hu2), the source of much of our local fish and crustaceans. The total size of Taihu is 2250 km2 (869 square miles). This journey was to West Mountain Island (西山岛 – xi1shan1dao3) but nearby is an equally beautiful twin, East Mountain Island. Our island of choice is popular with Chinese tourists and known for its scenic views of five-mast wooden fishing junks in sheltered bays, white painted houses on winding hilly lanes, wetlands with egrets and terns, and fruit farms and stalls with a glorious array of yumberries, juzi oranges, and succulent peaches. We pulled into a lakeside car park where a crowd was beginning to gather to discover Buddhist monks, both male and female, in black livery and with shaved heads. They were arranging blue plastic tanks of live fish, freshwater crabs, and turtles.

On inquiry, it turned out that this was the Fang Sheng celebration, not of animals in our region, but of fish. The fish had all been purchased from local restaurants for the "catch and release". Soon the prior, abbot, or equivalent chanted prayers, and the fish and other species were taken to the edge of the lake, and the contents of the blue tanks overturned. Some of the fish could sense the lake water and freedom and flipped and flopped into it. The children present were encouraged to push the recalcitrant's into the lake. Buddhist or not, it was hard not to cheer these fortunate fish escaping execution. Lunch was at a family farm restaurant, some of the best places to eat in China. The fish, unsurprisingly, was marked as sold out, but there was an abundance of chicken, goose, pork, and seasonal vegetables. It was also a time to muse on the status of the monks. They might have been pious, but they were undoubtedly not impoverished with their Apple phones and arriving in the monastery's Buick people carrier, presumably funded by generous donations. I have even heard of stories of Chinese monks having to be put on diets for becoming too tubby and similarly rotund to Friar Tuck. Unfortunately, unlike what I saw that day, this ceremony has caused debate about cruelty and precisely the opposite of what is intended. One example of this is unscrupulous dealers who bring captured birds to the cities for release, and few, if any, can find their way back to the countryside and perish.

It was 10 am on September 18, 2019, and I was sat outside on our balcony in the warm morning sunlight. Our newly acquired kitten stepped outside to join me. He's a playful British Shorthair and came to us with the apt name of "Pudding" (布丁 – bu4ding1 in Chinese with the same meaning). Suddenly he did the equivalent of a feline wheelie and shot indoors. The cause of his distress, and mine, was the blaring of multiple sirens at what I first thought must have been a colossal factory fire. I then realized that there were too many alarms, and they were too loud and jokingly said, "we must be under attack", and then quickly shivered as I realized the date. It was to remember the contrived invasion of Chinese Manchuria by Japan on this date in 1931. It was incredibly eerie and thought-provoking. You can still find relics of the 1931 invasion and the subsequent 1937-1945 Sino-Japanese War referred to by the Chinese as the Chinese War of Resistance Against Japan, and on one visit to Guangzhou, I found an old placard pointing the way to an air-raid shelter. Maybe someone had forgotten to take it down, always a possibility in China, or had it had been left there as a chilling historical reminder?

If you are visiting China, it is worth cross-checking your itinerary not just for the national festivals but also against the regional ones. Another reason for this is that many are not on a set date because they relate to lunar calendars. You will almost always be able to observe the events close up and quite often take part, so beware if you are concerned about strange food and drink or have two left feet when it comes to dancing.

Because I work in agriculture, one of my favourite festivals is the 3000-year-old Mid-Autumn Festival which is akin to the Harvest Festival in the UK or Thanksgiving in the US and of which variants are found over most of Asia. It is also called the Harvest Moon Festival and will occur on a full moon in late September or early October and is a national holiday. It has many facets, but the primary ones are to say thanks or prayers for a good harvest and pray for a good one next year, for the family to be together and for romance. After all, in older times, a poor harvest could mean the collapse of the village right up to the loss of an empire. There are also a lot of sometimes conflicting myths about the festival relating to Chang'e (嫦娥), the immortal female moon goddess and Hou Yi (后羿), her husband and accomplished archer. Some western readers with an interest in space exploration may recognize the first name. Chang'e 4 was the Chinese unmanned spacecraft that landed on the dark side of the moon in early 2019 (although the dark side of the moon isn't actually dark). Similarly, an integral part of the myth involves the Jade Rabbit (玉兔 – yu4tu4), the name of the lunar rover that landed on the moon in 2013.

One version of the story includes Hou Yi becoming a tyrannical king who commanded an elixir of eternal life to be made for him and which Chang'e stole and jumped out of a window to float up to her home, the moon.

In my favourite potted short, sad, and romantic version, ten suns rose in the sky together, causing the people to suffer distress from the heat. Hou Yi shot down nine of the suns, leaving one to supply light and warmth. As a gift for his marksmanship, an immortal, Xiang Wang Mu, gave Hou Yi the elixir of immortality. He subsequently gave it to his wife so they could be immortal together. Unfortunately, while Hou Yi was away hunting, one of his apprentices broke into his house and demanded the elixir. Chang'e refused to give it up, and she fled to the moon. On his return, the devastated Hou Yi, who had no way to get to the moon, displayed all the food Chang'e liked including cakes, which eventually became the ubiquitous and famous moon cakes. Fortunately, Chang'e is not lonely living on the moon because she has a friend there, the Jade Rabbit, which refers to the pattern of this animal to be seen on the moon and this shape has also observed by several other unconnected ancient civilizations.

In ancient times, people started to pray to Chang'e, asking for prosperity and security and asking for blessings on lovers. This part is why the red lanterns, often with riddles on them, are in the festival. If a man gives a woman a lantern and likes him, she can signal so by giving him a handkerchief. It's the ancient equivalent of "will you be my Valentine?" The one thing from this myth foreigners will be able to relate to is the moon cakes which for a few weeks before are piled high on prominent display in the shops and increasingly coffee shops. They have flaky pastry exteriors with an impress of the brand or other auspicious symbols on the top and are stuffed with treats. Typically, they are bought in boxes of six or more (even numbers), but you can buy individually wrapped ones. If you want to splurge, you can order costly ones; probably the best are from Hong Kong. So long as you have a sweet tooth, moon cakes are delicious, although savoury ones such as five kernel nut and roast pork or exotic seafood are available. My favourite fillings are hard to find snowy rose sugar pâté or the lotus seed paste ones.

A 150 gramme (5.3 oz) date stuffed moon cake packs around 600 calories, and on a good day, not in one sitting, I can eat three of them; the calorific equivalent of seven Mars bars and the fat equivalent of nine of them, for all three. Only the peculiar Scottish habit of deep-frying Mars bars can compete with almost the same nutritional values per unit. Moon cakes are not suitable for vegetarians, Muslims, or Jews. This also applies to people with allergies as the pastry often includes pork fat and sometimes peanut oil, or for those with cholesterol problems (because of the egg yolk and other inclusions). As I don't go to the gym, the calorific punishment for me of eating three is 80 km (50 miles) of hard cycling. It's worth it.

Next in line for space exploration is Tianwen 1, the search for heavenly truth, which travelled to Mars in 2021 and is named after a poem by Chinese poet Qu Yuan (c 340 to 278 BC), who's death is commemorated in the annual Dragon Boat Festival. The rover on the craft was named Zhurong, a mystical figure in Chinese folklore associated with fire, and the name was chosen by a public vote.

The Hungry Ghost/Zhongyuan Festival (中元節 – zhong1yuan2jie2) is firmly rooted in Buddhist and Taoist origins and takes place from mid-August to early September. It's the reverse of the Chingming Grave Sweeping Ceremony because, on this day, the spirits visit the deceased's living relatives. A few years ago, I went with a friend to her mother's grave on this day of remembrance. Little did we know that there was a new road to the cemetery, and we finished up trekking on steep country dirt tracks until exhausted. That's when a local farmer, realizing where we must be going, rescued us and bailed us into the bed of his tractor and trailer, called rather literally a drag- pull machine. (拖拉机 – tuo1la1ji1) and gave us a lift to the summit. This description, often the brunt of jokes, is also found in an amusing phrase, 拖拖拉拉 tuo1tuo1la1la1, literally push-push-pull-pull, which are the Chinese words for to procrastinate.

At the entrance to the multi-denominational and atheist cemetery was a welcome centre where you could buy flowers and other suitable paraphernalia. Next came a lane with a fork in the road passing the giant urns for burning incense and "ghost money", a sort of silver paper that burns very well. At a fork in a road was a surprise for me in the form of a statue of Comrade Lei Feng. Everyone in China knows this highly propagandized man and his young and handsome rugged features, usually wearing a military hat with cold-weather fur ear flaps. Contemporary posters of him are as iconic as the Athena Che Guevara posters from the 1970s. Lei Feng, a soldier, died, age 22, in 1963, not fighting but when a telephone pole from an army truck hit him as it was reversing. His diary extolling Mao became the centrepiece of an extensive propaganda campaign, "Learn from Lei Feng".

Academics dispute whether his diary was a forgery, but whatever the truth, it was a great success as a propaganda exercise. Lei Feng also has a memorial day (March 5) where students are taught about him, and volunteers go and clean up public spaces. This cemetery was multi-denominational, including for no denomination, but the Christian graves were in a plot together, each one marked with a small cross.

I will never be a competent poet, but that night, I was sufficiently moved to write on returning home.

Black on Red (红底黑字)

Below the autumn mists of
Huang Guan Mountain,
A gracious amphitheatre:
Seats occupied or reserved,
Stubby pines as armrests
Waiting for the show.

Next to the track by the pond,
A fork in the road
Christians to the left
Follow the crucifix of Jesus,
Others to the right
Past the bust of Lei Feng.

Seventy something steep steps,
A shuffle along the row,
Passing empty red etched graves.
The one we seek, the words
Are painted black: black on red.
Red for life, black for death.
Water and tears wash the stone

Tea to finally cleanse
Flowers and incense placed,
No festival food today.
We speak aloud our thoughts
Give our trembling thanks.

A setting pale sun
The twilight wind

Caresses the cheeks
Of the audience.
A poke from the gods
Wishing all goodnight.

Afterwards, we headed down the hill a short way to the monastery. Crowds had already gathered, and there was a courtyard with piles of rubbish bags full of ghost money and nearby paper horses and other paper effigies. The monks with shaved heads were carrying out boxes of relics on their shoulders, two to a heavy box. Then the two senior monks dressed in gold and vermillion, including similar coloured hats, delivered the prayers. Firecracker strings were then lit, followed by the lighting of the bonfire, which symbolizes releasing the ghosts from their suffering. The crowds strained to take photographs of the bonfire, and when it had subsided, several people came up to me to show their pictures of the bonfire smoke and the outlines of ghosts within the smoke. I politely muttered approval though I couldn't see the ghosts as they could. It's also traditional to have a feast with empty seats around the table left for the ghosts who are ravenous, as well as on the fourteenth and last day of the festival, releasing lanterns and paper boats onto water to help guide the ghosts back home.

If the date is September 9 and you see elderly people wearing sturdy shoes and some carrying walking sticks, frequently with flasks of tea, climbing hills and mountains, you will have stumbled upon the Double Nine or Senior Citizens Festival. Feel free to join in if you are age-appropriate. It's a 2000-year-old festival when on that day it was traditional to climb mountains and towers as a symbol of a wish to remain strong and healthy in old age. It's also normal to carry a sprig of dogwood, which it is believed can ward of sickness. Soon I plan to join the retirees and partake in this festival and enjoy the nine-layered Chong Yang "tower" cakes and chrysanthemum wine and have a good old-fashioned natter with my fellows.

As well as all these nationally celebrated events, the Chinese ethnic minorities also have their celebrations, and if you are visiting any of these areas, its well worth checking in advance what can be seen. Good examples are the Shodun Festival (雪頓節), August 4, in Lhasa, Tibet with the Giant Buddha Hillside display, Tibetan opera, dancing, feasts with yoghurt featuring, and yak and horse racing. For children, try the Dai minority Water Splashing Festival, (泼水节 – po1shui3jie2) April 13-15, in Xishuangbanna, Yunnan, with its dragon boat racing and massive water fight on the last day.

Chapter 7: Following the Diaspora (Cambodia, Indonesia, Malaysia and Singapore)

The Chinese Diaspora, the scattered ones, also sometimes wishfully called "the sons and daughters of China" by the Communist Party, comprises over 50 million people or about 3.5% of China's population. It's not even close to the largest Diaspora, which is generally considered the German Diaspora (not all from Germany) at around 150 million and the Irish Diaspora at around 90 million. However, it is unique in the degree of global spread. That is why it's easy to find a bratwurst and beer anytime in Texas or a green beer on St. Patrick's Day in the US, but you can find a Chinese restaurant in any far-flung corner of the world. It's been an arduous journey for many of the Chinese Diaspora.

Those lovely contributors at Wikipedia have come with the amalgamated table below on the Chinese Diaspora (selected for above 0.4 million). It is difficult to estimate numbers because of definitions and who qualifies by where they were born, inclusion or exclusion (especially in the Philippines) of mixed race, self-identification, etc.

Thailand*	9.3m
Malaysia*	6.6m
United States*	4.9m
Indonesia*	2.8m to 7m (unofficial)
Canada*	1.8m
Myanmar*	1.6m
Australia*	1.2m
Philippines*	1.1 to 27m

Peru	0.9m to 1.3m
South Korea	0.8m
Vietnam*	0.8m
Japan	0.7m
France	0.7m
Venezuela	0.4 to 0.45m
UK*	0.4m
South Africa*	0.3-0.4m
Russia	0.2-0.4m

I have marked with a * those countries that I have deliberately sought out or where I have occasionally stumbled upon the Chinese Diaspora. Sometimes, it was just I was homesick for a plate of noodles or a steamed bun.

The Chinese Diaspora is fascinating and especially how it has kept some Chinese traditions but also deviated in many ways. The Chinese have been building communities worldwide for centuries, often suffering from racism, bigotry, and jealousy. A small part of this was self-inflicted with secret societies, bloody gangs, and self-help groups not easily distinguishable to their adopters. Those perceptions, even today, have not entirely gone away. For example, the motives of the modern Confucian Institute, a sort of more propagandized version of the Goethe Institut, arouse suspicion, but today, the resentment is caused more by Chinese financial clout and has thankfully become less violent. Soft power, wherever possible, is the new mantra. It doesn't mean that there aren't some hostile outbursts, and not just in Asia, such as when in 2014 the Australian MP, Clive Palmer, went on national TV and described the Chinese government as "bastards and mongrels". Sometimes, the sheer weight of Chinese numbers and spending power can cause distress, such as in New Zealand, that gracious and peace-loving country, which in 2018 placed a restriction on overseas buyers of property, not exclusively aimed at the Chinese but certainly part of the consideration. I'm not singling out the antipodeans. One of the joys to me is on a cold day in Melbourne, Australia, is watching the Chinese and local students harmoniously sharing a table and eating a bowl of noodles and learning each other's culture and language.

Mass migration is more a product of the 19th Century onwards. However, the Chinese had settlers in most of Asia and even beyond much earlier, including Japan in around 210 BC. By the 7th Century, there was a Chinese trading settlement on the River Tigris. The more recent story in many countries is the same: start as mostly poor labourers (plus sometimes a few wealthier traders and artisans), the labourers often referred to as "coolies", derived from the Chinese word for hard labour (苦力– ku3li4), and move onwards and upwards by sheer determination and resourcefulness. You can see this effect easily in the table above: the indentured slave replacements of Peru, the cooks and chefs of Venezuela, the often-indentured railway grunt labour of the US and Canada railroads, and the farmers and tin miners of Malaysia.

The deviations are to be found everywhere, some from forced situations and sometimes voluntarily. They are easy to see in food, cultural adaptation, and habits and sometimes include the loss of the mother tongue. Twice in my life (in New York and Calgary), I have ordered food in Chinese, and the people at the next-door table, ethnic Chinese who have never been there, have told me they wouldn't know how.

Sometimes the level of persecution is unfathomable. In percentage, not absolute numbers, the country where the Chinese Diaspora has suffered the greatest isn't even on the above list. That infamy goes to Cambodia, where the Khmer Rouge regime (1975 to 1979) reduced the numbers by more than half from a high of perhaps 425,000. Nobody knows how many perished, escaped, or blended into rural communities.

In the earlier part of the regime, the Chinese were not particularly discriminated against for being specifically Chinese, and all perceived enemies of the murderous regime were persecuted. But the Chinese were an important part of the urban middle class as business people, traders, and merchants; all activities that were a key target for elimination under Pol Pot. As an offset, the Khmer Rouge was also receiving support from the People's Republic of China. This ended in 1979 when Vietnam (with tacit Soviet support) invaded Cambodia and displaced the Khmer Rouge, and China attacked Vietnam because of this, in an often-forgotten war. Two communist countries, Vietnam and China, fighting each other is hardly something either country wants to remember. Vietnamese troops didn't leave Cambodia for another ten years, with Chinese-Vietnamese skirmishes taking place during the entire decade, and the Chinese Diaspora remained in a precarious position. Many years after Pol Pot, they could speak their language at home (mainly Cantonese), celebrate New Year, and become key functioning members of the business community and government.

A similar situation existed in Indonesia from the point of the Chinese not being particularly sought out but being in the wrong place at the wrong time. In 1965-66, Indonesia President Sukarno perpetrated a series of massacres carried out by both the conventional military and death squads. Sukarno ostensibly was purging the PKI (communists) but with many other ethnic and factional grievances appearing. Nobody knows the total death count, but 2000 ethnic Chinese out of 500,000 massacred might be reasonable.

In 2019, I was working in Indonesia, Malaysia, and Singapore. Indonesia came; first, the economic powerhouse of emerging south-east Asia with a GDP of three or four times its nearest newly-industrializing counterparts (Thailand and Malaysia – South Korea is categorized industrialized). This wealth is much diluted when measured per capita by virtue of Indonesia's large population of 276 million people, down to £2600 ($3900/head). My overwhelming first impression was how little Chinese culture was on display. There were, I think, several reasons for this. Firstly, I was working in Jakarta and Selangor, whereas much of the Chinese Diaspora is in Sumatra. As I later discovered by reading, the second reason was I found my hosts very reserved in discussions of their history and that the Chinese in Indonesia have become reasonably well assimilated.

My overriding impression of Indonesia was of a quiet, conservative, confident, and polite Muslim nation but not as religiously oppressive as I have seen in many Middle Eastern countries. However, its history is littered with atrocities such as in East Timor and West Papua. There are even areas where very non-Muslim activities occur, such as the consumption of large quantities of alcohol in that other mecca, especially to the Australians, Bali, but gambling and drugs are outlawed. Because I work in agriculture, I was impressed to see the government making efforts in this sector which is essential by population employed (one-third of the people). To overcome shortages or unwillingness of rural labour, free tractors were being handed out by the government, something I had never seen before. They weren't just two-wheeled hand-pushed machines with motors not much bigger than a hair drier, but shiny new four-wheel machines from Japan and the west. The shortages of labour were caused by urban migration and the unwillingness of the younger generation to carry out the extreme back-breaking work of manually harvesting palm oil fruits and other plantation crops in Indonesia's steamy hot climate. As one commentator told me: "the free tractors do seem to go mostly to areas where votes are to be had, but at least they are good quality". Very droll. At that time, I was close to an important site for me on this visit, the Bogor Botanical Gardens, laid out by Sir Stamford Raffles, but work commitments precluded a visit. He is a key figure in this chapter and in the history of the Chinese Diaspora.

Next came Malaysia and then, inextricably linked through history, to Singapore. What a contrast to Indonesia. I wanted to hear the story, not from textbooks, but first-hand. The first reason is that it relates to British history. The second reason was more personal. My father had been conscripted into the Royal Air Force and was sent to the Malayan Emergency as the rear gunner in a bomber in 1952-53. He was a terrible soldier/airman by his accounts, failing his jungle survival training and finally returning to the UK at less than a featherweight wracked with tuberculosis only to be saved by the then-new sulphonamide drugs. He was regularly up on misdemeanour charges, mostly reduced because of his ability as a jazz pianist honed as an underage teenager in the smoky 1950's Manchester clubs. The British forces, and maybe others, usually seem to find some use even for its malingerers. He felt fortunate he hadn't, to the best of his knowledge, personally and directly killed anyone (there was nothing in the air to shoot at) although, at a stretch, some of the bombs may have hit people. The crews mostly blew up rice fields to try and starve out the communist opposition. In his late 40's, he went back to Malaysia on a short tour as a university lecturer in Kuala Lumpur and sent letters and cassette tapes to me describing a country he grew to like a lot.

On this leg of the journey, I was assigned a Chinese Malaysian colleague as the local company affiliate knew something of my background. His English, as is common in urban Malaysia, was excellent. Our first lunch together, he took me to an area of Selangor called Taman Intan, to an open-sided and packed restaurant called Teluk Pulai Bak Kut Teh (直落普莱肉骨茶) where we ate delicious pork ribs in a rich broth. Although there were several Chinese dialects spoken, Mandarin was well understood. I felt right at home.

My colleague was proud of his Chinese heritage, celebrated the main Chinese festivals, sent his children to private Chinese run schools, and we were soon discussing everything from the Malaysian love of motor racing (F1 and motorcycles), what we did at Chinese New Year, how to preserve the Chinese identity for children and more. He was more circumspect discussing the government's attitude to the Chinese Malaysians and other minorities, and I later found out why. The private schools, for example, that he described were out of necessity, and Chinese is not taught in the public sector schools. James Chin, University of Tasmania, Australia, and Hwok-Aun Lee, University of Malaya, in related articles from 2016, describe one of the most active affirmative-action initiatives in the world. Lee explains that Article 153 of the Malaysian Federal Constitution explicitly permits reservation of civil service positions, scholarships, training, and licenses for Malays and other native groups based on their "special position". He goes on to explain, "This policy essentially aims to boost the upward mobility of the 'Bumiputera', a group comprising Malays and other indigenous groups, to increase their participation in spheres of influence and power". and continues, "This legal authorization of ethnic quotas and preferential selection, derived from racialized policies and driven by socio-political pressures, renders affirmative action a policy imperative". Chin adds, "Second, the non-Malay population, comprising mainly Chinese and Indians, were oftentimes relegated to second-class citizenship, no longer able to rely on government help or attend institutions of higher learning due to the quota system. Many non-Malay businessmen were forced to employ 'Ali Baba' tactics to survive. In such an arrangement, the business belonged on paper to Malay ('Ali') while the business was actually run by a Chinese ('Baba')". Chinese Diaspora integration seemingly has been more challenging than in Indonesia.

My second conversation was on a lengthy taxi drive. The English-speaking driver, complete with taqiyah skullcap, was in a happy, talkative mood, as it was the last day of Ramadan, and that night, the special Eid-al-Fitr feast was due. He was fascinated to know I lived in China and that I was British by birth, and he asked me if I knew much of the history of his country, just as we were passing some abandoned tin mines. I said I knew a little but wanted to hear his version. I have not deviated from his account, which paid particular attention to the British and Chinese. It was a humorous conversation accompanied by much laughter from both of us. He explained that the Portuguese and then the Dutch in Malacca had been the first colonial powers looking for trade opportunities and particularly spices. Yan Yan had seen several colonial relics (including re-constructed ships and museums) on a visit to Malacca the day before while I was working. He explained that the British left a lasting mark (from 1786 in Penang and Singapore in 1819, as I later discovered). That was how the conversation had started: the British wanted the tin from those mines and later other natural resources such as rubber and palm oil. At this point, I asked if there was still a legacy of the British and, in particular, that overriding icon of colonialism, the railway station, such as can be found in Bombay (Mumbai nowadays) and Rangoon (Yangon nowadays). He laughed and said Kuala Lumpur Station was indeed a beautiful example of such. He said he didn't think that the colonial British were particularly interested in unifying Malaysia as one country as it was divided up "by the sultans" and that they, the British, were more set on trade and reaping natural resources.

When it came to the Chinese, he said that the British were very clever, and he wasn't referring to brainpower. I got the impression it meant conniving diplomats, militarists, and wheeler-dealers and, I felt, said with a certain amount of grudging respect. "First, they supported the Chinese, then turned against them, then supported them again". In the early colonial era, the British needed manpower to gather all those rich natural resources, and Chinese labour was an integral part of that story. Particularly after the British loss of Singapore to the Japanese in 1942, they then supported the Chinese Malaysians and others in their guerrilla tactics against the Japanese. That was before doing a complete turn-around in 1948 and seeing many of them as sympathisers of the attacking Malaysian and mainland Chinese supported Communist Party (hence the previously discussed Malaya Emergency). I asked the driver about Singapore. "In the end, we wanted our own national identity and gave the Chinese to Singapore as their home". He went on to explain that many Chinese people stayed in Malaysia and they are a well-respected part of the country and community and indeed it did feel a little bit that way, even with my previous caveats on racial discrimination, with signs in simplified Chinese, Chinese language newspapers and their own schools.

Hearing history taught or self-studied from a different perspective is a passion of mine, partly because I was brought up on a "very proper" British history of Asia. Although his account is likely somewhat biased, there are some truths in it and not so easily found in western history books. For example, the British did indeed carry out a volte-face from supporting the fledgling Malaysians and especially the Chinese in counter-insurgency against the Japanese to attacking the ethnic Chinese communists, but the earlier level of support for the communist insurgents is less clear. It also seems true that the Malaysians, as part of the country we now know today, were fearful of being overrun by Chinese immigrants fleeing the Japanese invasion from 1937. The British did try and create a "Malaysian Federation", but their first attempt was the botched Malayan Union Plan (1946). The Plan did not involve consulting the general population. It included granting citizenship to any person born in Malaya in the previous ten years, regardless of race or ethnicity, i.e., including the millions of Chinese and Indians living in Malaya. You can imagine what the majority Malay population thought of that idea. It was quickly replaced in 1948 by the Federation of Malaya, which restored the rulers and sultans to their former position.

It is patently untrue that the Malaysian Federation "gave" the Chinese their Singapore home. They expelled the ethnic Chinese from the Federation to Singapore in 1965 to preserve a more ethnic (and Muslim) Malaysia and because of intra-ethnic riots and disputes. The first Singapore Premier, Lee Kuan Yew, was vehemently opposed to it. I made a mental note to try and get hold of a Malaysian secondary school history textbook as I am curious to know what is written in it.

Over the coming days, it became clear that Malaysia was heading in a different direction to much of South East Asia. Agriculture, unlike Indonesia, was an afterthought. This was a country that had two indigenous car manufacturers (Perodua and Proton), a burgeoning electronics industry, a well-educated workforce, and a vision of the future. Malaysia is fascinating, alluring, and difficult to understand.

On to the last leg of this journey was Singapore. I arrived there aggravated by two incidents. As this part of the journey was a holiday at our own expense, I had purchased my wife and me the cheapest tickets I have ever bought (£18 each) from Malindo Air for the short one-way flight. That works out at 1/10 of a penny per mile, close to my all-time cost per mile record of 1/13 of a penny on a flight from London to Dallas in a half-empty TWA plane in 2001. A few weeks later, it was no wonder TWA went bust for a third and final time. I hadn't read the Malindo Air baggage allowance, which was zero, and was told that our baggage would cost an additional £120. So, I asked what it would cost to upgrade to business class, which had a substantial free baggage allowance. It turned out that this was much cheaper overall, and we switched, only to be told afterwards that we couldn't use the upgraded tickets we had just been issued, as the business class cabin was "over-utilized". It meant we would have to go steerage after all and pay the excess baggage. At this point, the check-in attendant could see that I was unhappy and that trouble could be coming judging by the voluminous stamps in my passport. I never raised my voice, which in Asia risks getting you sent to the back of the queue or ignored, and our baggage went onboard without a fee. Duty-free sales didn't help my demeanour. Friends in Singapore had told me that alcohol was expensive, so I tried to purchase a bottle of gin, only to be told that it couldn't be sold to me as I was going from Malaysia to Singapore, but that any other destination would not be a problem. It's one example of the testy relations between these two countries, with disputes about territory, freshwater, and shipping also never far below the surface.

This was my first and long overdue visit to Singapore. I was excited because I knew I would find a thriving Chinese Diaspora as it is the only nation globally, excluding China, with a majority ethnic Chinese population. According to the 2015 General Household Survey, 74.3% are ethnically Chinese. Although I have been to several Chinatowns worldwide, such as San Francisco, Sydney, London, and New York, I was hoping this experience would be slightly different as it was in Asia. I wasn't disappointed.

A visitor should have a basic awareness of some of Singapore's peculiar rules and regulations as the fines and punishments are severe: no jaywalking, no smoking except in designated outdoor areas, no bringing in tobacco products (unless declared in the red channel), never any chewing gum including for nicotine relief, no nicotine patches, no littering, no feeding the pigeons, no spitting, fines for not flushing a public toilet, and especially no stealing a person's Wi-Fi signal. The last one carries a jail term of up to three years. I think and hope tourists will often get off with a warning for these offences. Then there are the more serious offences that can easily land you in jail: no pornography including in your computer cache, no criticizing the government, and above all, I repeat, above all, no drugs including in your system on arrival as you may be asked to pee into a bottle. 500 grammes or more of trafficked cannabis will likely get you the death sentence, or if you are fortunate, life imprisonment, and in the case of even tiny amounts of heroin and cocaine beyond personal consumption, you will be executed. Executions, by hanging, are carried out on a Friday at dawn, making your last supper a Thursday evening.

With help from Singaporean friends, I had chosen a mid-price hotel on Arab Street. My first impressions were not favourable as the electronically magnified muezzin calling at all hours from the mosque was distracting and a mediocre meal in a nearby Lebanese restaurant was outrageously expensive.

The following day was different, and we spent a few days seeing Singapore in all its glory. Even though I am used to cleanliness in some modern Asian cities (Japan and China), Singapore gleams like a well-kept Scandinavian or Swiss city. The MRT subway system is immaculate (no eating or drinking of course) and whisks you around the island in air-conditioned comfort and all the signs are in modern Chinese and English. What fascinated me were the different ethnic areas: Middle Eastern and related, Chinatown, Little India, British colonial, Marina Bay/the "Sands", and the CBD. I am sure an extensive exploration would reveal more zones. The Indian area, with its exotic fruit and vegetable stalls, Hindu temples, a street selling Indian gold jewellery and saris, and the best curry on this side of Madras (now Chennai), all made the visit there worthwhile.

The British colonial area fascinated me with the famous Raffles Hotel and a lovingly re-constructed Victorian pub, "The Penny Black" at Boat Quay, where you can quaff a pint of Old Speckled Hen or a Pimm's cocktail and eat a SGD25 (£15) plate of fish and chips or a sandwich for SGD22 (£13). That's not too bad for a city where eating out can be expensive if you want to hang out with the in-crowd such as at the trendy Scandinavian inspired Zèn Restaurant on Bukit Pasoh Road where a tasting menu dinner will set you back SGD450 (£265) and a suitable wine pairing another SGD250 (£148). Other pubs were catering for homesick Brits missing blighty, such as "The Yard" and the "Dog and Bone" on Upper East Coast Road where you can eat roast beef and Yorkshire pudding washed down with a few pints of London Pride bitter. We settled for an al fresco crab dinner near the Penny Black and watched the sun go down over one of the most spectacular urban skylines in Asia. I couldn't help wondering which watering holes Nick Leeson got blind drunk in and spewed up on a nightly basis, but I am sure they would have been trendy and expensive places. Leeson, for the unfamiliar, was the rogue derivatives trader who in 1995, "top-drawed", as British traders like me call it, enough bad contracts to cause the collapse of the UK's oldest merchant bank, Barings, with losses of £827 million and who eventually was sentenced to a six and a half year stretch in Changi Prison although he was released early on medical grounds for colon cancer, something he survived from.

After dinner, "on spec", we took the MRT (Mass Rapid Transit) to the end of the line at Harbour Front and decided to take a stroll towards the Marina Bay Sands (MBS). The walk was pleasant enough, passing by high-end apartments on quiet streets. Some of the scenes from "Crazy Rich Asians" were filmed around MBS, and I did get to see something I had hoped for: my likely first example of one of the "Crazy Rich Asians" (book and 2018 film). It was a young man practicing his acceleration skills in a roaring, no doubt adrenalin-pumping, yellow Lamborghini. There aren't many places to wind up such a car in Singapore, except when the Formula 1 street race comes to town, but the streets on this evening were deserted and he let rip.

I hate shopping and would happily devote the rest of my life to be an online shopping recluse and was especially dubious when I read the retail area was called "The Shoppes" as though soliciting an acquaintance with medieval London or York. However, the MBS is something to behold and is a world-class pleasure palace. Its architecture and engineering are brilliant. Opened in 2010, the three towers for the hotels have more than 2,600 rooms and were designed by the rightly famous Moshe Safdie to look like decks of cards. Perched horizontally (cantilevered) on top of the 57 storeys was a 2.5-acre Sky Park that looks like a giant surfboard with gardens, restaurants, three infinity pools, and magnificent views of the CBD, harbour, and ocean. A separate fourth tower was planned, which will include a 15,000-seater music venue. As well as the retail outlets and restaurants, there is a massive atrium casino (the largest in the world), with 500 gaming tables and 1,600 slot machines, two theatres, an "ArtScience" Museum, an outdoor event plaza for 10,000 people, a conference centre/exhibition hall, and 16 hectares of outdoor space mainly used as tropical gardens to stroll around.

Visionary architects like Safdie also need great engineers. Here is a conundrum for you to ponder (answer at the end of the chapter). Water is heavy, which is why most swimming pools are built close to the ground. If you add up the 1.4 million litres of water in the three infinity pools, the weight of the stainless steel structure to support the water, and the weight of the 250,000 tiles, it is something of the order of 1600 tonnes. Now, build this structure 57 floors high so that on a windy day or with variable subsidence on the towers, the integrity of the pools remains intact with no unintended spillage. How the hell do you do that?

What makes the MBS so enjoyable is there is something for everyone. A lot of it is free with excellent access for the most part to the general public, including the SkyPark, the lush gardens with magnificent views, and there is plenty of free entertainment. On that particular evening, there was the daily spectacular harbour light show and a group of young Singaporean massed drummers playing Brazilian rhythms with ferocious intensity. Thought had been given to every type of food and drink budget from inexpensive food (for Singapore) in the basement food hall. Hint:

try the Laksa: a steaming bowl of noodles and peanut sauce. Upstairs and high above are expensive gourmet restaurants featuring the signature dishes designed by famous chefs: Puck, Ramsey, Boulud, Yamamoto, Kunkel et al. It's fun to window shop the jewellery and jewel-encrusted watches and the glitterati who buy them. The sales staffs are well-trained and not sniffy, unlike an unsavoury incident I once had in Hollywood, on Rodeo Drive, when I was asked to leave a very high-end clothes shop as I obviously had no intention or the money to make a purchase. My luck was in at the casino, and my success at the blackjack tables paid for most of the holiday, even though that was only 1/100 of the price of the Chopard watch I had admired earlier.

This Diaspora had created a paradise for themselves.

"Anything you can do, I can do better", and it probably shouldn't surprise the reader by now that the City of Chongqing in Southern China employed Safdie Architects to design Raffles City, the eight tower structure of hotels, restaurants, high-end residences, retail space, and offices (no casino of course – this is China), with an even more magnificent and higher signature Safdie cantilevered platform dubbed The Crystal. The horizontal Crystal is nearly the same length/height as the Eiffel Tower. The choice of the name Raffles City, Chongqing, seemed peculiar to me. It makes sense from the viewpoint that the joint developers are the Chinese management company CapitaLand and the Singaporean company, Ascendas (who also developed the offices where I worked in Suzhou). The developers and the Chinese seem to associate the word "Raffles" with quality. There is another Raffles City in Shanghai built in 2003 with shopping and offices also managed by CapitaLand.

Sir Stamford Raffles (1781-1826) was a highly controversial British colonial figure. He is credited with founding modern Singapore by signing a treaty with Sultan Hussein Shah of Johor on February 6, 1819, although he legged it back to Penang on February 13, not to be seen back in Singapore for another four years. He left the administrative functions to the Raffles appointed Governor, Major Farquhar, a man he then proceeded to undermine for his own self-promotion for the rest of his career until Farquhar was sent home to Scotland, never to serve in office again. Farquhar did a good deal to promote Singapore as a trading port at the expense of the Dutch. Raffles died early at 44, and a great deal of his glorification goes to his wife, Lady Sofia H. Raffles, whose book, *Memoir of the Life and Public Services of Sir Thomas Stamford Raffles* became a bestseller of its time.

Before his success in Singapore, Raffles had a patchy history as a cad and a bounder. In 1812, Raffles (the appointment supported by Lord Minto), appointed his friend of six years, Alexander Hare, an even bigger cad and bounder, as EIC (East India Company) Resident of Banjarmasin and later, Commissioner of Borneo. Hare was helpful to Raffles because of his local knowledge and his linguistic abilities. The Australian, Andrew F. Smith, produced an excellent literary review with personal opinions in 2013, called *Borneo's first "White Rajah": New Light on Alexander Hare, his family and associates*, and I have used several pieces of his material.

Hare, against EIC rules, had secured some 3300 hectares (6,500 acres) as his personal fiefdom from Sultan Suleiman and was even issuing his own coinage. As Hare was short of labour in such a large territory, Raffles assisted Hare in the transportation of convicts, other "undesirables" and coerced "volunteers" from Java to Borneo to provide the slave labour force Hare needed. The EIC transportation of slaves had been made illegal in 1811, but only in EIC territory. The numbers are disputed, but a figure of around 3000 slaves is reasonable (according to James Simpson, a contemporary lawyer in a later inquiry into the matter and discussed by Smith). Particular attention was paid to supplying women for Hare's harem, which was probably several hundred in number. Smith, in my opinion, is rather genteel about the events: "Nevertheless, the steps taken with Raffle's agreement for the supply of young women for Moluko are certainly unpleasant". In the modern world, this would have made Raffles eligible for trial for pimping, possibly aiding and abetting slavery, and sex trafficking. The issue of slavery here is controversial. Raffles, I believe, was a devout and high-profile anti-slaver and got into seriously hot water for freeing the EIC slaves in Singapore without EIC permission. Yet, his actions outside EIC territory are not consistent.

Raffles was also responsible for the 1812 overthrow, looting, and ransacking of the Sultanate of Yogyakarta as part of an effort for the EIC and against Dutch primacy in Java. Raffles' primary mission, however, was to make money for the EIC, and in this, he failed and was relieved of his post by John Fendall in 1816.

Yogyakarta remains the precursor in Asia of that other British colonial wanton looting and destruction, that of the Beijing Old Summer Palace (圆明园 – yuan2ming2yuan2) in 1860 by High Commissioner Lord Elgin. This was not the same Lord Elgin who purloined the Elgin Marbles; that was his father, so perhaps kleptomania was a family trait. Elgin, I suppose, had some sort of excuse for retribution as a peace delegation to the emperor was gruesomely tortured and 20 people murdered, including Times journalist Thomas Bowlby. Raffles had none.

Sometimes, as a British person, it is hard to cope with this history.

The Chinese connection relating to Raffles and the branding in Chongqing seems peculiar. I can only surmise it is because the Chinese today have forgotten or chose to forget their history. On January 8, 1819, Raffles wrote to his boss, Lord Hastings of the EIC and Governor-General of India, describing his opinion of Singapore:

"There is a most excellent harbour which is even more defensible and conveniently situated for the protection of our China trade and for commanding the Straits than Rhio".

theonlinecitizen.com, Singapore, 31/1/2019

The "China trade" referred to was, of course, the export of Indian produced opium that brought China to its knees and because the EIC was severely in debt as a result of several costly wars, including against the French in the Seven Year's War (1756 to 1763). Raffles was a substantial cog in this abhorrent trade.

Yet for all this, the Raffles name is everywhere, ad nauseam, in Singapore: on statues of him, on hospitals, on schools, on the Raffles Cup at the Singapore Turf Club, etc. "Turf Club" is the polite British way of saying "racecourse" and is designed to keep up dress codes and standards, to keep out the riff-raff or send them to a working-class greyhound race as the dogs run on cinder tracks and not turf (but not available in Singapore). Think champagne and strawberries and cream, and voluptuous hats and not flat caps, pints of ale and a meat pie. Even the wire mesh at the Singapore Zoo, well worth a visit, is made by the internationally renowned Raffles Wire Mesh Company. There is even a tongue in cheek, Sir Stamford Waffles café in Singapore, where you can buy fake lobster rolls and waffles with Pandan (a leaf similar to banana but with an aromatic flavour) and Kaya ice cream (it's a sort of sweet coconut jam). Raffles did indeed start the creation of what is now a jewel, Singapore, and Lord Elgin (the son), of course, has long been discarded by Chinese historians as evil, but Singapore still has the Elgin Bridge in Singapore named after him.

Even in death, Raffles was a controversial figure and was refused burial at his local church by the vicar of St. Mary's, Hendon, Theodor

Williams. His family had profited from the slave trade in Jamaica. It is an irony that the aforementioned Raffles Wire Mesh Company at the zoo does have some provenance. One less controversial part of the Raffles legacy was his ability as a botanist and zoologist. He was the first President (in 1826) of the royal-chartered Zoological Society of London, with several species named after him, including the Olive-backed Woodpecker (*Dinopium rafflesii*) and a species of pitcher plant (*Nepenthes rafflesiana*) and one reason why I was sad not to see the botanical gardens in Bogor, Malaysia.

The fascinating part of Singapore, to me, was Chinatown. It was a peculiar mix of familiarity and deviation from the original homeland. Arriving at the MRT station, a short walk reveals the Buddha Relic Tooth Temple, which looked very Chinese. It is actually almost new, finished in 2007, but built on Tang Dynasty lines. Nearby was the covered, as is customary, Maxwell Road Hawker Centre, and the food inside was superficially Chinese. I could see and smell home favourites like Hainan Chicken Rice, fried and steamed dumplings, and congee. If the Crazy Rich Asians are getting their sustenance at Zèn, hawker centres are where good value, stick to your guts food is to be had. They are all over Singapore, and each has its ethnic twist.

At the Maxwell, I suddenly realized that this wasn't quite like back home in China. Some of the stalls still had the traditional Chinese writing, not typical in Singapore, including the one selling Hainan chicken. Food mainly was eaten with forks, although I did get chopsticks on request from my stallholder, and he enjoyed chatting away with me in Mandarin as he made me an oyster omelette. Plates were returned in-person to a washing-up vat, unlike in China, where it would be seen as taking the work of a clearer away. A walk down one of the streets revealed touristic shops selling all manner of Chinese junk. I even bought a pseudo and cheap Panama hat made of paper because the sun and heat were oppressive; one size only available and, of course, made in China. There were no pushy salespeople, and I was starting to feel disorientated by this. Then on a street corner, we stumbled upon something that is so Singaporean and could never be found in China. The stall vendor was selling a selection of fruits, including Durian Fruit, but they were uncut, and there was no smell of puke in the street after a pub crawl, no whiff of decaying rubbish at the tip, no smell at all. Yan Yan loves the taste of this fruit even more than I hate it, and she selected one. We were ushered into a thankfully cool and air-conditioned room, something akin to a fish tank as outside passers-by could watch, given a knife and plastic gloves, the latter presumably not to offend the pedestrians with any stink after our departure (Eau de Dorian is a somewhat acquired perfume) and we're left to our private tasting. It was like a wine tasting complete with street observers.

Several years ago, I saw a documentary about two specific streets in Chinatown and wanted to see them. The first was a curiosity to me. Sago Lane (硕莪巷), is a major deviation by the Chinese Diaspora because of the death houses outlawed in 1961. I have searched everywhere to see if such an equivalent exists in mainland China, even in the places where the Diaspora mostly came from, and have concluded they do not. No big surprise to me as the Chinese are superstitious about death, but in old Singapore, it was a case of needs must. Sago Lane still exists, but the death houses have long since gone. The second was Upper Chin Chew Street (Tofu Street) with its former brothels, music halls and opera houses, gambling and opium dens, shops and eateries, and especially its association with the Samsui women. There is nothing left. It is now a part of the residential and shopping Hong Lim Complex. Singapore, like in many other matters, has sanitised some of its history.

Apart from being superstitiously unacceptable, dying at home with any dignity was well-nigh impossible in the overcrowded, impoverished homes. If those close to death carried an infectious disease such as cholera, it could quickly spread into an epidemic. Poorer people, with little dignity, were therefore sent to the death houses in Sago Lane. Upstairs were dormitories for the dying. You waited, fatalistically, in your death bed, knowing on expiry of life, your corpse would be moved downstairs for internment. It's in these places that many of the Samsui women died. Their story is a brave and tragic struggle.

Samsui women (almost always single but sometimes claiming to be married so as not to be mistaken as whores), came to Singapore (and Malaya) from the 1920s to the 1940s, primarily as construction workers and escaping the deprivations of China. Post-1930, due to the 1928 Immigration Restriction Ordinance, the colonial government put severe restrictions on male immigrants but not so on women. This was the thinking:

"Under favourable conditions the vast majority of immigrants find a ready market for their labour in the Malay States under British protection.

But when trade is stagnant and the local industries (tin and rubber) are depressed, large numbers of unemployed labourers stream into Singapore and abide there in the hope of obtaining employment.

The resultant economic distress and overcrowding in insanitary conditions is a grave menace to Singapore, which, from its geographical position, is not merely a conduit pipe, but is forced to play the role of a filter bed to intercept and retain very undesirable elements".

(The Singapore Free Press and Mercantile Adviser, January 21, 1928).

The Samsui women were certainly not "undesirable elements" and met a pressing need, primarily in construction. They survived on the most meagre of rations, mainly rice, tofu, and a few vegetables so that they could send money back to family in mainland China.

They would assemble at Upper Chin Chew Street (Tofu Street) and work as low-paid day rented labourers and were easily identifiable by their red headscarves. If there was no work, there was no pay, and I am sure some work days were lost because of the inclement weather in Singapore with its violent tropical storms. Work hours were in Dickensian proportions. I felt compelled to tell this story out of admiration for the "red scarves" and the sacrifices they made for family, a very Chinese and Confucian trait. There are only a few left alive now. In a way, their legacy remains in a different way. 95% of the 9500 housekeeping staff at the MBS hotel are from mainland China, no doubt remitting money home as their predecessors did.

Did I like Singapore? In a way, yes: for its cosmopolitan vibrancy, its (especially Chinese and colonial) history, and its architectural beauty. I also suspect another, possibly similar story could be told or novel to be written about the lives of the Indians in Singapore.

Ah, the answer about my question on the infinity pools. First, you hire one of the best contractors (Natare Corp) and then pre-fabricate the lining. As their manufacturing is based in Indiana, US, hire 30 ships to bring the pieces to Singapore. Then, hoist 500 hydraulic jacks to the top of the towers and assemble the pool lining on top of the calibrated jacks, keeping the wall to within 4 mm over the entire 146 metre (478 feet) length.

Chapter 8: Following the Diaspora (Thailand, Philippines and North America)

In many ways, the most successful Chinese Diaspora in Asia is in Thailand and the Philippines, and although the journey is slightly different, the result is similar. The reason for this is because the Chinese have been so successful in integrating themselves.

For Thailand, getting royal protection and patronage and holding political sway helped the Diaspora become one of the most successful. The current Thai royal dynasty is descended from the Siamese King Rama I (1737-1709), whose father, Taskin the Great, had a Chinese father and Thai mother and actively encouraged Chinese immigration because of skilled labour shortages in his kingdom and for trade purposes. Taskin died by beheading in a coup d'état, and although his ashes are to be found in Thailand, there is an important temple dedicated to him in Shantou, Guangdong. Ten former Thai prime ministers are of at least partial Chinese descent.

This level of integration and patronage is significant because the Chinese-Thais have become influential in politics, in the military, and overwhelmingly dominant in business which in many countries could have led to violent reprisals. There have been some bumps in the road, such as discrimination during the 1930s to 50s lead by the dictator and Prime Minister Plaek Phibunsongkhram who was allied with Japan despite having some Chinese ancestry. Many Chinese commodity trading businesses were nationalised during this period.

When you go to Thailand, and if you haven't been, I highly recommend you do, it doesn't feel so "Chinese" such has been the level of integration, although Bangkok does have a large, vibrant Chinatown (Yaowarat) with signs in both languages. The "old" language, principally a dialect from Chaozhou in Guangdong Province, has been lost to the younger generations. Driving on the open highway, almost all the cars seem to be Toyota and Suzuki. In the fields, the tractors and rice harvesters are most frequently Yanmar and Kubota – Japanese machines in both cases. Japan is the biggest overseas investor in Thailand, with China currently second and rapidly catching up. Now, the mainland Chinese are buying property in Thailand as well.

Despite the large Diaspora, there aren't signs everywhere in Chinese. It takes more digging to discover the associations. Many of the Diaspora have Chinese names but identify as Thai and use their Thai names. Here is one example of a man I know of, 李建發– Li Jian Fa. Mr. Li, for daily usage, calls himself กมลศิษฐ์ทวีอภิรดีฝา – Kamolsit-Thawi Aphiradifang. He has a special number on his ID card dispensed from the King and has become completely integrated into Thai life. Although Mandarin is a complex language, I suspect Thai is as well. For those not familiar with Thai names and places, they are frequently long and difficult to write and pronounce. Try: Krungthepmahanakornamornratanakosinmahintarayutthayamahadilokp hopnopparatrajathaniburiromudomrajaniwesmahasatharnamornphim arnavatarnsathitsakkattiyavisanukamprasit (and variants), which is the official name for Bangkok. It beats anything the Welsh or New Zealander's can come up with by more than 100 syllables and try putting that, as only part of the address, on a postcard.

The Chinese had started settling in the Philippines from the ninth century onwards. They married local Filipinos (and Spanish colonizers), explaining the vast range in the earlier table (the Philippines* 1.1 to 27m). The 27 million represent this early migration, whereas the 1.1 million represent the more typical later 19th-century migration found in most countries from Fujian and Guangdong. These later migrants can still speak the languages of their homeland, such as Hokkien. They rarely intermarried. The younger offspring of this group speak English and Filipino, and rarely Chinese. As with Thailand, the business and political success of this latter group is impressive.

Outside of Asia, the Chinese Diaspora has a fascinating tale to tell. For example, one of the early destinations of the Diaspora was to South Africa and it gave support to Mahatma Gandhi in his earlier years in his struggles for equality in that country before returning to India.

I am going to concentrate on the biggest non-Asian group of the Diaspora: in the US.

I had first become interested, accidentally, in the Chinese Diaspora in the 1990s when I was working in Sacramento, California, as an expert adviser on noxious and invasive plant species. I decided to stay out of town in Auburn. It's a beautiful sleepy old city founded around 1848 with many wooden "cowboy style" buildings on the main drag. There is little obvious to suggest a Chinese influence as you munch on a chopped salad and sip a glass of delicious chilled Californian chardonnay.

On an evening walk, I discovered the beautifully sculptured statue of a gold panner at the bottom of the main road. I knew of the Californian gold rush of 1849, but I was curious to know more of the logistics behind it. Where were the panners from, and how were they fed, clothed, shaved, and provided with other basic needs which in the Wild West surely included gambling dens, houses of ill repute, etc.? The Chinese in the initial gold rush, 325 of them in 1849, were mainly used as labourers. Still, by 1870 there were over 100,000 west coast and mostly Chinese immigrants, almost all men, numbers swollen by the demand for labour on the under-construction trans-continental Union Pacific Railroad (completed 1869), in factories, and on the land. Discrimination was rife with the Page Act (1875), essentially restricting any women from immigrating. The Chinese Exclusion Act (1882, repealed 1943), with very few exceptions, also banned any Chinese immigration for ten years. Canada also enacted similar legislation with the Chinese Immigration Act (1923). Little wonder then, with such racial tensions, that Chinese labourers were picked on or even killed. In the Rock Springs Massacre in Wyoming in 1885, white miners killed 28 Chinese miners and injured another 15 of them. In the Snake River Massacre in Oregon, 1887, 34 Chinese miners were killed by seven whites on horseback, although this may be because the Chinese were carrying gold as much as because of their race. A significant portion of the press at the time blamed the Chinese. These are just two of many discriminatory events of the time. The Qing Emperor supported the anti-immigrant legislation because of labour shortages in China, and several Californian businessmen were against it because they were losing a cheap source of labour.

When the Titanic sunk in 1912, there were six Chinese survivors (of eight), all of whom were travelling in third class. It seems they didn't understand the instructions to remain in their cabins and therefore made it to the lifeboats. On arrival in New York, and no doubt traumatized, they were locked up and deported within 24 hours. After World War II, more flexible immigration policies brought about a relatively peaceful period and better integration, and it's only recently in the Trump era that anti-Asian (not just Chinese) hate crimes have increased exponentially.

By and large, the relatively small numbers of Chinese immigrants to Europe, mainly to France and the UK, fared much better than those in North America. In France, a significant community making ceramics came from Wenzhou and Zhejiang, and later refugees from Vietnam arrived. The British story is sometimes amusing, and I am not sure how true it is, but it sounds about right. There have been several waves of migration to the UK, mostly from former colonies and possessions like Hong Kong, and one occupation in the UK, as in the US, was in the Chinese laundry, probably poorly paid, requiring little skills, language, or otherwise. As the story goes, with the advent of the electric washing machine in the 1950s, the Chinese in this industry became redundant, and they switched to another occupation: cooking. The British liked the food so much that it became one of the stalwarts of their diet along with fish and chips and curry. In both France and the UK, the Chinese Diaspora is considered well integrated.

Chapter 9: Food, Glorious Food!

This section on the wonderfully exotic food of China was one of the most popular in *The Lure of the Red Dragon*. I did receive some criticism along the lines of "show us the pictures of the final dishes", which wasn't a practical possibility. One day I would like to write a recipe book with colour pictures, but it's on the backburner at the moment. If you have read my earlier book, you will have a pretty good idea of Chinese table etiquette, food hygiene, and related issues, but this basic information can be found elsewhere with a bit of diligent research. Appendix 2 provides a brief summary of the dishes I previously discussed.

Attempts at the categorization of Chinese food are complex because it is based on regional ideas, who conquered whom, religion, the importance of different tastes, and the medicinal usefulness of the food. It's helpful to have a basic understanding of the concepts, techniques, and history. It will guide you to the suitability for your palate or even dazzle your Chinese host over dinner with your newfound knowledge. I try and put Chinese food into ten boxes, although it's not a categorization I have found elsewhere. It is based on the eight traditional cuisines plus Beijing Fusion and Western Chinese Style. I have discovered categorizations of up to 58 different styles, but few would have the ability to remember them all. A second helpful categorization comes from the "five tastes" in Chinese cuisine: sweet, sour, bitter, salty, and pungent.

By the Tang and Song Dynasties (770-207BC), food was already categorized into four distinct regions, one in the north and three in the south. The region is superseded by the symbol 菜 (cai4), which here means "dish", although it is also the word for vegetables. The three southern are called 苏菜 (su1cai4) from Jiangsu Province, 粤菜 (yue4cai4) which roughly equates to modern-day Guangdong Province and Hong Kong and is sometimes called Cantonese style and 川菜 (chuan1cai4), Sichuan style. 鲁菜 (lu3cai4) in the north, from Shandong Province, makes up the quartet. It wasn't until the Qing Dynasty (1636-1912) that the full deck was identified and is a required prerequisite of knowledge, tastes, and skills for any aspiring chef in China. The new additions were Hunan (湘菜 – xiang1cai4), Fujian (闽菜 – min3cai4), Anhui (徽菜 – hui1cai4), and Zhejiang (浙菜 – zhe4cai4), all southern or central provinces. That leaves northwest China out of the categorization, and it is why I have added two new categories, Beijing Fusion and North West Style. Here is a potted version of the different styles.

Shandong (鲁菜)

Shandong is blessed with a long coastline and a cold sea (Bohai and Yellow Seas) as well as rivers, including the Yellow River, and fish is an important component of the cuisine. The famous Chinese philosopher, Confucius (551-479 BC), was a native of Shandong and he is less well known as an early foodie. In his writings, "The Analects", he offers practical culinary advice which is as valuable today as it was 2500 years ago. He concentrates on matters as the correct blending of foods and condiments to ensure a harmonious dish. He also advises eating only at mealtimes and never to excess and eating meat in moderation, and regularly consuming fresh seasonal produce. As Confucius placed family and friends at the heart of his philosophy, he also recognized the congeniality of sharing food. His views on alcohol are that it does not need to be limited but not to reach a point of confusion. It seems like the old boy might have enjoyed a tipple or two. Shandong-style food is technically very healthy, especially the flash fry technique where the ultra-high temperature oil is often discarded and braising is also used. It is lightly seasoned, often with onions and garlic (Shandong is still the centre of garlic production). Still, it then disappoints on the health front by producing thrombosis on a plate by ridiculous amounts of salt and vinegar. The effect is similar to that found in Scotland when eating a salty herring and then drinking a glass of whisky, creates a desire for more salt in a never-ending cycle. Shandong drinkers are known throughout China as heavy drinkers, especially white spirits (baiju) and beer. Any of the braised seafood dishes and chicken dishes are excellent, as are the soups, and you can always ask the chef to go light on the seasoning as Shandong dishes should always be cooked to order from the freshest ingredients. Shandong gets cold in winter, and there are always steaming wheat noodles, buns, and cornbread.

Jiangsu (苏菜)

This is the food from my home region of Jiangsu Province, and I have included Shanghai, already an important trading and fishing town by the Middle Ages. I do not include notes here on a special variation called Huai Yang, which is discussed in the section on Beijing Fusion and is the most refined food from this region, and of all China. It's a region of natural abundance with a long coastline and a myriad of lakes, rivers, and man-made fishponds. It has plentiful rainfall, and it's warm enough to double crop, to grow one crop of wheat and one crop of rice in the same field each year. Although there are many variations in the styles of cooking in this culinary region, to my mind, the thing that binds them together is the variety and freshness of the produce and especially the sauces and crystal clear consommés which can rival the French ones in their unctuousness and depth of flavours. The only disappointment is that some of the sauces are quite sweet, especially in Shanghai, but it is a minor criticism. Jiangsu style cooking is all about preserving the flavours and balancing them, and making sauces, so flash frying is less common and braising, steaming and stewing have more prominence.

Well worth searching for is "Lion's Head" which are giant braised pork meatballs in brown sauce (狮子头 – shi1zitou2), Jinling Salted

Dried Duck, a speciality of Nanjing (盐水鸭–yan2shui3ya1) which is good plain cooked or with a ginger and spring onion sauce, the rather prosaic "Farwell my Concubine" (霸王别姬-(ba4wang2bie2jie1): soft-shell turtle in a mushroom and wine sauce, and sweet and sour Mandarin Fish in a squirrel shape (there is no squirrel in it – it squeaks like a squirrel when after cooking the hot sauce is poured on it (松鼠桂鱼 song1shu3gui4yu2). Seasonality brings new and delicious produce to the markets, such as the much-prized and expensive sweet hairy crabs (大闸蟹 – da4zha4xie4) caught in Yangcheng Lake close to home in September and October. Although considered a lake crab, they behave more like salmon, only breeding in the ocean and returning to the inland lakes to spawn. They are traditionally served with dark vinegar and ginger dipping sauce. For those with a sweeter tooth, sticky rice and lotus root served with fragrant and fresh Osmanthus flower sauce is a summer and autumn delight. I have lost count of the number of available fruits, nuts, and vegetables for carnivores and vegetarians alike, but it must be several hundred.

Cantonese (粤菜)

The Cantonese food from Guangdong, Hong Kong, and partly Macau is one of the most well known in the west because of the modern history of early trade concessions, particularly to the British, and subsequent migration. It is the stuff of many a western TV dinner. Those stalwarts of the takeaway: sweet and sour pork with fried rice, Chow Mein, and spare ribs with a hideous red coating all have their origins in this region, although they are often cheap, greasy, and unrecognisable from their roots. Cantonese food should never be greasy. It uses very modest amounts of seasoning and sugar and is seldom spicy. The Cantonese takeaway menu might well have the fiery and spicy Kung Pao Chicken, but that is to suit the western palate and stop desertions to the curry houses. This dish is from Sichuan. Cantonese food is often described as bland, but this belies its purpose: to bring out the flavours of the produce. All the main cooking methods are used, but stir-frying is widespread, and the major sauces such as Hoisin and oyster sauce can be found in almost every western supermarket. Long before I had ever visited China, I ordered the dish of the day at a Cantonese restaurant in San Francisco only to discover it was snake. Cantonese cuisine uses just about everything that moves or breathes, so be careful what you are ordering. With this sole proviso, I have found Cantonese food an excellent choice for people who don't think they like "Chinese" or spicy food. I have some friends like this and took them for a weekend Cantonese brunch. Brunch is popular in this cuisine, and I chose a classic to start (点心 – dian3xin1 in Mandarin, dim sum in Cantonese), those tasty dumplings filled with shrimp or beef, and often vegetables, served in bamboo steamers. I included (肠粉– chang-2fen3 in Mandarin, cheung fan in Cantonese) which are rice dumplings with similar fillings but wrapped up in a thin and slightly sticky crêpe. I followed this up with roasted duck (叉燒 – cha1shao1 – in Mandarin, char siu in Cantonese), also the name for smoky barbequed roasted meat of any type, with a side of plum sauce. I finished up by appealing to the western sweet taste, and Cantonese food is good for this, with some steamed buns with oozing sweet milk custard inside (奶黃包– nai-3huang2bao1 in Mandarin, nai wong bao in Cantonese). The pickled diced radish, a personal favourite (菜脯– cai4pu2 in Mandarin, guai shu in Cantonese) even rated as agreeable. The result: "this is bloody delicious". The only let down was there was no coffee with brunch, and dim sum has a long association with tea drinking, but there was a coffee house downstairs for a takeaway to carry upstairs.

Cantonese style with its vast array of seafood and crustacean dishes, its availability outside China (the dim sum in Sydney, Australia are legendary), and the availability worldwide of many ingredients, plus the often-straightforward cooking techniques are suitable for the aspiring home chef as well.

Although a bit of a misfit within this cuisine group is the food from Macao with its Portuguese and other Asian and African influences. Try Galinha à Portuguesa (葡国鸡 – pu2guo2ji1 in Mandarin, po kok gai in Cantonese), chicken in a mild yellow coconut-infused curry with lemon, olives, and chorizo).

Sichuan (鲁菜)

The colour of Sichuan is red, at least when it comes to the food. It's exceptionally spicy, and asking for "not spicy" in a restaurant (不辣 – bu4la2) will help but not save you from burning lips, sweating, and a later bum burning. It starts at breakfast with red noodles and progresses throughout the day with more lashings of the red stuff. Once you have got used to it, it becomes addictive.

In the southern and inland provinces of Sichuan and Hunan, the food gets much hotter and spicier. Sichuan food is unique in China because of the use of one ingredient, the seeds of the prickly ash tree, which is also used in Indonesian, northern Indian, and Nepalese cooking. These seeds create a curious numbing effect on the mouth and lips (麻 辣 – ma2la4), a little like a spicy equivalent of the American Pop Rock candy. Add to this fiery hot chillies, which were introduced to the region about 300 years ago, and you have an explosive mix. The most famous dishes using this base are the Sichuan hotpots which are popular all over China. This consists of soup or broth such as chicken, although there are many variants, with the spicy ingredients added. It then bubbles away at the table on an adjustable electric ring while the chosen ingredients are added and cooked. The choice is extensive, but some of my favourites are thin strips of lamb, fish balls, Enoki mushrooms, hard tofu, taro root balls, and shrimp. Any type of cabbage cooked in the broth tastes terrific. A table of ingredients to make your own dipping sauce mixture usually is to hand. Garlic, green onions, creamy peanut sauce, ginger, and salty fish

XO Sauce are commonplace. A couple of tips: Sichuan hotpot is oily and too spicy for some. If you ask, many establishments have a divider to split the pot in half. You can put a less intense or less oily broth in one half or use it with a mushroom or similar broth for cooking only vegetables. The prickly ash seeds are also used in oils in a wide variety of dishes, including beef and rabbit. Another variation is Sichuan's spicy equivalent of Spaghetti Bolognese called ants climbing up a tree (蚂蚁上树 – ma3yi3shang4shu4). The ants are tiny balls of pork, and the glass noodles are the twigs on the trees.

Hunanese (湘菜)

Hunan cuisine is one of the Qing Dynasty additions. Staying in the south and landlocked, if you like a fiery hot Indian Vindaloo or Phaal curry, you are going to feel right at home. The neighbouring food from Guizhou Province is, if anything, even spicier. The key ingredient of this cuisine is fresh chillies and lots of them, and rice to accompany. There is even a well-known old song and, more recently, a caricature video of pretty and slightly provocative young Hunanese young ladies eating chillies. A girl allegedly sings to her lover:

辣妹子
辣妹子辣
辣妹子辣妹子辣辣辣
辣妹子长大不怕辣
吊一串辣椒碰嘴巴
辣妹子辣
抓一把辣椒会说话
Hot spicy girl
Sassy young girl
Spicy and sassy, hot, hot hot!
Fearless when growing up

Hang up some chillies and touch my mouth
Sassy young girl
Let's grab a chilli and talk.

There is little respite. Even the sugary version of the flower bun (花捲 – hua1juan3) often eaten at breakfast time is packed with chillies in Hunan. Signature dishes of the province include pulled pork with fresh green sweet/bell peppers (青椒肉丝– qing1jiao1rou4si1). Hunan people also ferment foods to enhance flavour and texture in dishes such as fermented black beans with pork ribs (豉汁排骨-chi3zhi1pai2gu3), along with, you guessed it, a liberal quantity of chillies.

Fujian (闽菜)

Back on the southern coastline is Fujian, a well-known culinary style in the west from migration to Taiwan and to a wide-dispersed Diaspora. If you like Japanese food and would like to try an exciting alternative, this is your go-to style, although raw fish is not used. I think most South Americans, Spanish and Portuguese would also like this style and especially with the accompaniment of the speciality fermented red rice (koji – べにこうじ in Japanese, 红曲米– hong2qu1mi3 in Chinese). The food has a Japanese taste of umami (うま味 in Japanese, 鲜味 – xian1wei4 in Chinese), classy soups, a multitude of seafood dishes and even like Japan, chefs with dazzling knife skills. There is certain healthiness from much-reduced stir-frying and a heavier dependence on stewing, braising and steaming. Saltiness often comes from healthier fermented fish sauce rather than table salt, and spicing is subtle. Rice wine in cooking (like dry sherry) also pleasantly enhances many dishes. Food is frequently served with dipping sauces, allowing a novice to learn what is desirable. Fujian also has a mountainous interior, and wild fungi and bamboo often supplement fish, poultry, and pork.

Here are two stand-out Fujian dishes of many. Jumping Monk Soup or Buddha Jumps Over the Wall (佛跳墙– fo2tiao4qiang) is a sumptuous dish. The name relates to a story of a monk, a vegetarian by faith, who walks past a house and smelled such a delicious aroma that he jumps over a wall to eat some of it. When caught, he explains that even the Buddha would have jumped the wall to eat it. The base of this thirty-plus ingredient one-pot dish is a soup made from hours of simmering of a stock of black chicken or duck, pork or ham with rice wine, and sometimes brandy. Next, come vegetables such as mushrooms and bamboo. The top layer is reserved for the showy and expensive items that can be seen when the lid is taken off the pot, and usually is seafood such as sea cucumber, fish maw, abalone, scallops, and shark's fin. A sumptuous version can take three days to make. The second dish is a "skin" of finely minced pork mixed with sticky rice and starch (燕皮– yan4pi2) which has been compared to Japanese surimi. The skins are then used to make wontons (肉燕-rou4yan4) and can be eaten as they are, or added to a celebration soup (太平燕 – tai4ping2yan4).

Anhui (徽菜)

Anhui is the home of big mountains and food legends. What on earth could be the culinary connection between Aveyron, France, and Huangshan, Anhui, China? The answer relates to exceedingly smelly and mouldy food that was discovered by accident. In French legend, a young man was eating his lunch of bread and cheese in a cave when a beautiful maiden passed by. He abandoned his food and went after her, and only when he returned months later, he discovered mouldy and delicious Roquefort cheese had been created. The Chinese legend has a Qing Dynasty scholar from Anhui, Wang Zhihe (王致和), who went to Beijing and, after failing the imperial examination, became a tofu salesman. He wasn't very successful, and one day he chopped up his unsold stock and placed it in an earthen jar. A few days later, he opened the jar to find the tofu had fermented and developed a green mould and was very smelly. To his surprise, the taste was delicious, and this stinky tofu (臭豆腐– chou4do4fu1) even became a favourite of the Qing imperial court. If, like me, you love Roquefort, Blue Stilton, Gorgonzola, and others, you will love stinky tofu. For the rest, better learn the Chinese words to avoid distress. It is not used in many Anhui complete dishes and is preferred as a snack food.

Anhui, as a mountainous inland province, draws on a wide variety of ingredients found in the wild: foraged herbs (often dual-purpose edible and medicinal), fungi, bamboo shoots, nuts and berries, tea leaves, dates, poultry, freshwater fish (wild and farmed) and even wild boar feature prominently. These ingredients are often incorporated into hearty stews or served slightly sweetened or with very oily and sticky sauces. I think outdoor types and sportspeople might find this food tasty. Another disputed legend is that the common American and Canadian dish, chop suey, came to the west via Anhui. When the Qing diplomat and militarist, Li Hongzhang, visited the US in 1896, he hosted a dinner for his American counterparts. Perhaps worried about rumours of Americans' huge appetites, he instructed his three travelling cooks to create a substantial fusion dish using up everything in the kitchen, and this became the popular restaurant dish, chop suey. Whether true or not, there is plenty of historical evidence that after the national spread of this dish, the migrant Chinese working in the US at the time wouldn't eat this non-authentic restaurant dish, and I can hardly blame them.

If you can find it, the epitome of Anhui dishes is first-grade hotpot (一品锅 – yi1pin3guo1) which isn't a traditional hotpot as it is cooked away from the table and is really a combination of a stew and pie. It follows strict rules based on ancient precepts and Chinese medicine. The bottom layer needs to be healthy veggies such as bitter winter melon, carrots, bamboo shoots, and turnip. Next comes a layer of seasonal meat, but wild boar or duck would be a good choice for genuine authenticity. Then comes a fish layer, again whatever is seasonal, and can include seafood. Next is the fungi, and Anhui excels in this as it has a wild shitake mushroom (香菇– xiang1gu1). The pie "crust" is tofu puffs or similar. A final garnish is a green herb or vegetable. Also worth seeking out is Yellow Mountain sausage (黄山香肠 – huang2shan1xiang1chang2) cooked with bamboo shoots and dried mushrooms which produces a fragrant chunky soup, or for the more adventurous steamed stone frog (清蒸石蛙– qing1zheng1shi2wa1).

Zhejiang (浙菜)

Prosperous Zhejiang is the "Bordeaux of China". Like Fujian next door, if you like Japanese food, it's a good cuisine choice, and its abundant seafood is eaten both lightly cooked and sometimes raw. It's also famous for its Shaoxing rice wine that is readily available worldwide and tastes like sherry and is almost as indispensable as soya sauce in Chinese cuisine. The Chinese name for this sherry is yellow wine (黄酒 – huang2jiu3). Finer vintages are prized, and like wine from grapes, it has different levels of sweetness and age. Zhejiang is also famous for some of the best green tea in China, Dragon Well Tea (龙井茶– long2jing3cha2) grown close to quite possibly China's most beautiful city, Hangzhou (Han), although my home city of Suzhou (Su) in Jiangsu Province competes. The natives of both provinces know the phrase, 上有天堂, 下有苏杭 which translates to something like, "above is heaven but below is Su-Han". The coastal areas use abundant seafood, but Zhejiang's inland capital, Hangzhou, not too far from the coast, also uses plenty of it.

The inland areas use lake fish, and poultry and one of the most famous dishes is the 1000-year-old Beggar's Chicken (叫化鸡– jiao4hu-a4ji1). There are many legends about this dish and several with imperial origins. The one I prefer is a beggar, who stole a chicken from a farm, and lacking a cooking pot, wrapped it in lotus leaves and clay and put it in a wood-burning hole in the ground, buried to cook for six hours. Another inland Hangzhou dish is West Lake Grass Carp in Vinegar Gravy (西湖 醋鱼– xi1hu2cu4yu2) which traditionally uses no salt as this lake fish is already salty. There's something profoundly satisfying about dining al fresco on a warm spring or autumn day on the highest terrace of several ancient restaurants surrounding the stunning Hangzhou West Lake and eating these sumptuous dishes washed down with a medium-dry sherry or a local tea. A gentle stroll on paths and over ancient bridges around the lake is the perfect conclusion to a memorable day.

One part of Zhejiang has gone in its own direction for centuries, namely the "sweet and salty" port city of Ningbo. Here brining of sea-food and vegetables is widespread and no more so than in the Ningbo (Raw) Salty Crab (宁波咸膏蟹– ning2bo1xian2gao1xie4). After brining, the crab roe creates a pretty orange sauce. Two other signature dishes are steamed turtle in crystal sugar soup (冰糖甲鱼 – bing1tang2jia3yu2) and Yellow Croaker Fish in Preserved Cabbage and Bamboo Shoots in a Sherry Sauce (雪菜大黄鱼– xue3cai4da4huang2yu2), which is a good choice for those that don't like many bones in their fish. Ningbo residents also enjoy confectionary and none more so than Sweet and Sticky Ningbo Rice Balls (宁波年糕– ning2bo1nian2gao1), traditionally stuffed with black sesame or red bean paste.

Beijing Fusion

Technically, Beijing is part of the Shandong style of cuisine, although the city doesn't quite have a border with this province to its east. The four provinces to the north of Beijing, namely Inner Mongolia, Liaoning, Jilin, and Heilongjiang, don't get a separate culinary categorization, probably because they have not always been part of China and because they have also been influenced over the centuries by Beijing Fusion and Shandong style. Go to a fish restaurant in the port city of Dalian in the northern Province of Liaoning, select your live seafood, and the cooking style is often Shandong Style. Go to the border city of Dandong in the same province, and the food is heavily influenced by Korean cuisine.

Although Beijing is ancient, it changed hands (and name) many times before the Yuan Dynasty (1271-1368), the Ming and Qing Dynasties (1368 to 1911), and the Republic of China (1911-1928) made it their capital. There is the first bit of Beijing Fusion because the Muslim Yuan Dynasty was Mongolian and descended from Genghis Khan, more used to mutton hotpots and hearty meat noodle soups on the go on horseback as they conquered a good slug of the known world. You can make a note of the following or point at these words: 清真菜館 (qing1zhen-1cai4guan3) or Muslim (halal) restaurant. No pork served. The Yuan influence is easily seen to this day in the delicious lamb kebab street stalls.

The second part of the fusion is that a subdivision of Jiangsu 苏菜 (su1cai4) cuisine is called Huai Yang (淮揚) and has nothing in common with the salty food of Shandong. Huai Yang is named after the Huai and Yangtze rivers and is considered the most refined cuisine in China. Chinese food presentation isn't the best compared to the elaborate Thai and Japanese styles and often has more than one meat or fish dumped in the same pot or plate. Huai Yang is the opposite. It typically glorifies one featured ingredient in an elegant presentation. A good example is the Qing Wensi Tofu (文思豆腐), a soup made of soft tofu, dried day lily, black fungus, mushrooms, and bamboos shoots. Presentation is vital, and a single block of tofu must be cut into a seemingly impossible 5000 tiny shreds. The emperors knew this and "volunteered" (better than losing your head for insubordination) the best Huai Yang chefs to serve at the imperial court in Beijing. Even the Peking ducks, enjoyed on the imperial table since the Yuan Dynasty, are a species from Nanjing in Jiangsu Province.

If dishes like Wensi Tofu sound healthy, they are. The imperial physicians, chefs, and advisers were charged with using the finest ingredients and healthy ones and sometimes rooted in traditional medicinal ingredients. The near-immortal emperor had to be protected. This is in marked contrast to the leadership, royal or otherwise, who became globular and spherical, which likely often contributed to their death (Emperor of the Carolingian Empire, King George IV of England, Chancellor Helmut Kohl of Germany, King Eglon of Moab, President Idi Amin of Uganda, etc.) and in some cases died as a result of overeating at a single meal (King Adolf Frederick of Sweden and maybe King Henry 1 of England). The record of longevity of some of the Chinese emperors, especially for their era, is impressive: The Qianlong Emperor (18th Century-87 years), Emperor Wu of Liang (5th Century-85 years), Emperor Zong Li Ren Xiao (12th Century – 69 years) are such, but the most incredible era for longevity is Emperor Wu of the Han Dynasty (2nd Century BC – 69 years). If you look at Chinese imperial portraits, don't be fooled by the bulging yellow gowns but instead look at the often-slender faces, although the Yongle Emperor (1360-1424) does look a bit tubby but still had a long time in this world. In Europe, few can compete with this record of longevity, although Louis XIV at 77 and Queen Victoria at 82 are noteworthy, and Queen Elizabeth II is going to smash all records out of the park. There are also a few Middle Eastern and Asian Monarchs in history with decent levels of longevity.

By the Ming Dynasty and into the Qing Dynasty, meals were still sumptuous with more than 100 dishes for a state banquet, but red meat had become a much less important part of the imperial table replaced by fish and poultry. Even the world-famous imperial dish Peking Duck (北京烤鸭– bei3jing1kao3ya1) produced from the Imperial Kitchens (there were two) uses a healthy technique of roasting in a hanging oven. One word of warning, though: it is little known many of the ducks are force-fed towards the end of their lives and if this offends, better choose something else.

It's still possible to taste the imperial foods in Beijing but be prepared to be disappointed as a foreigner if gastronomy is your interest. Some of the themed and costly (think hundreds or even thousands of RMB if you desire), imperial restaurants have spectacular settings and non-more so than Fang Shan (仿膳) Restaurant in Beihai Park. The food will probably be as authentic as you can get, but it may well not satisfy modern taste buds. Many of these restaurants only offer a tasting menu of typically eight to fifteen courses. Some famous imperial restaurants aren't even offering much authenticity at all. There are some things you can do to mitigate, including choosing the more expensive a la carte to try something you know you like rather than discovering a few hidden gems, finding a restaurant that offers a group tasting menu to defray costs, or do a bit of research to find restaurants that incorporate some authentic imperial dishes. The opposite goes for a Peking Duck meal, and the best establishments are genuine, authentic, and affordable. My favourite is Quanjude (全聚德) in Qianmen, established in 1864, which can definitely claim authenticity as the original head chef was a retiree from the Imperial Kitchen. I also ought to mention Xianyukou Bianyifang.

(鲜鱼口便宜坊), established in 1855, also in Qianmen, but with origins 600 years old. There are plenty of other good duck restaurants, but beware of those masquerading as the real deal and go to one with provenance and be ready to queue and share large tables (rectangular or circular) with others and enjoy the bonhomie.

Many of the centuries-old beliefs of eating seasonal and medicinal produce abound today. For example, at our home in winter, we eat Chinese radish to protect the lungs, and in summer, bitter melon and ginger, both of which cool down and detoxifies the body (ginger only in the morning). It's a complicated subject, but fortunately, there is a valuable rule of thumb for vegetables and pulses: white ones are for the lungs, purple and black ones for the kidney, and red ones for the heart.

There are some foods that Beijingers consider their non-imperial own, and often they are street or fast foods such as at Qingfeng Steamed Bun Restaurant (庆丰包子铺), a popular chain where, in December 2013, a well-known resident of Beijing, stood in line and paid cash for steamed buns, fried pork liver, and mustard greens and chatted with the astonished locals. It was President Xi and with virtually no security. It's the equivalent of an American president wandering from Pennsylvania Avenue to order a Chick-fil-A. I was a little surprised he paid cash and wondered if he has an Alipay account?

Western Chinese Style

The Qing Dynasty classifications of eight culinary techniques exclude the west of China, probably because the categorisation is essentially a Han Chinese invention. The vast mountains and deserts of the most westerly region, now predominantly Xinjiang Province, wasn't finally conquered by the Qing Dynasty until 1759 after one of the most comprehensive genocides in history, with the almost complete destruction of the nomadic Tibetan Buddhist tribes of Dzungaria. It was carried out by a Manchu army and Uighur Muslim allies under the Qianlong Emperor (1735-1796). After 1759, the area was settled by a mixture of Han Chinese, Hui and Uighur Muslims, and other colonist farmers. The second large area of the west is Tibet. Even to this day, it is an impoverished mountainous region, and food is simple: barbequed meat such as yak and mutton, sweet tea, yak butter, and tsampa (糌粑– zan1ba1): roasted mountain barley flour used in tea and gruel. The food is suitable for the high-altitude, calorie demanding, Himalayan lifestyle, and some of the curries with their Nepali and Indian origins are tasty, but it is limited in scope.

The food of Xinjiang is the best-known food of the west. It is radically different from any other found in the rest of China and heavily influenced by culinary techniques coming down the ancient Silk Road from Persia, Arabia, Turkey, and beyond. It's easily recognizable to most foreigners by its Turkish-style kebabs, naan bread, pilaf lamb, and rice dishes with dried fruit and vegetables, and it's popular all over China. It's easy to find the restaurants. Look for Arabic style script (it's not actually Arabic but a Turkic language) and pictures of camels, Islamic art, and men with elaborate costumes and large swirly moustaches carrying the signature dish, "big chicken plate" (大盘鸡 – da4pan2ji1), a classic Hui dish with potatoes, carrots, peppers, and noodles. Both wheat and rice are eaten in Xinjiang, but wheat predominates because of its use in bread and noodles. With the Qing colonization and the growth of sedentary agriculture, and the more recent use of irrigation in the arid climate, an extensive array of fruits, spices, and vegetables are available and used such as Hami melons, Turpan grapes (fresh and dried), pears dates, apricots, tomatoes, aubergines, cucumbers, as well as all the spices you would find in a Middle East bazaar. In recent years, dry dairy farming has also become important.

Some dishes are spicy, but there is usually fresh pomegranate juice, rice pudding, or soothing yoghurt to hand. You won't find wine or beer on offer in every restaurant, although this region does export wine and alcohol is readily available, and no pork dishes and halal prepared meat are the norm. The inhabitants also have a comparatively sweet tooth, and no better example is the street food, Matang (麻 糖– ma2tang2), a chewy concoction of fruits and nuts like a superior granola bar.

The remainder of the western region is in Shaanxi and Gansu Provinces. Many visitors who got to Xi'an to see the Terracotta Warriors will encounter both Xinjiang and Shaanxi food. If you find yourself in Xi'an, you may discover signs for noodle houses pronounced biang2biang2mian4, written something like this, as there are several variations:

The name "biang biang" is onomatopoeia and comes from the sound the thick wheat noodles make as they are stretched and banged on the table. When Chinese people see this sign, they smile as these are considered the most complicated symbols in the language, and the first two symbols have up to 62 strokes each and would take some considerable time to write. They are not real symbols; although each component is, hence the smiles, and there is an interesting story behind this. Once upon a time in Xi'an, a hungry student heard people in a noodle house shouting "biang biang". After chasing down the noise and ordering, he realized he had no money on him. Thinking quickly, the student asked the chef if he knew how to write the symbols, and he said he did not. The student grabbed some paper and wrote out the symbols we know today. After spontaneous applause by the clients, the chef gave the student his meal for free. History does not tell if he was an art student, but it beats washing the dishes. Another famous hand-pulled noodle in beef broth from the west comes from Gansu Province called Lanzhou Spicy Noodles (兰州拉面– lan2zhou1la1mian4). Lovers of Vietnamese food should seek this one out at it is similar to phở bò, although there is no known connection between the two.

New Discoveries

On top of the dishes in Appendix 2, taken from *The Lure of the Red Dragon*, I have had the opportunity to explore some new and exciting foods.

<u>Restaurant Dishes</u>

- Lao Wang Hot Pot (捞王). Region: All of China in big cities. I'm not generally in the business of promoting individual enterprises, but this medium-sized chain is unique, with 80 establishments worldwide. This Shanghai business has a unique proposition, and 捞– lao1 means to dredge up, which is appropriate. It's a hot pot with an accoutrement table similar to all hot pot establishments but after that has little in common. There are various base broths, but the famous one is with ground white pepper, chicken, slightly chewy pork stomach and mushrooms. The base stock is filled up from giant black urns with spouts as often as is necessary, but I have never been able to get the secret recipe. There is a little bit of etiquette to the order of the subsequent additions to the broth; first the chosen meat and then the vegetables. It seems the savoury doughnuts can be eaten pretty much at any stage. This food is sensational.

- Braised and Caramelised Pork Hock (猪蹄膀–zhu1ti2pang2). Region: All of China. This dish is popular at celebrations, and there is a reason why. The hock can easily weigh in at over 3 kilogrammes and needs a large number of people to consume it, although it can be reheated in the boiling liquor. It's the perfect dish for homesick Germans and others and much better than the anaemic Schweinshaxe at the local Meister Bräu. The marinade is usually a mixture of black or sometimes rock sugar, dark soya sauce, black bean paste, garlic, ginger, sherry, black pepper, star anise, and vegetables and mushrooms. Cooking time is a simmer of four to eight hours, depending on the size of the hock.

- Korean Style Barbeque. Region: All of China. Of course, originally from Korea, but it is so popular that it has been adopted.

The restaurants are easily identifiable by Korean writing with its ellipses and straight lines (한식당) or by greeters wearing silk powder blue and pink dresses. The setup is different from Chinese styles, using a table with a sunken middle with searing hot coals under a cooking rack. In many cases, little dishes of pickles, often free, are served while you wait for the main event, and there are usually five or six dipping sauces available for the barbequed food and lettuce to make a wrap. It's a good idea to supplement the barbequed food with something more filling, such as rice or pancakes.

- Hainan Chicken Rice (海南鸡 – hai3nan2ji1). Region: All over China and Singapore, Malaysia and Indonesia, and other areas of the Diaspora. This dish originates from Hainan Island, the only tropical part of China. The semi-organic Wenchang chickens are fed on a diet of shredded coconut, peanut meal, cooked rice, bran, seeds, and caltrop and is China's equivalent of the French Poulet de Bresse. The chicken is poached and then put into iced water to get the perfect tenderness, and the rice is cooked in the poaching broth and chicken fat. Typically, there are three small dipping sauces to accompany the dish of chilli, garlic, and sweet dark soya sauce.

- Tea Smoked Duck (樟茶鸭– zhang1cha2 ya1) with Crescent Buns (割包 – gua4bao1). Region: Sichuan and hard to find elsewhere. It is a complex gourmet dish worth seeking out. The duck is marinated in, amongst others, a rub of Sichuan pepper, strong alcohol, garlic, ginger, camphor leaves, and salt, then blanched and dried and smoked in fermented (black) tea, then steamed and finally fried to get a crispy skin. The duck is served inside the buns. This is one Chinese dish that deserves a full-bodied red wine to accompany it.

- Shredded Meats (肉丝– rou2si1). Region: All of China. The meaning is silken meat and equates to pulled meats cooked in soy-based and often glutinous sauce. There are many types, such as Sichuan shredded chicken or a Beijing variation as a street food wrap with pork and leeks. Still, my favourite is what I like to think of as poor man's Peking Duck because it is pulled pork with all the other additions: pancakes to make the wrap, spring onions, cucumber, and sweet bean sauce. It is delicious and very affordable, and I always order double and bring some home in a takeaway box.

- Cold Noodle Dish (凉皮 – liang2pi2). Region: Xinjiang and Shaanxi. The noodles are generally made from wheat flour. The dough is soaked for up to a day, and the milky water, which is mostly starch, is then discarded to leave a cold skin (the meaning of liangpi) of mostly gluten. Then it is boiled and then chopped into long rectangular noodles as the basis of the cold dish. Vegetarian ingredients are now added depending on the different recipes and include chilli oil, vinegar, sesame paste, cucumber, bamboo shoots, peanuts, garlic, coriander, tofu, etc. It's a perfect dish for a hot summer day and has a similar cooling effect to Spanish gazpacho cold soup.

- Clay Pot Rice (煲仔饭 – bao1zai3fan4) with Lap Cheong and Pork Belly. Region: Hong Kong (and Guangzhou) but there are many other variations. Just as with the moon cakes in Chapter 6, Hong Kong beats out the competition for deadly and addictive deliciousness, and this dish should come with a health warning on the bowl. It's a clay pot dish where the lid should only be opened to add new ingredients and whose origins are 2000 years old. The combination of sweetened smoked sausage (腊

肠 – la4chang2 in Mandarin, lap cheung in Cantonese) and fatty cured pork belly and sometimes a few greens is delicious. The rice on the edges and bottom is the best part and is sticky brown and crispy, just as in the rice pudding your grandma made. The problem is that per serving, it is over 4000 calories and 685% of the daily saturated fat allowance, 176% of the cholesterol, and 68% of sodium, based on a 2000-calorie diet.

- Buddha's Delight (罗汉全斋 – luo2han4quan2zhai1). Region: All of China, but the origins may well be Indian. As the name suggests, this dish is vegetarian, and quan zhai means entirely of vegetables, and traditionally eggs and dairy products are not allowed. It is common as a vegetarian dish in general restaurants. In many Buddhist monasteries in China, it is available for a few coins or sometimes free, and served as a refectory meal in the monastery. There are different versions, but the one I describe traditionally has 18 different vegetables and fungi, which are stir-fried in oil and then a sauce of pickled tofu, soya sauce, ginger, vegetarian oyster sauce, and sugar, but there are many other combinations. The noodles in the dish are made from glass noodles which are starch-based from beans or potatoes. It's a hearty and healthy dish but beware as even monks like a soupcon of MSG.

- Sliced Mutton in Aspic Jelly (羊肉冻/羊肉膏 – yang2rou4dong4/ gao1). Region: All of China. This is a food that is brought home, often after having waited in a long line to buy it and have it cut by the vendor into wafer-thin slices. It can sometimes be found in restaurants as a cold appetizer. It is also found in restaurants. I once fed it to an Italian delegation that then started waving their hands in excitement at this gelatinous treat.

Street Foods (and Drinks)

I classify street food as food and drink from stalls, street vendors, snacks, and establishments too simple or small to be called restaurants. The Chinese are inveterate snackers and consumers of street food.

- Little Fat Sheep (小肥羊– xiao3fei2yang2). Region: Inner Mongolia and elsewhere. This is one of those dishes often found in "hole in the wall" establishments, perhaps with a few low-lying plastic stools and chairs outside and not to be confused with the 450 strong restaurant chain Little Sheep Hotpot. The authentic item is a lamb stew with noodles, vegetables, mushrooms, goji berries, ginger, etc., and is aromatic and never spicy.

- Bubble Tea (珍珠奶茶– zhen1zhu1nai3cha2). Region: Taiwan but found all over China and especially in malls. The fruit juice and tea blends also have bubbles, also called pearls or boba, and are tapioca balls that sink to the bottom of the plastic cup, and usually, the cup is sealed with cellophane with a straw provided to pierce it so you can shake up and blend the ingredients. Some bubble tea doesn't even have tea in at all. After that, the variations are enormous. I like a tea-based concoction with mangoes and whipped cream on the top.

- Breakfast Noodles. Region: All of China. Although noodles are eaten day round, they are particularly associated with breakfast. They are consumed in millions of small eateries with just a few tables, and the turnover is rapid. It's not polite to linger: slurp and be gone. If you don't like the dishes on offer, so long as one person is eating them, it's perfectly acceptable to bring in food from elsewhere, but do be prepared to get a little cup of the broth to taste for free to entice you to try the whole dish next time. Also, pay attention to hygiene and choose a clean establishment as some are indescribably filthy. I like thin strips of beef in chicken broth with chives, coriander, and I add a little vinegar and hot chilli sauce (these are always found in the table condiment set) on a cold winter day. Wontons with a meat filling in the same broth are also popular.

- Street Crêpes (煎饼馃子-jian1bing3guo3zi). Region: Northern China but found everywhere. It's breakfast food for hungry workers on the go. Look for a towed food truck or an umbrella with a cook underneath and follow your nose. To order, the vendor will swirl batter onto a pre-heated round griddle, add an egg cooked to medium, and some seasonal vegetables. A brushing of savoury, or if desired, hot sauce completes the job, but there are always extras available for the ravenous, including very poor-quality sausages. But hey, it's cheap and filling. The crêpe is rolled and wrapped in a plastic bag and consumed in the office or on the way there if you can't wait.

- Osmanthus Lotus Roots with Blossom Syrup (桂花莲藕 – gui4hua1lian2'ou3). Technically this dish with Jiangsu origins qualifies as street food, but few in their right mind would eat it in the street as it's one of the stickiest foods on earth. It's sometimes served in restaurants as well. Much better to take it home or even make it at home. Lotus roots are an off-white colour, but the finished product is pinkish. The holes in the lotus roots are stuffed with pre-prepared sweet rice and boiled in a soup of black (brown) sugar, red dates, and goji berries to give the new colour. Lashings of the tiny yellow Osmanthus flowers mixed with honey are then poured onto the roots.

- Popcorn. Region: All of China. Now hang on, surely pop-corn is as American as cheesecake or chocolate brownies, and the Chinese surely didn't invent this when they got bored with gunpowder? I believe commercial popcorn is an American in-vention from the 19th century and an imported idea to China, but it has been around for a long time, and there is some evi-dence that maize appeared in China as early as 1505 AD. I have certainly encountered it in several 19th-century Chinese novels. As in the US, it was considered a cheap treat popular in tough times. What is different is Americans mostly like salty popcorn, whereas the Chinese taste is for sweet additions. I've read several intelligent theories on this, including that salty popcorn stops you from going for a pee during a movie, as do in-flight peanuts. My ideas are a bit different. Salt creates thirst, and thirst sells litres of soda. The Chinese do not much like butter or can be allergic to it, just as foreigners have some allergic reactions to peanuts. Desirable Chinese popcorn flavours includes strawberry, choco-late, and "black sugar" (really Demerara brown).

- Sweet Cream Buns Topped with Meat Floss. Region: All of China. I discovered this snack by accident one day when I was late to go and get some coffee and a light bite for breakfast, and this was all that was left. I'd always shied away from these buns because, frankly, Chinese sweet cream isn't so good and tastes synthetic. However, as I bit into what I thought was some sort of candy topping, it was salty and combined with the sweet cream, it was shockingly good. What I had stumbled upon was meat floss (肉鬆 – rou4song1). It is a dried and very finely pulled pork or beef that has been stewed in sweet-ened soya sauce. The floss is much used in Indonesia, Malaysia, and Vietnam, but I have never seen it in a cream bun in those countries.

Home Foods

Thank you as always, my dear wife, Yan Yan, for these delicious dishes. She always serves them with a portion of rice and often a healthy steamed sweet potato in your personal bowl.

- Asparagus Lettuce. This vegetable, *Lactuca sativa var. augustana* et al., is not well known outside of Asia and deserves more prominence. It is most prolific in summer. Preparation of the stem is simple, and the leaves are also edible. Strip the stem and slice the remainder into julienne strips, heavily salt to draw moisture, and then wash thoroughly. For a cold salad, add sesame oil, a little sugar, and spring onion. It can also be stir-fried, but either way, it is satisfyingly crunchy.

- Chinese Red Toon Sprout. This vegetable (*Toona sinensis*) is the young leaves of the Chinese Mahogany Tree and appears all over Asia at the start of spring. The leaves can be either red or green, but the red ones are considered tastier and need blanching in boiling water to remove any minor toxins. My wife mixes the chopped leaves and stems with diced tofu, chopped preserved salty duck eggs, and a dab of chicken stock powder. It's a creamy vegetarian dish with a nutty and mild onion taste and incredibly addictive. Vegans can leave out the egg.

- Aubergines with Salty Fish and Fermented Black Beans. The Chinese aubergines are mostly long and thin and cut easily into bite-sized pieces. This quite oily dish is a mainstay of Chinese cooking.

- Spring Rolls with Garlic Chilli Sauce. There's nothing like a piping hot plate of home-made spring rolls filled with ground pork mince, chopped bamboo, and shepherd's purse *(Capsella bursa-pastoris)*, a weed I have spent half my life trying to kill in agricultural crops in the west, and dipping sauce, and cooked in small batches as a TV dinner. Spring rolls must be made fresh and eaten immediately to have the desired crisp exterior and soft middle. Those bought at a takeaway or frozen from a supermarket in the west won't cut it, and even those served in a restaurant need to be on the table in less than one minute with the hot oil still bubbling on the outer surface.

- Stuffed Savoury Buns (油面精– you2mian4jing1). The buns, ready for stuffing, are customarily purchased as you would buy puff pastry in the west, and they have the raw texture of a slightly oily choux and very light pastry, which goes a little soggy on cooking. Make a small hole and fill them with your filling of choice. We like minced pork, wild greens and seasoning, and a dash of vegetable oil. The completed buns are then boiled in seasoned chicken stock, which makes the soup.

- River Snails Stuffed in their Meat Mixed with Ground Pork in a Rich Onion Soup with Fried Egg (田螺塞肉–tian2luo2se4rou4). These river snails are much larger than the French escargots, but everything about this dish tastes French. Once the blended seasoned ground pork is mixed with the snail meat, it is re-inserted into a hole in the snail shell. The rich onion soup is enhanced with Chinese sherry.

- Baby Lake Clams with Young Leek Rings, Winter Bamboo, and Ginger. I am sure there is some master chef who can explain why this flavour combination works, but it does.

- Braised Pork and Chestnuts. I have a love-hate affair with this dish. The hate part is if I am giving the job of blanching and skinning the chestnuts which is fiddly and time-consuming. The love is for the delicious winter stew which ensues. Call me a heathen, but a dash of Worcestershire Sauce is an improvement.

- Baby Lake Fish similar to whitebait with egg, salty sauce, green onions, and light soya sauce. It's the Chinese version of the Italian Frittelle di Gianchetti and just as tasty.

- Octopus Stir Fry. Octopus is notoriously difficult to prepare and cook, and I have had several disasters in my life creating something similar to chewing gum. In this dish, the octopus needs parboiling with seasoning, but every single one is different, so chef skills are paramount. The latter stages are a stir fry with red onion and spring onion, finely chopped celery, sherry, and at least one type of soya sauce. Fortunately, it is possible for the incapable to buy perfectly parboiled octopus in a bag from the supermarket. It's close enough to the real thing to satisfy, so give it a go.

Army Food

I was carrying out some research on why Chinese people eat so much Spam, called by the more refined name of luncheon meat in China (午餐肉– wu3can1rou4) and the brunt of many jokes, including the name for the rubbish you get in your computer inbox. Almost every Chinese food store and supermarket sells it. The original brand Spam was unleashed on an unsuspecting world by the American food giant Hormel, in 1937 and rose to prominence during World War II. Today, in China, Spam is still a premium brand along with Tulip from Denmark, but there are several competing local brands. As it is pork, China's meat of choice, convenient to use in a can, meaty, and suitable for many Chinese stir fry dishes, it remains popular. That's when I discovered that luncheon meat is a mainstay of the Chinese armed forces, with a potential 2.3 million consumers. They tend to be supplied with the local brand, Lingxiang made in Chongqing, and the ingredients are pork, water (potable), sugar, salt, MSG, and unspecified spices. I'm not sure if the Peoples Liberation Army, the PLA, has nutritionists, but the addition of sugar seems ill-advised. China has already had to redesign some of its frontline tanks because the new generation of porky recruits couldn't fit into them and they have also been castigated by the government for their terrible eyesight, as they are always playing games on their phones. Perhaps more carrots in the diet would help?

My interest was piqued because, in my youth, I was a member, under compunction, of the British CCF (Combined Cadet Force), and I wondered what modern armies, including China's, were eating today. All I remember when in the field were little tins of curry with a briquette warmer, making you want to evacuate your bowels, and Army Biscuits (Plain), which were like concrete and stopped you shitting for a week. I left the CCF as soon as I could to escape any potential hormonal desensitization from bromine in my tea, although I did enjoy the range shooting, and I am a marksman.

After a bit of further research, I discovered that these military rations are not a secret, and I have to thank Steve Thomas (search on YouTube – Steve1989), an American blogger who is an expert in this culinary area. This guy has even tasted hardtack from the American Civil War and lived. I had expected to find pork luncheon meat in the Chinese dishes given the considerable volume of purchases, but although there were a few MRE (Meals Ready to Eat, also known in the colloquially as Meals Refusing to Exit and others), Chinese menus with regular pork such as Type 09 Infantry Ration Menu 9, Pickled Vegetables with Shredded Pork and Noodles, and Menu 10, Pork and Mushroom with Noodles, were rare examples. Chicken and particularly beef were more common. In China, I can only surmise that the enormous volumes of pork luncheon meat must be used in field kitchens and mess halls and not in MRE, and perhaps by having less pork in the field rations, it simplified logistics. There aren't a lot if any, Hindus or Jews in the PLA. On subjective taste tests by non-Chinese, the Chinese ration didn't fair too badly.

	Chinese 09/Type 09 Self-heating in the Bag 2015	US Menu 23 MRE Separate Flameless Heater and Hot Beverage Bag 2017
Calories	1065	Aprox 1250
Main Dish	Steamed Rice and Red Beans, Spicy Sauce	Pepperoni Pizza with Cheese and Sauce*
Snacks	Beef Egg Roll	Italian Bread Sticks with Jalapeno Cheese Spread Oatmeal Cookie
Dessert	Peaches in Syrup Sponge Cake	Cherry/Blueberry Cobbler
Beverage	Citrus Vitamin Drink	Chocolate Protein Drink Instant Type 2 Coffee, Creamer, Sugar

	Chinese 09/Type 09 Self-heating in the Bag 2015	US Menu 23 MRE Separate Flameless Heater and Hot Beverage Bag 2017
Extras	Spoon	Spoon
	Napkin/Toilet Paper	Matches
	Water Measure	Chewing Gum
		Salt
		Napkin/Toilet Paper
		Moist Towlette

*The pizza is small: about half the size of one slice from a normal one, presumably why extra snacks are provided.

One surprise to me was that the Chinese version had a spoon and not chopsticks which I thought might have been useful for poking the enemy eyes out. On commercial flights in China chopsticks are never used.

So, what about the French? Surely, they wouldn't fight on this junk? The French philosophy is different as they provide a full day's MRE compared to the Chinese and American ones, which are supposed to be supplemented by local resources but would just about keep you going if there were none. That makes sense in hostile climates where there may be no local supplies. In the Afghanistan War (2001 onwards), a French MRE could be traded for five, part complete for the day, American ones.

	French Ration de Combat Individuelle Rechauffable (RCIR) Menu 4 –Separate Flameless Heater/ Example (2017)	**French Ration de Combat Individuelle Rechauffable (RCIR) Menu 9 –Separate Flameless Heater/ Example (2017)**
Calories	3200 or more	3200 or more
Hors D'Oeuvre	Chicken Liver Pâte	Venison Terrine
Appetizer A	Sauté of Rabbit	White Bean, Sausage and Duck Cassoulet
Appetizer B	Whitefish, Rice and Vegetables	Créole Pork with Rice and Pineapple
Snack/Dessert	Cheese or Crème Dessert	As for Menu 4
Beverage	Purified Water	Purified Water
Extras	Chocolate	As for Menu 4
	Caramels	
	Chewing Gum	
	Nougat	
	Fruit Gelée	
	Tea	
	Coffee	
	Cocoa	
	Milk Powder and Sugar Cubes	
	Paper Towels	
	Water Purification Tablets	
	Matches	
	Waste Bag	
	Eating implement	

There is no powdered beverage, and purified water for tea and coffee are the available options, though it's not that long ago that a miniature of wine was included, although the date of removal (if ever) is disputed. On top of their daily gourmet package of 1.5kg, the French also have the heaviest general assault rifle (FAMAS at 3.61kg), with the Chinese QBZ-95B (2.9kg) the lightest of the three countries. Sacré bleu, I hope these French Rambo's do plenty of weight training, and although they might leave a few corpses on the battlefield, at least they take their waste food home in a little bag. I've always thought of Chinese and French cuisines as some of the finest in the world, but the French win by miles when it comes to the military.

Chapter 10: New Places

In *The Lure of the Red Dragon*, I suggested that the following were worth visiting: Ancient Towns (many), Mount Putou, Hainan Island, and the Mountains of South West China in Yunnan Province.

I now have some new suggestions to whet the appetite of the wanderluster.

Chengdu, Sichuan Province

Sichuan has something for everyone and non-more than the provincial capital of Chengdu. We finished up on vacation there somewhat by accident as Yan Yan had won an expensive Swiss Longines watch on DouYin, but it required personal collection with free flights provided and both of us assisting with a promotional video to get it. When we showed up at the flashy jewellers, I had fortunately chosen to wear some elegant and branded European clothes, including patent leather white shoes and a Panama hat. We were chauffeured around in a large black Mercedes with the insignia MO (my initials) on the number plate. I'm not so old to be impressionable.

There are multiple suitable entry points into Sichuan. Those moving at a more leisurely pace could consider a dual visit to Chengdu via the municipality of Chongqing using the high-speed train, which takes two hours. Chongqing is a mountainous and beautiful Tier 1 city with many tourist attractions. Those with even more time might well consider a three-day luxury boat cruise down the Yangtze River to the Three Gorges Dam at Yichang, something I highly recommend. Chengdu is both an ancient cultural and culinary centre as well as modern and is considered to have some of the finest shopping in China, in the upmarket

IFS (International Finance Square) area (think Gucci and Prada) and the artier Taikoo Li area with both international brands and local boutiques.

Here are some of the treasures of Chengdu:

The Jinsha (金沙) Site Museum, which includes a covered area and a multi-room exhibition hall and outside landscaped gardens, is a national treasure. It doesn't take long on arrival to realise that this is something of exceptional historical importance, and the site is starting to cause scholars to rewrite parts of ancient Chinese history. It was discovered in 2001, by accident during work by building developers. It is likely that only a fraction of the site has so far been unearthed. I highly recommend that this is the first historical site to visit in Chengdu as the chronology becomes easier to follow in subsequently suggested places to visit. Until this discovery, most of the scant information about the ancient Kingdom of Shu (possibly 1000 to 316 BC) came from a site at the ancient walled city at Sanxindui (三星堆), founded around 1800 to 1600 BC and excavated from 1986 onwards, but was known about since 1929. That city was lost to the Qin in the violent Warring States Period. Unfortunately, many of the earlier pieces found on that site were sold to private collectors. At some point around 1200 to 1000 BC, Sanxindui waned, possibly due to persistent flooding or outside conflict, evidenced by the royal artefacts found at the unwalled Jinsha site, a place where the monarchy migrated. Although much less well known, and in archaeological discovery terms relatively new, the site is comparable in importance to the much better-known tomb of Qin Shi Huang (259-210 BC) in Xi'an with its terracotta warriors. The excavation unearthed both burial pits with hundreds of artefacts and around 500 elephant tusks, and even more numerous wild boar and deer teeth. There are also ceremonial, spiritual wooden and bronze trees, many produced in local workshops. Not only were the inhabitants capable of defending themselves judging by the jade daggers, axes, and swords, but the level of craftsmanship and art in the peach coloured jade crafted into religious ceremonial zhang and gu, the gold masks, the jewellery, and above all the bronze work, are astounding given the dates. The most important discoveries are the bronze masks covered in gold foil and especially the exquisite Gold Foil of the Sun and Immortal Bird, with the originals on display.

The Shu were also long-distance traders but to what extent is still unclear. I managed to find a cowry shell in one of the displays, quite a surprise for an area 800 miles (1300 km) from an ocean (now) and even further for one that had cowry shells. Current thinking is that trade was extensive within most of modern-day southern China and Thailand and with some credibility with ancient Mesopotamia. Shu-style tree and sun worship were also an essential part of those other civilizations, and historians have struggled to explain how China's Bronze Age developed compared to the west. The oldest known bronze artefact in China is a primitive knife found in Gansu Province dating from around 2800 BC, but the level of sophistication in the mysterious Kingdom of Shu is exponentially higher, and perhaps this is the missing link?

The museum is well suited to children because of the life-size mockups of what Shu life was like and because of the spacious gardens to run around in. The Shu were finally conquered and absorbed into the State of Qin in 316 BC, which by 221 BC had conquered all the other states during the Warring States Period (475 to 221 BC) and the first true universal Emperor of China, Qin Shi Huang of the Qin Dynasty, ascended (he of Terracotta Warrior fame). That entire dynasty only lasted less than 50 years. It disassembled after a series of life-sapping revolutions and treachery. It is also one of the bloodiest periods of Chinese history. There was technically still left one Emperor, Emperor Xian of the Eastern Han Dynasty during the Warring States. He was a puppet to the warlord/king Cao Cao of the Wei who was defeated at the critical Battle of The Red Cliffs in 209 AD to an alliance of Liu Bei of the Shu Han and Sun Quan of the Wu, thus splitting China into three and called the Three Kingdoms Period (220 to 280 AD). They weren't really kingdoms but competing warlords or "little emperors". All three little emperors were clever men. Cao Cao was a brutal thug, excellent militarist, poet, and skilled calligrapher. Sun Quan was an accomplished and affable diplomat, a delegator with a military pedigree, and was directly related to Sun Zu/Sunzi, the author of *The Art of War*, a book still studied by tacticians today. Liu Bei is discussed below as he is directly related to this narrative on Chengdu.

This potted history will provide you with enough basic information to make the next logical trip after the Jinsha Site Museum, the Jinli area of Chengdu, and the Wuhou Temple. I hope it is helpful because the foreign language information in the Wuhou Temple is lacking, perhaps because there is no realistic way to label exhibits to explain such a complex history. Chinese tourists from other regions will fare better as they will almost certainly have studied this period of history at school. The temple was built in 223 AD in memory of Liu Bei of the Shu Han (courtesy name Juande – 161 to 223 AD). I was excited because I had read the translated version of *The Romance of The Three Kingdoms* by Luo Guan Zhong, written much later in the Ming dynasty. The crucial Battle of the Red Cliffs is a classic in how to defeat an enemy when outnumbered twenty to one or more. Although Liu Bei was a winner in this battle, he also suffered several crushing defeats in his lifetime. This extremely tall, 1.82 metres (six feet), giant of a man for his time, had a generous spirit and formidable intellect, believed in Confucian morals and Taoist principles. He was also ably assisted by Zhuge Liang (courtesy name Kongning – also called Crouching Dragon), a genius hermit who was eventually persuaded by personal visits to join Liu Bei. He became an organizer that kept supplies and troops coming to the war front from Chengdu. His statue is also prominent at the temple. Liu Bei spent much of his life defending his kingdom, especially against the ever-dangerous Wei, but in an act of betrayal, he also had to fight his supposed ally, Wu. In 219 AD, war broke out between Wu and Shu Han after a surprise attack by Wu (with a secret alliance with Wei in place), leading to the capture and execution of Shu Han general Guan Yu and the loss of Jiangling to Wu. The Shu Han-Wu alliance against Wei wasn't restored until 223 AD. In 222 AD, Sun Quan renounced his suzerainty to Wei as King of Wu, although it wasn't until seven years later that he declared himself Emperor of Wu.

Liu Bei died in 223, the year he declared himself Emperor of the Shu Han and was succeeded by his son Liu Shan with Zhuge Liang, now Marquis of Wu District, acting as a father figure and regent to the teen-age Liu Shan. Cao Cao had already died in 200 AD and was superseded by his son, Cao Pi. One of his first acts was to usurp the throne from puppet Emperor Xian and established himself as Emperor of Cao Wei, thus ending the Eastern Han Dynasty. This pitted the two sons of their fathers' kingdoms, Liu Shan (Shu Han) and Cao Pi (Wei), against each other.

One by one, the kingdoms collapsed, and Shu Han was the first to fall when in 263 AD, the massed Wei attack saw the taking of Chengdu, and Liu Shan surrendered, ending a brief 43 years of the Shu Han Kingdom. He was given an honorary but superfluous title and survived. Next to fall was the Kingdom of Wei in 249 AD, when the last of the Cao family, the young Cao Shuang, suffered a coup d'état at the hands of the regent, Sima Yi, and was executed along with his entourage. Sima Yi's grandson, Sima Zhao, took the 263 AD surrender of the Shu Han. The Wu went into decline after the death of their charismatic leader, Sun Quan, and in 280 AD, the last of the Sun line, the vicious tyrant Sun Hao, surrendered to Sima Yan. Sima Yan, the son of Sima Zhao (236 to 265 AD), had become de facto Emperor of all but Wu in 266 AD and honoured his grandfather with the posthumous title of Emperor Xuan of Jin. This is why the next dynasty is called the Jin Dynasty and not the Sima Dynasty. After 300 bloody and turbulent years, China was once again unified.

Within the walls of the Wuhou temple is a tranquil garden with lakes and waterfalls and an extensive collection of bonsai. It's the perfect place to walk around and sit and contemplate life on a warm spring or autumn day. Outside the walls is a famous street and pedestrian area, Jin Li (锦里) Street, whose origins go back to the Qin period. Nowadays, its buildings are mock Qing Dynasty style, and if you are planning to go there, it's better to go to the temple in the late afternoon because this area comes to life in the evening. It's pretty enough with its tourist shops, restaurants, teahouses, and bars. People like to grab overpriced snacks from a plethora of stalls, and the food is very average, and not particularly Sichuanese. On the opposite side of the road to the main gate is an area of several blocks that many visitors might miss. I recognized it immediately from the signs and language as I had lived briefly in Nepal. ཞལ་ལག་མཇེ་མ་པ་དང་ག : Bon Appétit! in Tibetan, and there are several eateries and Buddhist monks wandering around in their saffron and amaranth coloured robes. Unless you plan a trip to Lhasa in Tibet, this is a rare chance to try out this type of food. The yak for handpicking and sucking off the bone, the pea and broccoli salad, and sweet yoghurt were all authentic, cheap, and delicious, although Yan Yan balked at the idea of trying the buttery tea.

If you aren't interested in temples or bonsai or non-authentic street food but want to see an old street, a much better sojourn in Chengdu is the Wide and Narrow Lanes area (Kuanxiangzi – 宽巷子 and adjacent Zhai Alley – 窄巷子). Built during the Qing dynasty, the streets of elegant residential houses were converted to an upmarket tourist area in 2003, and it's where you can find shade in courtyards with banyan trees and purple flowering jacaranda and eat a light dish or drink tea. You will hear the banging of drums and see greeters adorned in costumes and encouraging you to see Sichuan opera shows, and there are several haut couture establishments and high-end art galleries. For those unfamiliar with Sichuan opera, its trademark is the ability of the characters to switch faces in the blink of an eye and magically. You won't discover how this is done as it is a closely guarded secret passed down over centuries.

The most visited tourist site is the Chengdu Research Base of Giant Panda Breeding, on the not to be missed list for many and surely for most children. It is not to be confused with Chengdu Zoo, which has 300 species, including pandas. The former is all about only pandas and unrelated red pandas. Sichuan is the home of the wild giant panda, although a few are found in two neighbouring provinces. I wanted to go to the Research Base because firstly, I had never seen a real panda, but also a couple of years ago, I had seen a Chinese documentary on the difficulties of breeding captive pandas filmed in one of the outlying mountain stations. These adorable and fascinating animals have everything going against them for survival, not just due to the deforestation of bamboo forests but because of their inefficient lifestyle attributes. Pandas will not easily breed in captivity, and experiments have been tried in the past to encourage them, including giving the males the little blue pill, with no success. In the tragicomedy documentary, several female pandas had come into heat. When they were introduced sequentially to young males, the boys showed no interest in the females and sat munching away on bamboo in the corner. The breeders did manage to coax them towards the females with long poles and an orange attached as pandas love this fruit. A couple of them did try and mount the females but couldn't get the position right, but most just weren't interested, and the aroused females started screeching in sexual frustration. In the end, and much to the relief of the females, and this viewer, an older experienced male panda was introduced, and there was a happy ending, but the breeders had failed in their task because a vital part of the programme is to increase genetic diversity. To make matters worse, giant pandas seem to have the odds stacked against them in the wild, where they primarily live as solitary animals. Females regularly have twins but usually abandon one to starve. They also need to consume up to 15 kilogrammes of ligneous low-energy bamboo stems per day, leaving them little time in a day except to eat, defecate and sleep. It's essential to go to the Research Base as soon as it opens in the morning, and you can watch the pandas stripping bamboo shoots with great dexterity using their peculiar pseudo thumb and eating the finished product. By noon they are asleep for the rest of the day, with further feeding in the evening. Both the conservation efforts for wild giant pandas and the captive animal breeding programme have been successful both in the wild and in captivity. They are now removed from the global critically endangered list. In the wild, numbers have been increasing to perhaps 2000 individuals.

One final excursion to put on any itinerary is Luodai Ancient Town (洛带). According to legend, during the Three Kingdoms Period, a Shu Prince, Liu Edou, dropped his jade band in a well while fishing for carp, and that is the origin of the town's name. "Dai" in Chinese means a band or a belt. The town itself is a little bit worn, full of plastic knick-knacks to take home, and touristic food is everywhere. On the edges of town, there are some shaded areas where you can drink tea (your own or purchased), buy a bag of pipa fruit (loquat), and watch the locals play mah-jong. There are four interesting and well-preserved guildhalls from the 18th century Qing Dynasty (1644 to 1911), with spacious courtyards. Many of the guilds came to Sichuan as traders from Guangdong, Jiangxi, Chuanbei (part of Sichuan), and Huguang (Hubei, Hunan, Guizhou, etc.). 90% of the inhabitants of the town are of Hakka origin.

As busy as the old town was, on the day of our visit, the all-important Hakka Museum was virtually empty, and I wondered if people ever found it or were even interested in it, even though it is only a short walk from the town centre. The museum reconstructs a large fortified multi-family

Hakka roundhouse (土楼 – tu3lou2), although genuine versions can be found in Fujian Province at Chuxi Village and elsewhere. The Hakka are generally considered a sub-shoot of the Han Chinese confirmed by genetic testing and are also not considered one of the 55 ethnic minorities. They do, however, retain a separate language or dialect and distinct cultural identity. Their origins are an open question with at least six theories from which to choose. In Mandarin, Hakka people are called 客家人 – ke2jia1ren, which means "people from the guest families", which alludes to them in history as often being considered strangers because of their frequent migrations under persecution, but sometimes as encouraged settlers. Although "Hakka people" are regularly used words, they do need to be used with a bit of caution as it also has the connotation of "poor gypsy from somewhere else". There is an excellent map in the museum with the suggested progression of the multiple wave migrations, but it is not definitive. The Hakka story is as epic as that of the dispersion of the Jewish Diaspora or the Native American Indians being pushed westwards in the Trail of Tears.

My preferred pieced together theory is a seven-wave migration with the first wave possibly starting in present-day Shandong Province. Under persecution by the first emperor, Qin Shi Huang, the Hakka fled to the mountains of now Henan and Anhui Provinces and remote parts of Shandong Province, although this is heavily disputed. The second wave seems to have occurred during the Jin Dynasty in the Sixteen Kingdoms of the Five Barbarians period from 304 to 439 (五胡十六國 – wu3hu2shi2liu4guo2), forcing the Hakka and other refugees to cross the Yangtze River and flee south to Jiangxi and also escaping to Zhejiang and later to Fujian. The third wave occurred in the lawless years toward the end of the Tang Dynasty (618 to 907) with further dispersion to the relative safety of the mountainous parts of Guangxi and Fujian and onwards to Guangdong. The fourth wave occurred in the Song Dynasty (960 to 1279). From 1127 onwards, further Hakka migration occurred after the dynasty's loss to the Jurchen Army by the sacking of the capital Kaifeng and relocation to Hangzhou in 1271. Eventually, Kublai Khan, grandson of Genghis Khan, invaded and pushed the rump of the Royal Song household into a corner in parts of Guangdong Province before they committed mass suicide in 1279. These events were a general movement of a fleeing population from north to south and included the Hakka people.

The fifth wave is unusual because it wasn't just based on fleeing from oppression. In 1644, the rebel Zhang Xianzhong (Yellow Tiger) captured all of Sichuan, including Chongqing and Chengdu, from the collapsing Ming Dynasty and initiated a reign of terror and genocide, which along with famine and plague, saw the depopulation of Sichuan by perhaps one third. It wasn't until 1670, when one of China's greatest emperors, the Qing Dynasty Kangxi Emperor (1654 to 1722), addressed this problem by offering silver to any impoverished Hakka in the south if they would relocate to Sichuan, including Luodai. Some Hakka also took the opportunity to settle the coastal strip after the 1669 ordinance allowing this area to be repopulated after being left devoid of people to impair any possible invasion from Taiwan by the then Ming loyalist, Koxinga. Settlers were also encouraged by free cattle, seeds, and tax exemptions. The sixth wave relates to the cataclysmic events for the Hakka of the 19th and 20th centuries and connects to international migration. The First Opium War (1839 to 1842) saw the first opportunity to emigrate from a previously shuttered China, and the Hakka took advantage of this. The Taiping Rebellion (1851-1864), which left 20-30 million people dead, started with a peasant revolt lead by a Christian Chinese Hakka. Many key leaders of the rebels, also Hakka, suffered random executions and persecution and caused a significant Hakka international migration, often via Hong Kong. Finally, the Punti-Hakka Clan Wars (1855-1867), leaving one million dead, was a consequence of the much earlier Kangxi Emperor's coastal strip depopulation. The Punti were the disenfranchised who wanted their land back from the Hakka, many of whom fled. As a consequence of these events, Hakka people are now found all over the world.

The seventh and final migration is also unusual, but it is a type of Hakka migration. It's small in numbers but historically significant. On one of the staircase walls in the Hakka Museum is a black and white photograph of an army officer with the Nationalist flag on the wall, pointing an accusatory finger at a terrified Hakka youth. Many Hakka took to the communist cause, and the Chengdu area from 1932 to 1935 was home to the East Sichuan Soviet. During the Long March (1934 to 1935), the main body of 86,000 communist soldiers (7,000 survivors) were 70% Hakka. If it had not been for the free passage granted by Hakka warlord Chen Jitang to the fleeing Communist army, the history of modern China might even have been different. Zhu De, the People's Liberation Army founder, was a Hakka born in Sichuan. Deng Xiaoping, the paramount leader of the PRC of China from 1978 to 1992, was also a Hakka born in Sichuan. In 1984 half of the Standing Committee of the Politburo was Hakka. Although the Hakka have been fleeing throughout history, they have a fearsome reputation as fighters. The Nationalist pursuer of the Long March soldiers in the Fifth Encirclement Campaign, General Xue Yue, was also a Hakka. A further example is the Communist Hakka, Marshal Chen Yi, also from Sichuan, who in the War of Resistance against the Japanese (1937 to 1945) commanded the New Fourth Army and led the forces that defeated the nationalists in the Huaihai Campaign. In 1955, he was made a Marshall of the PLA, became Mayor of Shanghai from 1949 to 1958, and China's Foreign Minister from 1958 until his death. When Chen died in 1972, Chairman Mao attended his funeral, the last time Mao was seen in public. These are just a few of a very illustrious Hakka military roll call.

The museum, set in beautiful gardens, offers a unique insight into Hakka culture. It is set on four circular floors, each with an interior balcony. There are rooms full of agricultural implements and other tools, pottery, arts and crafts, and other artefacts, and it is fun trying to guess for what purpose they might have been used. My favourite room was a Qing Dynasty school room where you could sit at a low desk watched by a stern bronze teacher complete with ruler presumably to whack uncooperative students. Or you could sit in the teacher's sumptuous chair at the front of the class, with a portrait of Confucius behind you. There are many photographs and pictures of Hakka life and books of each family's genealogy to inspect.

One of the good things about Luodai is that access to the old town, and the museum is free, something increasingly rare in China, and if you sit at a tea house with your own comestibles, no one is going to hassle you.

There are many other things to do in Chengdu, but I ran out of time and, to my regret, missed the Du Fu thatched cottage, park, and museum where this giant of literature wrote some of his best poems.

Qingcheng Mountains, Sichuan Province

The flat plains of Chengdu are surrounded by a ring of active volcanic mountains. Many visitors will combine a visit to Chengdu with a trip to these. It is quite possible to spend an entire vacation in one or both of the well-known ones: the Qingcheng Mountains to the northwest and Mount Emei in the southwest, as there is so much to see and do. Although it is possible to get to either area by high-speed train and use local buses, this is a good time to employ a knowledgeable local guide and driver that speaks your language for at least some of the time, because their knowledge will enhance your trip. It's typical to travel in groups of four to ten people, but you will have ample opportunity to find your own space. In this narrative, I will concentrate on the Qingcheng Mountain area. However, the higher 3099 metres (10,167 feet) Mount

Emei and the nearby Leshan Giant Buddha, the largest stone-carved Buddha in the world that took 90 years to complete (713 AD to 803AD), is considered by many to be even more spectacular. Both are UNESCO world heritage sites. In either case, if you like the great outdoors, pure mountain air, like hiking and climbing (up paths and steps, not on ropes), you will be enthralled. You also need suitable clothes, even in summer, for a wet weather climate, chills from altitude, and sturdy non-slip shoes. I'm going to discuss a small part of Qingcheng Mountain to whet your appetite. The best starting point for this is north of the mountain at the Dujiangyan Irrigation System (都江堰).

We had been paired up with an amiable couple of similar age from Shandong Province and travelled for two hours with a driver/guide from Chengdu. I could have happily spent a whole day at the irrigation system, and this is from a guy who hated hydrology at school and wading through frigid rivers determining water flow rates. The entry point is a viewing platform at the top of the gorge of the Min River with the mountains in the background, and essential for supplying Chengdu downstream with water. This was another good reason for a guide as he proved to be an accomplished photographer and took photos of us at the very spot where Mao Zedong, Deng Xiaoping, and Jiang Zemin all had their pictures taken. It's at the top of a tower to assist with the descent that was rebuilt after the 2008 earthquake. Towards the bottom of the tower is a frieze dedicated to Li Bing (circa 230 BC), Qin governor of Shu during the Warring States Period, and one of the most extraordinary hydraulic engineers ever considering the dates he was working. Considerable credit is given to his second son's work, Li Erlang, on the project. The three-part system Li Bing devised is still in use today. In winter, the Min River is pregnant with fast-flowing mountain water that caused flooding, but there was a shortage of water for nearby farmland in summer. First, Li Bing constructed a levee called the Fish Mouth which split the river into two parts. In dry times, the deep inner channel continued its course, but in times of flood, 40% of the water was diverted by the levee to follow a course away from the Chengdu Plain and eventually join up with the Yangtze River. The concave Fish Mouth was designed to ensure that most of the silt in the water could be carried down the fast-flowing inner channel to the second phase. To do this, Li Bing designed a woven open interlaced bamboo tube filled with round stones that were thrown into the river until a natural barrier was made. These were then supported from behind by bamboo screens, and local cedar wood tripods and examples are shown at the site of the method used. After four years of building work, he had split the river into the two channels. At a curve in the river below the Fish Mouth, the next stage was to create The Flying Sand Weir, an escape channel so that as the fast-moving water swirled around the bend, the turbulence created at the riverbed dumped sand into the escape channel. The sand would be dug out periodically and used to reinforce the Fish Mouth. This method stopped the inner river from silting up. It also functioned as a secondary overflow in times of extreme flooding. The final stage was to create a new course for the inner river. As Mount Yulei stood in the way, and without gunpowder, which was not invented until the 9th Century and using abundant local timber, Li Bing had his workers heated the rocks and then doused cold river water onto them to split them apart, although some sources suggest vinegar was used. This narrow 20 metre (60 feet) breach is called The Bottleneck. Using hammers and chisels would have taken thirty years, but the entire project, all three phases, took only fourteen years to complete. Legend has it that no one was brave enough to make the final hammer blow to breach, and so his daughter stepped up, only to be overwhelmed by a wall of water and die. As Li Bing was a military governor, he was also charged with keeping the river navigable at all times for the transport of troops, something his system also achieved.

Once you have descended to the river, you can walk the length of the project of several miles. First, though, you have to cross a 320 metre

(1050 feet) suspension bridge. The original ancient bridge was built of bamboo rope and rattan, but this was destroyed in warfare towards the end of the Ming Dynasty. In 1803, a couple, He Xiande and his wife, proposed building a bamboo chain bridge with stepping boards and named it the Anlan Suspension Bridge (Anlan means couple). Although the bridge was rebuilt and moved slightly in 1974, the bridge still keeps its "couples" name and implied romanticism and is a favourite spot to be photographed. On one side, the walk along the riverbank, a cedar forest on one side, and on the other, the river, is beautiful. It includes a stone walkway through the Guanlan, Wave Watching Pavilion to observe the raging inner channel. About halfway along the walk, our guide pulled us onto a track in the forest, and there was a giant rock that had been dragged there in recent times. It became a modern tradition to take a branch and place it against this rock as a symbol of holding it up and permanence and wish against future earthquakes. He explained that the rock had become a place where men place a branch to wish for virility in even more recent times. My male Shandong compatriot duly placed his branch and then looked at me and handed me a tiny twig to do the same as he seemingly judged I didn't need much help. Wives mock blushed, and we all could be heard laughing from a distance.

The final part of the walk is through the Li Pile Park with its formal gardens and several important temples and halls. If you have time, there are many discoveries to be made and extend my short history. One object, though, is worth special attention. It is a stone statue weighing 4.5 tonnes of Li Bing found in the river when a new sluice gate was built in 1974. The writing indicates it is about 1800 years old, making it the oldest known stone carving in China. The 2008 earthquake cracked the now concrete Fish Mouth, but it survived.

On the drive south to the Qingcheng Mountains, our guide talked tearfully about the massive Wenchuan earthquake of May 12, 2008, which killed or left missing over 70,000 people, injured 375,000, and left 4.8 million homeless. It occurred very close to where we were travelling. One of his now guide colleagues had been a teacher at a rural school in the area, and the school was virtually buried by a landslide, one of more than 200,000 that were recorded. His colleague managed to get 10% of the children out to safety and blames himself for not doing more. He is scarred for life and never went back to the village and never taught again.

To appreciate the buildings within the mountain area, you need to know a little about the mythical, legendary Yellow Emperor (皇帝 – huang2di4), allegedly 2697-2597 BC, the first of the three sovereigns or god-kings of the era. Although he was a prominent cult figure in the Warring States Period (475 BC to 221 BC), with the founding of the Qin Dynasty and future imperial dynasties, his cult following became unfashionable, although the modern Chinese name for any emperor is "Huang Di". He also became a symbol of Han nationalism against the Manchu in attempts to overthrow the Qing Dynasty. The Yellow Emperor in mythology is considered the father of all the Chinese people and, in particular, easily the most populous, the Han. The "three emperors" are deemed to have brought outstanding innovations to their people, such as fire, sedentary agriculture, medicine, the calendar, and house building techniques. He is also the subject of many early Chinese scholarly works, including Sima Qian's (circa 145 to 86 BC) *Records of the Grand Historian*. While the founder of Taoism is often considered to be Lao Zi, some Chinese Taoists believe the Yellow Emperor to be the instigator of the religion. Furthermore, the mountain is associated with Zhang Daoling, the first Celestial Master of Taoism (something like a cross between a pope and a preacher), who in history is recorded as having died on the mountain in 156 AD). The title was still awarded to the next Zhang in line of succession until the 64th, Zhang Yuanxian, who died in 2008 and after which a squabble arose over the future line of succession as he had no male heir.

So, in every way, the Qingcheng Mountains are connected with Taoism, and it is why visitors will find so many references to this religion in the temples and shrines, including the stone statues of Celestial Master Zhang at the Tianshi Cave and those of the "three emperors" at the San Huang Palace. It also explains why Taoism is one of the five great-grandfathers of modern religions with Christianity and Muhammadanism relative newcomers.

The Qingcheng Mountain is spectacular and has 36 peaks, with the highest, Pengzu Peak, at 1260 metres (4134 feet). Although I have a greater love of the much drier and taller mountains of Yunnan, it is a wonder of mixed coniferous and deciduous vegetation, and there is a lot to see and do on both the mountain and in the surrounding area. For those who don't have the time to do both, a choice must be made between the front mountain and back mountain route to the summit. Our new Shandong friends chose the former, and we chose the latter, and we waved goodbye. Whether your interests are more in buildings, temples, etc., or prefer a more scenic ramble in the countryside is influenced by this choice. In both cases, a cable car is available to take you to the summit. The whole mountain is a major tourist draw, and queues of Chinese proportions, especially for the front mountain cable car, are to be expected. At busy times, that would also probably make the back-mountain route a better choice.

The back-mountain route to the prosperous ancient town of Tai'an (泰安) takes you on winding minor roads with overhanging trees with shafts of sunlight penetrating the canopy. There are steep drops to the pounding river and waterfalls in the ravines below. Several small groups were cycling. The thought did occur to me that apart from the apparent diversity of vegetation and wildlife, this would make a world-class motor rally stage if properly supervised and then retracted such a thought in deference to the verdant and tranquil countryside. Along the route were clusters of mountain farmhouses with basic and very affordable rooms from as little as 100 RMB (£11.50) per night and even cheaper, some of the monasteries on the mountain will give you a bed. Down by the main entrance and town, there are a range of hotels, including the luxury and furiously expensive Howard Johnson with its private hot springs and screened private balconies with Jacuzzis. Howard Johnson is a premier brand in China and has nothing in common with the sometimes-grungy hotels of the same name in the US.

On arrival at Tai'an, in my opinion, it's better to leave until later the town as a place to rest after the excursions to follow. The cable car ride is the longest of the three available; front and back mountains, and takes 13 minutes to the top, although a two-hour steep uphill walk will get you there as well. I observed many things, including the fissured rocks and wild vegetation, but I was most fascinated by a cliff covered in what I recognized as beehives. I know Sichuan people are well adapted to mountain climbing and some children still have to do this every day to get to school, but being lowered on ropes off the cliff edge to collect the honey seemed extreme. On arrival at the top, it's still a significant hike up more steep steps to reach the summit and the Laojun Pavilion (老君阁), with its panoramic views. It is dedicated with a statue to Laozi, the founder of Taoism, and is approachable by both front and back mountain routes. Many choose to hike down the mountain rather than return by cable car because of the beautiful scenery. On your return to Tai'an, hopefully now happily tired and hungry, enter across the wooden slatted suspension bridge. Ignore the dire warnings of bouncing up and down and swinging side to side. I saw a whole uniformed party on a youth trip try it all simultaneously, and at that age, nothing would have stopped me from making it gyrate violently. Tai'an, through history, has been an important town on the "post house road" to get from the Chengdu plain to Jinchuan and Xiaojinchuan. The town and its Tang Dynasty temple also suffered badly in the earthquake, but both have been rebuilt. Next to the temple is a path that delineates the old post road. After a mountain excursion, if the weather is fine, it's deeply satisfying to sit and have tea or a cold beer next to the swift stream below and enjoy a bag of still warm and well renowned barbequed bacon.

There is easily enough to do in this part of Sichuan for a much longer holiday. Other sites that are suggested include the Dujiangyan Panda Base and the Wenchuan Earthquake Memorial Museum at Qushan. The memorial is designed as a huge crack in the ground that acts as a sunken pathway to large underground buildings topped with green roofs. Nearby, the ruins of the town of Beichuan have been preserved and left for people to visit and remember. Another possibility is China's largest private museum, The Sichuan Museum of Jianchuan, at Anren Old Town. It has four themes: World War II, Folk Customs, Communist Era and the Earthquake and more than 8 million items on display. Sadly, you won't be able to see the Museum's most famous resident, a pig named Zhu Jianqiang, "strong-willed pig". The pig survived 36 days trapped under earthquake debris in 2008, surviving on charcoal and rainwater, and had lost two-thirds of his bodyweight before being rescued. At 14-years-old, at the time of writing, he is on his last legs..

Xiamen, Fujian Province

Xiamen has a population of 3.7 million and has an agreeable subtropical climate and low pollution. It's a major tourism and conference/ exhibition centre and specializes in high-tech electronics industries and banking. The climate has led to the establishment of many fine gardens within the city, and a stroll or climb if you want to do the rocky parts through the two square mile (4.5 sq. km) Xiamen Botanical Gardens, is highly recommended. You will find manicured lawns, lakes and temples, and subdivided sections such as The Fir Garden, Rose Garden, Cactus Garden, and indoor glasshouses for more tender species such as orchids.

It is big enough that several visits would be needed to see its entirety. Xiamen is also an important city for music. Its ancient Nanyin, Gaojia, Gezai, and Dazuigu opera and musical styles are still performed today along with a more modern layer of western music.

Xiamen, in my opinion, is one of the most beautiful cities in China. Nixon called it "the oriental Hawaii", a bit of a Tricky Dicky exaggeration that, as Hawaii is genuinely tropical. To my mind, it is more like Nice in France, especially with the red-tiled roofs, Jacksonville in the US, or Busan in South Korea. The central city is divided into six districts, each with its points of interest. Two, Siming and Huli Districts, are on an island connected by four main bridges and a seven kilometre (four mile) undersea tunnel, and form the city's centre. Parts of the island are elevated terrain giving both sea and hilly views all in one vista. The natural restrictions of the terrain and an abundance of parks, green areas, and beaches, lead to an open and pleasing effect. Xiamen is a vibrant, growing city, and its future expansion will have to be on the mainland as space for building on the island is running out. The growth can already be seen in Haicang District on the opposite bank of the estuary, with some fine modern buildings appearing, such as the Science and Technology Museum.

On the island, the roads are wide and landscaped with an abundance of specimen flowers. In summer, pink oleander, orange mimosa tree, and purple jacaranda compete for the eye's attention. The southeast part of the island has a continuous coast road and cycle path (Huandao East and South Road), which is also the location of the January held Xiamen International Marathon. The route is marked by multiple bronze statues of runners in various poses, including pouring water over their heads and cameramen at the finish line.

Everywhere, the new blends in with the old. Adjacent to the exclusive and expensive yacht club is an ancient fishing village and temple with a statue of the god of the sea in this region, Ma Zu (妈祖), for sailors and fishermen to pray for protection. The southwest part of the island is also a hub with its commercial and tourism areas, ferries, ocean liners, and military ports. Its centrepiece is the pedestrian Zhongshan Road which starts at the Swiss Grand Hotel on the Xiamen Bund.

This stretch of coast is still a potential military flashpoint in the narrow chokepoint of the Straights of Taiwan at 180 kilometres (110 miles) wide, and there are reminders everywhere. Foreign navies (especially the US) like to assert freedom of navigation through the straits of Taiwan, something that regularly keeps tensions high. The massive new airport under construction in Xing'An District near the last battlefield site of the Chinese Civil War will double up for both commercial and military purposes.

It was on a trip to Golden Beach with its soft sand and wave polished stones protruding from the water, that I realized just how close the nearest parts of Taiwan are to the mainland at the Kinmen Archipelago, only 1.8 kilometres) (0.7 miles) away. No wonder there was a radar station on top of the hill in mainland China. This whole stretch of coastline bristles with artillery, uncleared mines, pillboxes, and anti-landing barricades on both sides. Kinmen Island saw extensive artillery bombardment from the PRC in the First and Second Taiwan Straights Crisis in 1954 and again in 1958. Above the beach is a retirement home for the PRC military, although it is not marked as such, one can imagine old soldiers and sailors sipping tea and reminiscing as they look out to sea.

Part of the history of this area is the Three Island Battlefield Site, and I was duped by our guide, who likely got a payback for his efforts. There is a well-reviewed exhibition hall and 87,000 square metre sightseeing park on Dadeng Island, which I never go to see. It boasts:

"Top of the World – Large Horn", "August 23 Battlefield Ruins", "Hero Sculpture Square", "Battlefield Tunnel", "Three-island Military and Civilian Historical Hall", "Military Weapon Exhibition Ground", "National Defense Educational Hall", "World Weapon Model Exhibition Hall", "Motherland Peaceful Reunification Exhibition Hall", and "Air and Ocean Drift History Exhibition Hall". Airplanes, cannons, tanks, patrol boats, warships, and other various light and heavy weapons with great contributions in the battle are displayed in Battlefield Sightseeing Park".

From Visit Xiamen (visitxm.com)

I was appalled at the place I was taken to. The paid site had an undersized jet fighter outside, which had nothing to do with the battle (it had double tail fins), a tank with a gun barrel so rough it would have blown up the occupants inside and decorated in modern camouflage (large squares), and a helicopter inside of dubious origins. The trenches, which were an important part of the battle, were made of modern concrete. The anti-aircraft guns, although real enough, had been mounted on concrete but were actually from naval vessels (not part of the battle). Children were firing plastic machine guns with laser sights at targets, clueless of the meaning of the patriotic songs being sung over the loudspeakers. There was no information about what happened at this important site. I can only assume that no senior military member or politician has ever been near this place because they would have razed it to the ground. It is an insult to the people on both sides who died there and, of course, a supposed celebration site, as this was the Communists finest hour, as Chiang Kai-shek and the Nationalists were finally vanquished to Taiwan.

Apart from Siming and Huli districts, there is a third part of central Xiamen: Kulangsu/Gulangyu Island (鼓浪嶼/鼓浪屿), which is part of Siming District but stands alone. It's the most popular tourist attraction by far and a deserved UNESCO World Heritage Site, and only accessible by several ferry routes. If you are travelling during the day, you must use the 25-minute tourist ferries, but you can use the five-minute workers' ferry at night. On the approach, on the seaward side, there is an appropriate nearly 16 metre (48 feet) statue of the self-styled aristocrat and scholar, Zheng Chenggong (鄭成功). The Encyclopaedia Britannica describes him as a pirate (although his father, the Marquis of the House of Zheng certainly was) and yet describes Sir Francis Drake as an English admiral. His father, Zheng Zhilong, was baptized in Portuguese-controlled Macau and obtained his notoriety plundering the Dutch. Calling his son a pirate is a little harsh, and remarkably in today's world, he is considered a hero in China, Taiwan, and Japan (his mother was Japanese, and he was born in Hirado in 1624 and he lived there until aged seven). Later, Zheng Chengong was given the royal name Zhu and, in 1646, adopted the name Koxinga (in Dutch), (國姓爺 – Guo Xingye in Chinese), which means "Lord with an Imperial Surname". He remained loyal to the Zheng clan army in the embers of the Ming Dynasty, unlike his father, who defected to the Qing, Manchu Dynasty, although his father was later executed in 1661 by them. This event made Koxinga the head of the clan, and immediately he renamed it House of Koxinga. His mother, who he had great affection for, was killed in the Qing attack on Xiamen in 1645 and was either raped and killed or possibly died by suicide, one year after leaving Japan for China. In 1656, Koxinga's army got to the gates of the then Qing city of Nanjing before being badly defeated in a failed siege attempt.

Koxinga is most famous for his attack in 1661 on Dutch Formosa, now Taiwan. He attacked with around 25,000 troops and persuaded the local natives of the island to switch sides, including catching any unwary Dutch and beheading them, and destroying their Protestant school textbooks, which were part of compulsory education for the indigenous people. Koxinga is also credited with bringing new farming methods and tools to Taiwan. On February 1, 1662, Frederick Coyett, the Dutch governor, surrendered Fort Zeelandia to Koxinga, and the Dutch were conquered. In the same year, Koxinga then went after the Spanish in the Philippines but died of malaria, age 37, before his invasion of Manila had commenced. There is a museum and garden dedicated to him on Gulangyu.

Xiamen (Amoy in English at that time) became a treaty port of the British shortly after the First Opium War in 1842, and Gulangyu was their choice of residence. However, they mostly remained in separate areas to the locals. Shortly after, many other countries had homes and consulates there, and the population was also bolstered by the largest contingent, returning overseas and often wealthy Chinese. It had its own municipal council, British organized police force, local taxes, churches, and a Christian cemetery, schools, and hospitals, including the Hope Hospital designed and built by the Dutch American, Dr. John Abraham Otte and opened in 1898. It's clear from the substantial buildings that fortunes were made and lost here. There is a four-floor mansion that was lost in a gambling debt and another one at the corner of the so-called Foreigner's Football Field (人民体育场) that was once owned by a hairdresser who came to the island and eventually made his fortune as a sugar trader, although this house is not marked as such, but the locals can point it out to you. When I saw the "football field", I was taken aback because I have rarely seen a more beautiful and manicured cricket pitch in my life and could not imagine that the British would have neglected a place to put willow onto leather. After some digging, it turns out that it was designed as a cricket pitch and lawn tennis courts in 1876, and football only started there in 1910.

Gulangyu, along with Shanghai, had the earliest modern amenities in all China, including telegram connections to Shanghai and Hong Kong (1871 – run by the Danish-owned Great Northern Telegraph Company), telephones (1924), electricity (1928), and tap water (1932). The architecture is high Victorian with an eastern twist with opulent villas and narrow hilly streets as space is tight. The island is only 1.8 sq km (1.2 sq miles). Many of the villas have, or are in the process of, being converted into hotels and guest houses. This is slow work, not least because no cars or bicycles are allowed on the island, and building materials, suitcases, food, etc., are moved around by prized licensed hand-pulled carts of which the owner can only work every second day. It's probably as well, as the effort to pull the carts up the hills, especially on hot summer's day, is backbreaking.

There is a lot to see on Gulangyu, and some visitors choose to spend the night or have a more extended stay in these converted villas rather than returning to the mainland. Wandering the streets and visiting the gardens would be a good choice for a whole week. Of the gardens, the jewel, of many, is the Shu Zhuang Garden (菽庄花园), part of the Piano Museum complex. It was built in 1913 and donated to China in 1955 by the Taiwanese-Fujian rice tycoon Lin Erjia (林爾嘉). It is a glorious combination of two gardens. The serene Bushan Garden purpose-built with many hidden elements that please the eye as they come into view, and there are twelve man-made caves in the cliffs which are perfect for children to play in. The Hidden Sea Garden impressed me more. Ancient China has an architectural history of stone walkways and bridges over freshwater ponds, but over a shallow saltwater bay with waves crashing against the rocks is most unusual. I tried to get into the mind of Lin Erjia. His 44 walkways, to match his then age, are over the shallow parts of the sea with suitable pavilions to hear the crashing or lapping waves. Indeed the name of the island (鼓浪嶼 – gu3lang4yu3) means "drum waves hitting the inlet", and his creation could hint at the power of music, something loved on this island.

Music, and especially classical music, is part of Gulangyu's life. Above the cliffs at the site of the former Wave Listening Pavilion is the Piano Museum. Tickets cover both the gardens and the museum. One of the nicknames for Gulangyu is "Piano Island". There are more than 100 pianos, many of which are valuable and rare, including 40 donated by the pianist Hu Youyi, a native of Gulangyu who now lives in Australia. Of the 20,000 or so residents of the island, they also own more than 600 personal pianos. In the museum are to be found, amongst others, the oldest four corner piano in the world, and an 1801 piano made by Muzio Clementi (1752 to 1832), the Italian-born English composer; rare because he was both piano maker, pianist, and composer. There are also several rare barrel organs on display. Gulangyu also boasts an organ museum also designed by the previously mentioned Dr. Otte, a modern 600 seat concert hall, a famous music school with master classes in your chosen instrument starting at around RMB 6800 (£780) including accommodations, for four 45 minute sessions. Famous musician residents of Gulangyu include composer and pianist Yin Chengzong, the 1962 runner-up of the International Tchaikovsky Piano Competition, and arranger/composer of The Yellow River Piano Concerto. In other years he might have won, but in 1962 the joint winners were no less than Vladimir Ashkenazy and John Ogden. Also associated are the famous opera singer and actress Ivy Ling Po, violinist Jing Yang, pianist Xu Feiping, and conductor Chen Zuohuang.

It would not be right to move on from Gulangyu without mentioning an exceptional lady, Lin Qiaozhi (林巧稚), whose career spanned the Qing dynasty and well into the PRC era (1901-1982). Her statue holding a baby is in the Yu Garden, and she was born on Gulangyu. She received a western education (London, Manchester, Vienna, and Chicago) and revolutionized Chinese gynaecology and obstetrics based at the Peking Union Medical College Hospital. Lin never married, and on each baby's name tag, she wrote "Lin Qiaozi's Baby", something she did more than 50,000 times in her career, one for each delivery she supervised.

The life for foreigners on Gulangyu abruptly ended with Xiamen's Japanese occupation in 1937, and by 1938 the island became flooded with refugees. The island was finally occupied in 1941, and the foreigners were expelled, and the Japanese language and education system were temporarily adopted.

Another aspect of Xiamen worth exploring is its distinctive architecture, of which four are the most noteworthy: Hakka tulou, southern Fujian style, Kah Kee, and modern.

Several of the Hakka tulou clusters are accessible as a day trip from Xiamen. Although I have explained the form and function of these roundhouses in the section on Chengdu, these are the real deal, and 46 of the sites became UNESCO World Heritage Sites in 2008. They were built from the twelfth century onwards. Some such as those at Yongding County, three hours drive from Xiamen, are easily accessible by public transportation or in more comfort with a tour guide and car. The second style is the South Fujian traditional red brick houses, which were also exported as a concept to Taiwan. This style can be traced back to the Tang Dynasty (618 to 907), especially in the Ming Dynasty (1368 to 1644), and continuing into the Qing Dynasty (1644 to 1911), and there are many variants. Typical characteristics are red brick walls and a wooden interior roof, swallow-tail ridges on tiled roves, small rectangular windows with bars giving a "jailhouse" effect, colourful decorations, a central uncovered courtyard, and often an ornate family temple nearby for veneration and keeping of family records. In recent years, in Xiamen and other southern Fujian cities, there has been a deal of effort to restore these quaint and historically valuable buildings and realize they are tourist attractions. Visitors are faced with a choice. Most will prefer a fully restored area such as in the Wudianshi (five shops) district. I chose something different: a restoration project in its infancy where it was possible to talk more freely with the locals and understand the traditions and construction techniques reusing ancient materials. There were few tourists, but the villagers had set up a small shop and a fish restaurant hoping for better things to come. The third distinctive style is called Tan Kah Kee (陈嘉庚 – chen2jia1geng1). Born in Xiamen in 1874, Tan made his fortune in Singapore, where his father emigrated as a teenager. His first successful enterprise was canned pineapples before becoming a multi-business tycoon and philanthropist, often giving to causes in mainland China. He was considered Hokkien (Min language speakers) and leader of the general Chinese community in Singapore. He was a strong supporter of Sun Yat-sen and became disillusioned with his perception of Nationalist corruption under Chiang Kai-shek, and later espoused the Communist cause. After hiding out the Second World War in Indonesia, he tried to return to Singapore in 1950 but was denied entry by the British because of his views and returned to the PRC, where he held several prominent positions. He had a particular interest in architecture, combining western and Chinese styles with local materials such as the glazed red bricks and orange tiles. His greatest influence can be seen at Xiamen University (take a short detour from a visit to the Nanputuo Temple (南普陀寺), but also the Lujian Hotel in Xiamen, and the Chinese Chamber of Commerce Building in Singapore. The university is probably the best example of Kah Kee style and is sometimes called "wearing a business suit with a bamboo hat".

What is so pleasing to the eye is that the modern buildings in Xiamen have extended this cultural heritage. The city is adorned with many fine and innovative modern buildings with more under construction. Some buildings look like an upside-down musical pitch tuning fork, several skyscrapers with holes in the middle as if someone took a bite out of them, some made to look like sailing yachts to reflect the maritime tradition. The weirdest of all and hated by the locals is a tower that looks like Jenga blocks that are about to fall over. For me, this one had a grotesque fascination, and it is the Chinese equivalent of Prince Charles' "monstrous carbuncle" when describing the proposed National Gallery extension in London. It is also the epitome of the type of architecture that President Xi rails at. When Xiamen is lit up at night and enhanced by colourful moving projections onto the buildings, it is beautiful, especially seen from on a boat in the estuary or from the sunning highways that loop out over the ocean and back over the beaches into the city.

For many Chinese and foreigners alike, they won't ever get the chance to visit or have the time to visit Taiwan. Still, Xiamen provides a rich source to understand the Taiwanese origins as well as the taste of it: literally. We finished up one weekend evening at what was once a fishing village, but it is now a raucous night market with street food called Zeng Cuo An (曾厝垵), although there are several similar areas as well as inexpensive indoor restaurants and more fine dining establishments on Zhongshan Road with its tributaries and street hawkers. There was something to suit every taste, but to me, there are three dominant features of this street food, namely, fish, meat, jelly, and fresh fruit. I'm not too fond of the texture of jelly, but for those who do this is jelly heaven, whether it be from the jelly fruit flavoured candies, the gelatinous noodles in the signature peanut (satay) soup, the sticky tapioca balls in bubble tea, or even the popular jellied sea worms/lugworms (for real) that are purported to have aphrodisiac qualities. I don't care if the last one was a favourite of Koxinga, I baulked at this dish, but I will admit that the strawberry flavoured jelly candy didn't taste too bad, and an adult version with sweet strawberry liquor inside could make it sensational. The fish, crustaceans, and meat had the opposite effect on me and are often grilled on a stick, and the shaved ice with fruit toppings or platters of exotic fresh fruit was delicious. Other specialities to look out for are misua noodles, oyster omelettes, spicy ginger duck, deep-fried tofu dumplings, and Tong'an wrapped pork. Another group of foods seems to be coming back in the opposite direction from Taiwan in the modern era. Cheese and fish stuffed baked potato and waffles with sweet fillings aren't typical mainland Chinese food.

Sweet Xiamen, I'll be back soon, I hope.

Harbin, Heilongjiang Province

The first time I went to Harbin (哈尔滨 – ha1'er3bin1) was in winter, and I was warned by a client that "in this world there is cold and there is Harbin cold". I wasn't impressed: a few years earlier, I had been to Minneapolis on a cold day when it was -26 C (14.8F). I knew real cold. For this Harbin trip, I had packed a fake fur hat with earpieces, warm hunting style gloves, wool scarf, and a thick London Fog greatcoat, and I needed them. It was unimaginably cold. Appropriately, Minneapolis has been twinned with Harbin since 1992. On every climatic measure, Harbin is colder. Harbin has a lower coldest ever temperature (-42.6 C/ -44.7F compared to -41.0 C/-41.8 F), a lower average January temperature (-22.9 C/-9.2) compared to -13.6 C/7.5F), and a cooler average July temperature (27.8 C/82.0F compared to 28.6 C/83.5F). The significant difference is Harbin has little snow in winter. It's bone dry, and face and moisturizer is a recommended addition to items packed. On the other hand, Minneapolis has lake effect snow and an average of 138 cm (54 inches) annually. One of the reasons Harbin is described as the coldest city in the world is that if you look on a map, it is north of the more temperate coastal Russian city of Vladivostok. Harbin and Minneapolis also have other things in common. They are important agricultural growing and processing centres with hinterlands as flat as a pancake. Harbin's hinterland is particularly blessed with rich black chernozem soils and abundant water, allowing the production of maize (corn), soybean, and rice.

Harbin is also famous for its language. It is considered by many academics and linguists to have the British equivalent of Received Pronunciation: pure or standard Mandarin.

Although best known as a winter venue, Harbin is also attractive in summer with its cool and pleasant climate and Summer Music Festival.

The world-class tourism venue, and visited by more than 15 million people annually from all over the world, is the Harbin International Ice and Snow Festival in January and February and keeps becoming lengthier. However, there are finite limits at the spring end as the structures become unstable and a hazard. 10,000 artisans and workers assemble it. The centrepiece, Ice and Snow World, opens in the evenings. Ice from the Songhua River is sawed into 700 kilogramme (1540 pounds) ice bricks up to one metre thick. The ice bricks and advanced lighting are then used to create illuminated structures, sometimes over 40 metres (120 feet) in height, and every year the buildings are different before it all melts away in summer. Some of the buildings are replicas of famous landmarks such as the 2019 Rome coliseum or the giant Egyptian Sphinx. Some are fairy tale fantasies of castles and palaces complete not with Mickey Mouse greeters but pandas instead. A second evening venue is Zhaolin Park, where master sculptors create spectacular works of art in ice and snow. Popular subjects from previous years include a giant pagoda and the 2013 sculpture "woman dancing with child", a stunning piece of original art. The final main venue is a daytime excursion to Sun Island. This is Harbin's main recreation area and is open year-round with various means of access, including a cable car and an electric tram ride around the island, which is advisable in winter, as most people can't take the cold for more than a couple of hours. It also has many giant ice sculptures in winter, but many are smaller and more intimate, and there are some indoor sculptures to avoid wind chill. Children and grown-up children will love the long toboggan run and snow tube fast rides, the Siberian Tiger Park and Polar Bear Park, and near the cable car is a reconstructed Russian village with shops selling souvenirs and comestibles. If you get fed up with walking on land, you can buy some cheap crampons from street vendors and walk home on the river.

There are other elements of the Ice Festival, and an important one is skiing at Yabuli International Ski Resorts (five of them), 125 miles (200 km) east of Harbin. Prices seem cheap to me compared to the west: two hours on the piste is about RMB 200 (£23) or RMB 500 (£57) for a full day, and a two-hour beginner lesson starts at RMB 260 (£30). As I have been a liability to both myself and all others within several miles when trying to ski, I had to do a bit of research on the quality of the skiing as I have no intention of ever going to Yabuli. I had to resort to online reviews such as this one which is gobbledygook to me, but it sounds OK:

"China's best ski resort, for now. 4 black runs, 5 blue/red slopes all deviations of one route. Sun Mountain resort best field to visit, one gondola and 3 lifts. Not bad overall but nothing compared to best of Europe or Japan. Worthwhile for 1 or 2 days if happen to be in Harbin anyway or even if living in Beijing. Otherwise not worth a specific trip".

I suspect the resort will be eclipsed in the future, and people will gravitate to the sites near Beijing being built for the 2022 Winter Olympics, hence the "for now" comment.

There are also opportunities to go skating, curling, snowmobiling, dog sledding, and watching the Saturday morning winter swimming club, bathing in the freezing river in Harbin. Taking your UK Outdoor Swimming Society or Brighton Swimming Club (English Channel) accreditations for the annual Christmas swim, even if translated into Chinese, isn't going to cut it here as you will likely die of hypothermia, so participation is not usually allowed.

Today, when you walk the streets of central Harbin, you are walking along streets rich in history, much of it tragic. The explanation why is a little convoluted and I have tried to condense it as best I can. Your walk and you should walk it if able, will take on a new life.

In the 20th Century, Heilongjiang and its capital, Harbin (population today 10.6 million), had critical strategic implications as the most practical way in times of war to access Beijing and all of China beyond, something that has been applied through history. Harbin, for example, would be directly in the firing line from the north of any attack from the Russian north. Although most westerners are aware of how World War III could have started in the 1962 Cuban Missile Crisis, they are probably less familiar that it could have started in Heilongjiang in 1969. By 1961, Mao's ideals wholly departed from the USSR with the renunciation of Soviet communism, and relations continued downhill thereafter. Matters came to a head when on March 2, 1969, after a border altercation on Zhenbao Island on the Ussuri River and probably started by China. Although the Chinese suffered the more extensive casualties, they were able to capture one of the state-of-the-art Russian T-62 tanks, which became incapacited in the river. First, the Chinese soldiers tried to rescue it but failed under constant heavy fire. Then the Chinese navy was called in to drag it out, but the Russians fired on their tank and sank it. Finally, when the Russians had left, satisfied the T-62 was unrecoverable, the Chinese somehow managed to secure their beaten-up prize. It was sent to the Lüshun (now Dalian) tank factory, one of the old terminus cities of the China Eastern Railway. The Russians tried one last time and sent a spy to blow up the factory, but he was caught and executed. This T-62 can't be seen in Harbin as it now resides in the Military Museum of the Chinese People's Revolution in Beijing. It is a worthy candidate to be the second most famous tank globally after the world's first, British 1915 "Little Willie" Mark 1 Tank, which has also been preserved in the UK. I am sure the Chinese army picked the T-62 apart nut by bolt in attempts at reverse engineering.

By the end of the 1969 summer, Russia was readying a nuclear attack on China, although it had been signalling quite openly its intentions to do so much earlier. It would have been an asymmetric war, as China had minimal nuclear weaponry and detonated its first nuclear test bomb in October 1964. However, it was going to be a bloodbath as China had its massive army, which was well dispersed by this stage, had its aircraft concealed, and had made great efforts to produce a string of underground bunkers. Chairman Mao had already taken refuge in Wuhan and his de facto number two, Lin Biao, in Suzhou. What averted the possibility of global war was the attitude of the US. On August 20, the Russian ambassador in Washington, Anatoly Dobrynin, and reporting to Brezhnev, informed Kissinger (and thereby President Nixon) that it planned a nuclear attack on China and asked the US to remain neutral. The US response was twofold. It threatened to unleash nuclear missiles on 130 Russian cities, and it also leaked the story to the great repository of leaks, the Washington Post, for the August 28 edition. China was saved from catastrophe and the wider world by the threat of a global war, by a most unlikely source, the US, who feared the USSR and not so much China. In China, Nixon is still remembered fondly for this and his 1972 visit to China, which ultimately broke China's isolation. The Washington Post, of course, was less than helpful to Nixon when it exposed him in the Watergate scandal in 1972.

The battle on the border in Heilongjiang continues to this day. On July 1, 2020, a video recording went viral of two giant brown bears sparring along the barbed wire fence line, one on each side of the border. In the ensuing mayhem, the fence posts were clawed into matchsticks. As in the Zhenbao Island case, it is unclear which side started the altercation, but there were no ursine casualties. Rare Amur tigers do better, and China and Russia have created a corridor for them to cross without let or hindrance. It's like a feline DMZ.

Russian influence in Harbin started in the early 1900s when the area was initially a string of villages, and today, Harbin is a Chinese city with some Russian characteristics. As it grew, more Russians were living in the city than Chinese, and even today, small parts of it are so Russian that you half expect a troika to slide out of a side street. There are plenty of street stalls selling rabbit, fox, and perhaps fake mink (judging by the price) fur hats, stacking Russian dolls, and restaurants selling distinctively Russian food. The catalyst for this expansion was the railway. After the 1894-95 China-Japan war, which China lost, in 1896, the weakened Qing Dynasty granted a railway concession to the Russian-owned China Eastern Railway. Russia was not a combatant in this war but was focused on imperialistic expansion. Harbin was the hub of this three-pronged railway system which linked the Siberian city of Chita to Vladivostok and onward into the Trans-Siberian railway. These were boom times for Harbin, and by 1913 in a census conducted by the railway, nearly half of the city's 68,500 residents were Russians (34,313 compared to around 23,537 Chinese of various ethnic groups). The Russians had their own schools, newspapers, orchestra (the oldest in China), and ballet. The next most prominent ethnic group was categorized in a census as Jews (5,032), but there were also Poles, Japanese, Georgians, Lithuanians, Germans, and a smattering of others. Russia occupied Manchuria from 1900-1905, of which Heilongjiang was a part, as a result of Boxers attacking the railway. It removed its Cossacks as a result of the Treaty of Portsmouth (New Hampshire, US) in 1905 as a consequence of the 1904-05 Russo-Japanese War, which Russia lost badly. Some historians believe this war marked the beginning of the end for Tsar Nicholas II. The treaty mediator was President Theodore Roosevelt, who was awarded the Nobel Peace Prize for his considerable effort. Although the Russians were forced into many concessions, they managed to keep the China Eastern Railway. It was finally sold by the USSR to the Japanese in 1935, another dangerous sign for the Harbinsty.

By 1917, Harbin had over 100,000 residents. Still, few would have realized the impending disaster that was to come as they sipped their smoky tea on Kitayskava Ulitsa, now called Central Street (中央大街

– zhong1yang1da4jie1 and pedestrian-only) with the original brick cobbles from 1898 still present. Postcards of the era show wealthy and immaculately dressed Russian adults, men in blazers and boaters, women in long dresses and white hats, with children dressed in western clothes, the boys wearing shorts and long socks, and the girls in brightly coloured dresses with lace ruffles. This street is a mix of European styles. In its heyday, it had elegant salons, urbane shops selling the latest French and Russian fashions, ice cream parlours (you can still buy delicious Russian ice cream all over China), perfumeries, and tea and coffee houses. The Russian influence is still easy to see in the Hotel Moderne (1914) designed by Sergei A. Vensan of St. Petersburg, and the Jiaoyu Bookstore (Education Bookstore), and in the preserved imperial dining room of Lucia Restaurant and Coffee House. There are also several examples of renaissance and art nouveau styles, including the Fu'er Shop for the former and the Daoliqiulin Shop for the latter.

The Russians and others also left behind their food culture, which sometimes became a fusion with Chinese food, and today there is still a legacy of other cultures' foods such as Korean and Japanese. As befits its history, Harbin also has numerous Korean and Japanese restaurants. The purely Chinese restaurants have their regional flavours that feature hearty dishes with many green onions, chives, and ginger. The signature dish is sweet and sour pork (锅爆肉 – guo1bao1rou4), where morsels of pork are fried in batter before adding the sauce, which has honey and ginger notes. There are plenty of restaurants in sumptuous surroundings serving something like the classics of Russian gastronomy: stroganoff, caviar blini, borscht, and the local Russian style specialities such as baked fish in sour cream sauce. Dig a little deeper and you will find the Russian-Chinese food a unique experience. First is the bread. The Chinese were never going to take to the rock-hard and bitter rye bread (I have some sympathy), so a little tweaking was needed. The solution was to use wheat flour and create a sort of sourdough cousin using beer hops as a natural starter, to create a loaf called dalieba (大列巴). "Da" means big in Chinese and "lieba" is a Chinese derivation of khleb (хлеб), the Russian word for bread, and in this case, each loaf is 2 to 2.5 kilogrammes (4.4 to 5.5 pounds). At the bakery chain, Bomele (est. 1931), you can buy this unique bread, including at the one on Central Street, which also has coffee, ice cream, and cakes downstairs and a restaurant upstairs. There are many fusion restaurants in this area, but I won't recommend an individual one, as exploring and choosing is part of the fun. It is worth looking out for Russian specialities, and some of the best is the street food. The most famous is a smoked red sausage (红肠 – hong2chang2), which comes with a thin layer of dust, giving the smoky barbeque flavour. Place it on a hunk of dalieba, and when offered, add the extra herbal spices and wash it down with an ice-cold Harbin Beer. Although not quite as famous as Tsingtao, the Harbin brewery was opened three years earlier in 1900. A good time to be in Harbin for beer enthusiasts is July and August for the Harbin International Beer Festival. The brewery is open to visitors year-round. Another worthwhile visit on Central Street is Madier (马迭尔 – ma3die2er3), a Russian ice lolly (popsicle) shop selling Russian slightly salty and creamy flavours. It is eaten even in the depths of winter.

A second street, no to be missed is Gogol Street (果戈里街 – guo-3ge1li3jie1), in the adjacent Nangang District to the east of Daoli District where Central Street is located. Built in 1901, it has the original horseshoe paving stones and slab marble historical friezes. Although there is abundant above ground and underground shopping, this is a place to consider visiting at night as it lit by more than 150 elegant converted European style gas lights as well as pretty ornamental lighting in the establishments, and there are plenty of bars and pubs to drink shots of vodka with glasses of local beer. Places worth a visit include the 1935 St. Alekseyev Church with its magnificent iconography, and the Churin & Co (Чурин и Ко) department store. This famous old company was started in Khabarovsk in 1882 but moved its headquarters to Harbin in 1904 and shortly after opening seven other stores across northern China. Also worth a visit is the Gogol Bookstore with its high back chairs and sofas, oak reading tables, portraits in oil paint, and chandeliers. You can browse and read all day here without interruption, and it has a feel of a 1900s St. Petersburg reading room.

The unforgettable signature building of Harbin is the previously Russian Eastern Orthodox Saint Sophia Cathedral. It's a half-mile walk from Central Street, and it needs to be seen twice, once in the daytime and once lit up at night. It attracts millions of visitors from all over the world. It now houses a fascinating art museum. Built in 1907, out of timber, and then improved in wood and masonry in 1923, the cathedral is a magnificent and tall Byzantine-style building tipped with a substantial green onion dome, with a mural of the last supper on the inside of the dome. The cathedral is surrounded by an elegant square complete with white doves and musical fountains.

Although one of the defining moments in modern history was the 1914 assignation of Archduke Franz Ferdinand in Sarajevo, Harbin, in one case directly, also had a role to play in the turbulent earlier part of the 20th century. The central station (松花江站 – song1hua1jiang-1zhan4) and bridge with the remains of the 1899 railway station that became Harbin Station in 1903 is an interesting diversion. Its art nouveau decoration, redeveloped in sympathetic style in the 1990s, hides a darker moment in history. Inside the station, you will find a memorial room, more like a corridor really, to commemorate the Korean, An Jung-Geung who hid a Browning semi-automatic pistol in his lunch box and assassinated Japan's first Prime Minister, Itō Hirobumi, in 1909. The exact spot of the assassination is marked with a plaque. An Jung-Geung must have been a capable marksman as he also managed to shoot and seriously injure three other Japanese diplomats and businessmen. The memorial room is controversial. At this time, Japan was in the process of colonizing Korea. To this day, in Korea, An is considered a hero, and the Japanese consider him a terrorist. He was captured by Russian guards and handed over to the Japanese, and requested to be executed by firing squad as a prisoner of war but was hung like a common criminal instead.

After the 1917 Russian Revolution, Harbin became a white Russian enclave, and the white Russian army secured the China Eastern Railway, and fleeing émigrés bolstered the Russian population to perhaps 100,000 people. Although demise was slow to come, Harbin also became a centre and hotbed for the Russian Fascist Organisation (RFO) with its central office in Harbin, which was later to have horrific consequences for the Harbinsty. The leader of the party, Rodzaevsky, developed strong ties to Japan and in particular the Kwantung Army that had been formed in 1906 to guard the South Manchuria Railway that Russia had ceded to Japan after 1904-5 Russo-Japanese War. The Kwantung Army later went on to have importance as the guardian of the puppet State of Manchuria (Manchukuo), created from the Japanese invasion in 1931 and later called the Empire of Manchuria, which survived until 1945. This is a classic definition of a puppet state because Japan installed Puyi as Emperor, the last Qing emperor forced to abdicate in 1912. Rodzaevsky was fervently anti-Semitic, especially against "red Jews" which may have spared the worst for "white Jews" in Harbin. He was helpful to the Japanese: his mostly Russian-speaking Asano Brigade, although commanded by Japanese officers, was capable of counter-insurgency against the Red Army. They were also able to round up suitable candidates for entry into the Harbin experimental Unit 731 programme.

There is a museum at 25 Xinjiang Da Jie (新疆大街), in Harbin dedicated to the Harbin 731 experiment. The level of depravity is so shocking that some may even choose not to visit, although the most appalling photographs, some of which I have seen, are not on display. Although not so well known in the west, Chinese children are taught in school about this place. With the innocuous name of Epidemic Prevention and Water Purification Department, Unit 731 was the most infamous of the Japanese World War II biological warfare facilities in China, although there was an extensive network of perhaps 15 related units, such as Unit 1855 (Beijing), Unit 673 (Sunwu), Unit 8604 (Guangzhou) and Unit 1644. The commander of the program from 1936 to 1945 (and based in Harbin Unit 731) was Lieutenant General Shirō Ishii. Although the main focus was on developing suitable biological warfare agents, other types of human experimentation were taking place related to trauma. Suitable subjects for experimentation were Chinese communists, Koreans, Mongolians, "red" Russians, and other prisoners and dissenters. Collectively, and presumably, to depersonalise the atrocities, they were known as "logs". At the Unit 731 museum, you can learn about the methods used and about how the most suitable biological warfare candidates were released onto the unsuspecting population at large. On the internal experiments, there are photographs, documents, and some life-size mock-ups of the experiments, which include:

- Trauma testing and efficacy from various weapons, including live fire at different ranges on inmates by pistols, machine guns, flame-throwers, grenades, and short-range bayonets and knives. Subjects included pregnant women so that the dead foetuses could be examined for injuries.

- Dropping heavy objects on bound inmates to observe crush injuries.

- Strapping adults and children into centrifugal spinners and increasing the G forces forcing a loss of consciousness and frequent death.

- Starving inmates and only providing saline water to drink to see how long they could survive.

- Hypothermia studies by placing limbs in frozen tubs of water and examining the effects of different types of re-warming.

- Exposing inmates to massive X-rays doses to determine burn damage and fatality.

- Vivisection without anaesthesia, including the amputation of limbs and re-attachment to the other side of the body, and cutting blood circulation to observe the effects of gangrene.

- Using syphilitic males to force rape both males and females to study the progression of the disease.

Apart from biological experimentation within Unit 731 and other related units, the biological agents were also released on the Chinese public. One experiment was to infect the inmates with *Yersinia pestis*, which causes pneumonic and bubonic plague and typhus. The sickest were kept alive for their blood to be transfused to infect others, and the least sick were shot. The final step for the last batch of infected prisoners was to expose them to vast quantities of fleas and their bites. The fleas were then packed in dust and inserted into bombs. On October 4, 1940, the bombs were dropped over Quzhou in Zhejiang Province. At least 2000 civilians died from the ensuing plague and another 1000 in nearby Yiwu. Another attack using anthrax killed around 6000 people in the same area. In a further example, more than 1000 wells were contaminated to study cholera and typhus. The estimates are around 30,000 dead; many after the Japanese had surrendered.

Another shocking part of Unit 731 is that no one was ever prosecuted by the allies for the crimes. There is documentary evidence in the museum that hints at the reason why in the form of a US report dated June reference WAR 99277 from the Legal Section of SCAP (Supreme Command Allied Powers) to WDSCA (War Department Special Staff Civil Affairs Division):

1. "The reports and files of the Legal Services Section on Ishii and his co-workers are based on anonymous letters, hearsay affidavits and rumors. The Legal Section interrogations, to date, of the numerous persons concerned with the BW (Biological Warfare) project in China, do not reveal sufficient evidence to support war crime charges. The alleged victims are of unknown identity.

   Unconfirmed allegations are to the effect that criminals, farmers, women and children were used for BW experimental purposes. The Japanese Communist Party alleges that: "Ishii BKA (Bacterial War Army) conducted experiments on captured Americans in Mukden and that simultaneously, research on similar lines was conducted in Tokyo and Kyoto.

2. None of Ishii's subordinates are charged or held as war crime suspects nor is there sufficient evidence on file against them......

3. None of our Allies to date have filed war crimes charges against Ishii or any of his associates.

4. Neither Ishii nor his associates are included among major Japanese war criminals awaiting trial…".

There were both American and British POW's at Unit 731 and even more in other units. Although never proven, part of the Japanese interest in Unit 731 was the bacteriological reactions to different ethnic groups, and they would have made good test subjects. The American government and their allies had basically turned a blind eye to cut a deal to get the intelligence on BW and never brought charges. Many of the Unit 731 group returned to academic life in Japan. Twelve members of Unit 731 captured by the Russians were put on trial in Khabarovsk in 1949. They received light sentences relative to the crime of between two and 25 years imprisonment, presumably having cooperated with the Russians. They were later repatriated back to Japan.

As the Russian forces closed in on the Japanese in 1945, Harbin was a scene of widespread panic. Where were the white Russians and ethnic groups to run to? Many, who had already had their property confiscated by the Japanese, chose to take citizenship of the USSR or were forcibly deported there. A significant number had already taken Soviet citizenship to avoid becoming stateless from 1920 when the Republic of China severed diplomatic relations with the USSR. 48,000 of the returning group were arrested as Japanese spies in Stalin's purge of 1936-38. Execution or being sent to the Gulag followed. A few, and especially Jews, fled to Japanese occupied Shanghai and survived, and you can read their unlikely and moving story of survival in *The Lure of the Red Dragon*. Some went to Tianjin and Palestine. Rodzaevsky's approach was to surrender in Harbin and appeal to Stalin that he was a patriot and nationalist and wanted to overthrow the "Jewish" influenced government in Moscow. It proved to be a fatal mistake. His appeal didn't do him any good. On his return to Russia with a promise of freedom, he was put on a show-trial along with several other party members. He was executed in the notorious Lubyanka Prison. By the late 1930s, Harbin's Russian population had dropped to about 30,000, and in the 1964 Chinese census, only 450 remained after a forced second wave of immigration to the USSR in 1952. Some avoided this second wave and managed to escape to far-flung destinations, including Brazil, Israel, Canada, and the US. The Cultural Revolution saw the final stab to the heart of the Harbinsty with the destruction of around 50 synagogues with only two re-purposed ones remaining today as well as the 1966 demolishing of the wooden Orthodox cathedral of

St. Nicholas, built in 1900. Today, finally, there is a solid movement to preserve Harbin's heritage.

I don't want to leave Harbin on this dark note because the future for Harbin is a bright one. It's a vibrant modern city with some spectacular modern architecture, such as the 2015 swirling Harbin Grand Theatre designed by Ma Yansong and a significant venue for the summer music festival. Today the Russians are back, trading their oil and gas and other hard commodities. The Russian ice cream remains ever-popular. The new trend you will find in many shops is the Russian "purple candy", a chocolate exterior with crushed almonds and powdered roasted peanuts inside (Kpokaht) in a purple wrapper. It's addictive and mandatory at Harbin weddings.

Chapter 11: New Heroes

I picked out four unusual heroes in the *Lure of the Red Dragon*: one American (Claire Lee Chennault) and three Chinese (Rang Guangqi, Ho Fengshan, and Liang Yijuan). Chennault, in his time, was justifiably famous, the others much more obscure. I deliberately set out not to re-gurgitate the biographies of larger-than-life characters in China's story, although in one case in the new heroes, Chairman Mao and George H.W. Bush both play a bit-part. The new heroes are William Taylor (American), Bernhard Sindberg (Danish), Dr. Wu Lien-teh (Malaysian), and Yuan Longping (Chinese).

William Taylor

The John Farrow directed semi-propaganda war movie, the critically acclaimed Wake Island (1942), the references to the battle in Quentin Tarantino movie Pulp Fiction (1994), and the frequently studied and re-lated attack on Pearl Harbour means that for many Americans, they are familiar with the events that occurred on Wake Island at the end of 1941. After the 1942 movie, the actor Macdonald Carey (Lieutenant Bruce Cameron) was sufficiently inspired by it that he joined the US Marines in 1943 and remained on active service until 1947.

I discovered the escapades of William Taylor by accident in a brief Chinese reference to a man of this name who jumped from a train near my home city of Suzhou. What I unearthed is a story of a surprising hero.

William Lorin Taylor (1917 to 2011) was born in Ogden, Utah, and as a 23-year-old took a contract as a builder, one of 1,045 men, including his brother Jack, and went to Wake Island in August 1941. By 1941, the

American military high command was almost sure that a Japanese attack would come in the Pacific one day. The 1937 oil embargo for invading China strapped Japan of this precious resource and almost guaranteed this. Although isolated, Wake Island, the largest of three islands in the coral atoll, had enough room to accommodate an airstrip within bombing range of Japan. Aviation already existed in Wake, on Peale Island, because it was an important refuelling point for the Pan-Am Clipper from 1936 onwards and allowed the journey from San Francisco to Hong Kong to be completed in six days rather than a month or more voyage by sea. The trip even brought tourists to Wake, seeking adventure and deep-sea fishing. The Pan-Am facility was serviced by 45 Chamorro men (native Micronesians) and a handful of expatriate staff. But the Clipper was a flying boat. What was needed was a war-ready airfield and logistical support.

Taylor's outbound journey and the beginning of his time on Wake were pleasurable. His employer, Morrison and Knudsen Construction Company, had negotiated a cost-plus contract with the US Government. The effect of this was that the company didn't care how many luxuries were provided. Uncle Sam was footing the bill. Part of Taylor's outward journey was in a first-class cabin on a luxury cruise liner while pulling three times the pay he could have earned back home. He was a child with a wandering family in the Great Depression and was impressed by the luxuriousness. He arrived on Wake on August 19, 1941, and set about his tasks. Many luxuries accompanied hard physical work, and to Taylor, it was an idyllic location. Although not a military man, Taylor observed the shoddily equipped US forces first, noting that the Americans were issued with 1913 bolt action Springfield rifles and World War I helmets. Defences were flawed and incomplete, and critically there was also no radar capability. During this period, the US Congress had also been fiddling around and arguing whether Wake deserved further funding.

What followed was a mixture of astounding bravery and military misjudgements by both the Americans and the Japanese. The Americans who were battle experienced from the European theatre felt the Japanese and their antiquated bi-planes and inferior fighting techniques presented only a minor threat. The Japanese were over-confident in their unproven and mighty navy and aircraft carriers which certainly weren't stocked with bi-planes, but lethal Aichi D3A Dive Bombers, Mitsubishi A6M Fighter-Bombers, and Nakajima B5N Torpedo Bombers. The US was also preoccupied with the war in Europe.

On November 28, Commander Winfield S. Cunningham arrived at Wake Island to assume overall command of a military contingent that by then consisted of 379 marines under the command of Major P.S Devereux, six army signals corps, 72 US Navy personnel, 12 Grumman F4F-3 Wildcat fighters with flying and ground crew, 59 in number, and an assortment of guns: six 127mm (5 inch) guns, 12 anti-aircraft guns, 18 Browning heavy machine guns, and 30 assorted other machine guns. The fighter planes carried no navigation or direction finders which meant they could only work when visibility allowed. The civilians numbered 1146 contractors and 70 Pan-Am employees. Taylor was already aware of impending danger, alerted by the passenger behaviour on the Pan-Am Clipper in November, where the window blinds were kept down as diplomats (both American and Japanese) and other dignitaries moved back and forth. One of the occupants in November, according to Taylor, was one Ernest Miller Hemingway. Hemingway, in February 1941, had pulled off a highly successful trip to China masquerading as the famous heavy drinking writer with his third wife, Martha Gellhorn, alongside him. He was working as a spy for the US Treasury Department, and the couple even managed to fly behind enemy lines in Guangzhou on the way to Chinese-held territory in Guangdong. On this trip, they met Chiang Kai-shek and his wife (who they did not like), and on April 14 in Chongqing, they had a covert meeting with Zhou Enlai (who they found charming).

The man who arranged this spying trip, I kid you not, was called Bond, but not with the first name James. Hemingway left Hong Kong alone on May 6. His marriage was already in trouble. The intelligence he had gathered would have been invaluable. He was never again seen in Asia, so why was he on Wake Island in November 1941? It seems an odd time to be doing a spot of deep-sea fishing.

Several American strategists in high command had concluded that Wake Island would be the first point of a Japanese attack, along with Guam, when the Japanese sprung the deadly and more head-on attack at Pearl Harbour, which started at 7.55 am on Sunday, December 7, in Honolulu, 5.55 am on Wake on Monday, December 8 (Wake is the other side of the international date line). In less than two hours, the US lost 2,335 servicemen with 1,143 injured, destroyed six battleships, and disabled the remaining two. The three aircraft carriers, which were the most important targets for the Japanese, were all out at sea on exercises. Simultaneous attacks were also carried out on Guam, which fell within two days, and Wake Island.

The first attack on Wake came at 11.50 am, local time, on December 8. As Taylor later described it:

"We got plastered…I was sitting on the back of a flatbed truck ready to go into lunch…and the Japanese came over the island and so I had a panoramic view of what was going on. They hit our aircraft".

Taylor reports seeing three groups of nine Japanese bombers, but there were, in fact, 36 planes in total. Only four US planes were spared as they were in the air at the time, but they couldn't engage because of poor visibility. The expatriate Pan-Am employees were immediately evacuated on a passing flying boat. Of the 45 Chamorro men, in the final death toll, 12 were killed, but it is unclear what happened to the remainder. Taylor never mentions them as a specific group.

Two more aerial attacks followed on December 9 and 10. The first destroyed the Pan-Am terminal and civilian hospital. The second was on the gun emplacements on nearby Wilkes Island. The Japanese reported to their commanders they had been destroyed, but they remained intact due to fortifications built by the army and the contractors. On December 11, the inevitable Japanese invasion began. It consisted of three light cruisers, six destroyers, three submarines, and two troop carriers with 450 special naval forces. Devereux played a good hand. He correctly suspected the Japanese thought they had destroyed the heavy gun emplacements, and he let the attacking vessels come close to the shore at 3700 metres (4000 yards) before opening fire. Seemingly, there was no need for the Japanese commander, Rear Admiral Sadamichi Kajioka, to commence with a bombardment out of range of the US heavy guns as he thought they were already destroyed. He likely felt emboldened by the stunning successes at Pearl Harbour and in Guam. Under the US close-range bombardment, the destroyer Hayate was sunk in two minutes, and the four remaining Wildcats sank the destroyer Kisaragi in both cases with almost complete loss of life. One of the features of the Wildcats were their ability to carry two 45 kilogramme (100 pound) bombs, and it was this that caused the loss of the Kisaragi. The light cruiser Yubari was allegedly also hit. The Japanese withdrew. The Hayate became the first surface naval ship lost by the Japanese in World War II. It was a huge loss of face for Kajioka and also because the Japanese press, also brimming with patriotism and confidence, had already reported a victory. After that, the Japanese continued bombing raids, with the US marines moving the guns almost nightly, a Herculean task that could not be undertaken without the accompanying sweat of the contractors. In his later memoirs, Taylor remained bitter that the contractors received no recognition for their bravery and immense work effort, although that was finally put to right many years later. The contractors were also dispersed and dug foxholes and latrines, and food was delivered around the island by food truck.

Taylor describes the different phases the contractors went through. They were sure the Japanese would return with much greater force to try and take Wake, and they knew how vicious the Japanese would be if captured. They didn't have an immediate problem with food, but a direct hit on the freshwater desalination plant would have been catastrophic, and there were only two available doctors. During this period, Taylor came close to losing his life, which would later happen with frequency. He was in a cramped dugout with five others when a bomb landed close by. As Taylor describes it:

"…there was a tremendous explosion right outside the entrance to the dugout. Sand, dust, and bits of coral filled the air inside the room… After about a minute, I heard someone calling me, 'Hey Bill, come on out and see this crater that was left by the last bomb.' I got up, moved through the dust and stuck my head out of the dugout, then I took a few steps up and I could see a huge crater, about twenty-five feet across and ten feet deep at its center. Now that might not seem like a really large hole until you realize it was coral sand. To make a crater that large in coral sand would require at least a five-hundred-pound bomb. I sat down on the edge of the crater and realized that if it had been about twenty feet closer to our shelter, I wouldn't have survived".

At first, there was a great deal of optimism that the US would mount a rescue. That was attempted by a force including the aircraft carrier USS Saratoga, put together by Admiral E. Kimmel in mid-December, shortly before Roosevelt fired him for not recognizing the threat to Pearl Harbour. His replacement, Vice Admiral William S. Pye, continued with the plan, but he knew he was only a temporary replacement and was risk-averse. He relinquished command on December 31, so he was correct about his interim position. Although the assembled got close to Wake, Pye recalled the relief force, thereby abandoning the defenders on Wake. It was a highly controversial decision. Some of the relief marines cried at abandoning their brothers, and Taylor believes the force would have beaten the Japanese to the atoll by one day and is scathing about the incident.

The second invasion of Wake began with a preliminary naval bombardment and a landing at 2.35 am on December 23 with a fortunate, humbled, and probably angry Kajioka given a second chance in command. The Japanese had a reinforced fleet and 1500 marines under then Captain Shiegematsu Sakaibara. Despite a spirited defence by the afternoon of the same day, it was all over, and the Americans surrendered. The battle again was not without controversy. This should have been a fight to the death as the Japanese Special Forces would have been expected to win or perish, and the US marines are expected never to surrender. In the confusion of the battle and after some poor military tactics by Cunningham, the shocked marine commander Devereux was ordered by Cunningham to surrender.

During all the hostilities, the US marines lost 49 men, with another 49 wounded and two missing. The US Navy lost three men, and 70 civilians were killed (including the 12 Chamorro), and 12 were wounded. The Japanese lost 144 men. The remaining captives were taken to a road running to the aggregate pit, stripped naked, and some were placed in gruesome contraptions made of phone wire that meant if you stretched your arms, a noose around your neck tightened. Machine guns were brought up, and Taylor was convinced they would all be killed. He observed Kajioka arguing with one of the landing party officers about what Taylor believed was their impending execution, and it appears Kajioka refused the request. If the subordinate (not proven as it may have been a man called Tachibana) was Sakaibara, as we shall see later, it makes Taylor's assertion very likely. After three hours, the sunburned and dehydrated survivors were told to dress and taken to the airfield by truck and given gasoline contaminated water which made many of them sick.

That night, after the arrival of heavy rain, they were stuffed into a hangar where many had to try and sleep standing and retching, and the process was repeated the following day. Finally, on the next day, they were moved to the barracks, which now had a barbed-wire fence. It was Christmas Day, 1941. This was to be their place of incarceration until January 12.

Several important events happened to Taylor during this period. First, he showed his survival instincts, something that would reappear many times over the coming years. Rather than accept the horrendously cramped conditions, he dug a small cave under a concrete slab which he eventually shared with his brother Jack. As the Japanese started to let the men out of the compound in small groups, Taylor recovered some food from previous foxholes and stored it in his cave. No one else tried to build a den. The second event was that during this period, he quit smoking and asked God for help. Although nominally a Mormon, Taylor had never been from a church-going family, and this was the start of a religious conversion. Any surplus cigarettes he acquired also became a valuable currency when he later became accomplished in prison trading.

On January 12, the Japanese separated 98 captives who were to be kept on Wake as forced labour. The rest were loaded into the bottom hold a former cruise liner, the Nitta Maru, bound for Shanghai via Yokohama. Again, Taylor nearly lost his life from being crushed between the transfer barge and the vessel and was rescued by a young Japanese soldier. The journey in the cramped hold was horrendous with insufficient food, and the captives were swimming in shit. During the first part of the voyage, there was a brutal beating for any infraction. At one point, Taylor managed to secrete a fellow's Ingersoll watch and Schaefer pen set in a search where the Japanese took anything of value. It became his property. He was starting to make Milo in Catch 22 look like a beginner. Significantly, during this time in the hold, Taylor was introduced to the Mormon "Articles of Faith" and the Beatitudes by a scriptorian, someone of knowledge, Oscar Rayand, and adopted them.

On the second leg of the journey, Taylor observed three marines and two sailors being taken for questioning. They did not return, which he discovered after the war was because they had been summarily executed by samurai sword as a revenge killing for Wake. On January 24, 1942, the Nitta Maru finally docked at the Port of Woosung, near Shanghai, and the POWs were marched seven miles in freezing weather to the prison camp. It was Taylor's first view of China.

There is a report called *Prisoner of War Camps in Areas other Than the Four Principal Islands of Japan* published July 31, 1946, by the Liaison and Research Branch, American Prisoner of War Information Bureau. It provides valuable information (and photographs) of both the POW camps that Taylor was incarcerated in, Woosung and Kiangwan. Woosung was not worse camp in China in the report (that would be Bridge House Jail, Shanghai), but it was a long way from the best camps, especially for those singled out as from Wake.

There were two features of incarceration in all of these camps outside of Japan. First, captured officers were treated much better than the rank and file and were usually kept separate. They were typically awarded the same pay rate as their equivalent rank in Japan, less deduction for "room and board", and were not required to contribute to hard manual labour. The report also says that enlisted men also received a tiny amount of pay for their work and the contractors even less, though Taylor said he never received any money. The second one was that the Japanese rarely provided any clothing, only occasionally shoes, and often insufficient blankets, although Taylor did receive some thin undersized khakis. This particularly disadvantaged the Wake contingent, who had arrived in tropical clothing. The captured marines, serving as guards from the US Embassy in Tientsin (Tianjin), fared much better and were allowed to bring clothing, personal belongings, and money, another source of potential trading revenue for Taylor. These marines had surrendered the embassy without a fight. The report describes the malnourishment, dire hygiene, and lack of winter heat in the early days. Taylor was apprehensive about the older American contractors aged 40 to 60 years and their lack of conformity. You have to go to Taylor's account to understand this. The first two days, they received substantial meals of curried meat and rice, but on the third day, the guards found that the inmates had thrown some rice away. The ration was soon changed to something meagre. The guards also provided wood-burning heaters, and the Americans tried to get warmer still by cutting down and burning the roof beams. So, the heaters were removed, never to be reissued. Taylor realised that the key to survival was to supplement his needs with traded extra rice, tins of vegetables, etc. Starting with his "seed money" from the sale of the watch and pen, he became the go-between with the Japanese guards, profitably trading cigarettes for cash. At this time, many prisoners thought they would be exchanged or repatriated, and morale in the camp in the report is described as good. Taylor correctly thought otherwise and bartered his cigarettes for promissory notes to supply the 20 cigarettes per week ration to him until they were released.

By and large, Taylor appears to have been a model prisoner and kept out of trouble, and therefore avoided much of the beating, face slapping and random collective punishments, removal of food, and solitary confinement. This was meted out by a man the report and Taylor identified as chief interpreter Ishibara. Taylor even learned a little Japanese and Chinese. From the beginning, he was already thinking about and discussing escape but could see no feasible way. Even if he could have got through the electric fence or slipped away from a work party, being a relatively tall white man with limited Mandarin in a city where cooperation by a local sympathiser would have been fatal for both was daunting. All the occupants and Japanese guards and staff of Woosung were moved to Kiangwan Camp on December 6, 1942. This camp had 1600 POWs, the Wake contingent, and the extras made up of 80 British and a few other nationalities. Conditions improved markedly.

At one point, Ishihara called Taylor to an interrogation. Fortunately, he only asked if he had ever traded with the Chinese, and not the Japanese guards, via the locally employed human waste removers called "honey bucket boys". Trading with the Chinese was punishable by death, and Taylor did not need to lie as he had not. Taylor did, however, have only good words for the senior Japanese doctor, Dr. (Captain) Ishiro, who managed somehow to balance his Hippocratic Oath with the criticism he was too soft on the POWs. Ishiro saved many men from death (including Taylor twice) by administering quinine for malaria and managed to get medicines for dysentery, typhus, and cholera, and smallpox inoculations. Food rations were much improved, although still only 2,150 calories per day; not enough for heavy labour, and sometimes supplemented by some Red Cross parcels and a few raised pigs, goats, and rabbits. An extensive library had been moved from closed consulates in Shanghai and there was access to radio for a while until the war news got too bad for the Japanese. There was some opportunity to send and receive mail. In early February 1944, Taylor was called to another interrogation with the underling translator, Morisako. There on his desk, to his disbelief, was The Book of Mormon that he had requested from his brother Dick. Taylor was on reasonable terms with Morisako, and it paid off on this occasion. After some questioning about why this bible wasn't like any other he had ever seen, Morisako let him keep this incredible gift.

Taylor finally managed to escape in May 1945. On May 9, the entire camp was being moved northward by train in boxcars with barbed wire over the windows, although several contingents had already been sent to Japan in earlier moves, including his brother, Jack, who was so mistreated nearly didn't survive. On May 10, five officers escaped, and on May 11, Taylor, with a compatriot, Jack Hernandez, managed to escape using some pliers Taylor had purloined to cut through the window wire. In the dangerous jump at night, Hernandez had to be left behind with a broken leg and was recaptured, but Taylor escaped.

His first encounter with a Chinese person, a farmer, was the following day as he had spent the first day in a wheat field hiding from searches and resting a swollen ankle. The farmer gave him water and directed him around a local Japanese barracks, walking with him for several hours to make sure he was safe. Avoiding villages where he could, the following evening, he had to get water from an old farmer and his wife, and this time the entire village turned out to greet or stare at him. These numbers and unwanted attention presented a great danger. On May 13, Taylor's luck had seemingly run out as he was caught in a field by two Chung Wei Hui soldiers, Chinese soldiers working for the Japanese, one with an old bolt action rifle and one with a pistol. Forced to his knees and stripped, non-combatant contractor Taylor saw an opportunity and tried to trip the rifleman but failed and finished fighting with him for control with the pistol man trying to get a shot in. The pistol man eventually got his gun close to Taylor's throat, and he let go of the rifle only to be clubbed to the ground. He wasn't badly hurt and feigned unconsciousness while the soldiers started to go through the contents of his Red Cross sack. He then proceeded to run zigzag style being shot at as he made his escape. By now, you might have started counting how many lives Taylor had: surely more than the nine lives of a cat with more to follow. Eventually, he found a village in the dark and freezing cold, and wearing only shoes and underpants, he entered a tiny hut where a man was snoring. Stealthily he stole the man's bedclothes and ran. The bedclothes turned out to be a thick coat and shirt, and when he put his hand in his pocket, Taylor found a wad of cash: the man's life savings, not an uncommon occurrence at the time. Shortly afterwards, he entered a village and was captured, but the soldiers welcomed him, fed him, and let him wash. He was in the hands of the Communist Eight Route Army, the Paluchun, and they found an English speaker to explain they were friends and treated him like a dignitary for the rest of the trip.

No other person escaped by this northern route during the war. What followed is a series of transfers across enemy territory, often on horseback or by donkey, all perilous and organized mainly by Brigadier General Wong and his able staff. Even the collaborationist Wang Jing Wei puppet army helped, not so loyal to their Japanese masters. The Japanese owned the lines of communication and especially the railroad and the Communists the countryside and trails. Every traverse of a railroad was a point of danger. During this part of the journey, three things happened that I think might have surprised Taylor. First, he met a young female and English-speaking soldier, San Leung. Her pictures show her to be beautiful, something only enhanced by her military uniform. There was no impropriety but undoubtedly strong feelings. This was a period of female emancipation in the Communist ranks and a different world from the foot-bound female farmers Taylor had observed on his journey. The second was the number of English speakers who had been drawn to the cause from all over the world, and particularly from Korea. The third was how organized and motivated the Communist army was.

Eventually, in Chinese Communist officer's uniform, Taylor made it to Tai Hung Shan. On June 22, 1945, he was only 560 kilometres (350 miles) away from Communist HQ at Yan'an. He was able to speak by radio to a sceptical American military at their base in Communist Party HQ there. Five days later, after banquets with the local senior military, Taylor, a hero, was flown to Yan'an in an American plane and observed a tall flagpole flying the stars and stripes at the airfield.

On June 30, he had dinner with Commander-in-Chief Zhu De. He was also taken to a warehouse and chose two captured samurai swords to take home and was taken to see Mao's sparse private quarters in his cave. Mao wasn't there. Finally, on July 6, Taylor was about to board an American C47 transport to Chongqing and onward to home when a car drove up containing Mao Zedong and Ju De. Mao gave Taylor a gift of two small hand-woven rugs. Taylor thanked Mao in Chinese, and the Americans asked for photographs, with Mao uttering the only words I have ever heard of him speaking in English: "Okay". Taylor found Mao likeable. A debrief was held in Chongqing before going to Calcutta and Miami. The Americans were both pleasant for the hero's welcome but also unpleasant as questions were asked about the motives of the Communists. What was Taylor supposed to say? As far as he was concerned, Mao had saved his life.

I mentioned that George H.W. Bush had a bit part in this story. In May 1944, he flew his first combat mission over Wake atoll.

One part of the story has a particularly tragic ending. On October 5, 1943, American aircraft from the Yorktown attacked Wake, and two days later, now Rear Admiral Sakaibara ordered the 98 forced labourers to be rounded up and machine-gunned. One escaped but was caught and beheaded by Sakaibara. Sakaibara was hanged by the allies for this on June 18, 1947, although his deputy, Tachibana, eventually had his death sentence commuted to life in prison.

Even though this story and that of Sindberg to follow, as well as the description of Unit 731 in Harbin earlier in this book, I think it is appropriate to remember the words of Taylor:

"Sometimes there are leaders of countries who lead their people along the wrong paths. But according to my experience, if you are able to become friends with a Japanese person, without any conflicts in the way, you are lucky, as the Japanese are wonderful people from a great nation".

(from *Rescued by Mao,* Taylor's book and used extensively in this section).

Dr. Wu Lie-teh

This section was added later than the rest of the chapter, which was written pre-COVID-19. It couldn't be more appropriate than during the COVID-19 pandemic Dr. Wu Lie-teh (伍连德– wu3lian2de2) came to my attention. His work, and the lives he saved in the early part of the 20th century in China, caused by a pandemic, have much in common with the current crisis. This includes mammalian species crossover, the appropriate use of masks, spread along travel corridors, the annual migration for Chinese New Year, lockdowns, and super spreaders. It's hard to imagine that many of the lessons from his work more than 100 years ago have somehow been forgotten and, if followed, could have saved many lives today. He was also active in condemning another scourge of modern society, namely narcotics.

Wu was born in Penang, part of the British colonies of the Straights Settlements, in 1879. His father was a newly arrived immigrant from Taishan, Guangdong Province, China, and worked as a goldsmith. His mother was a second-generation Hakka who had also emigrated from China. Wu was the star pupil at one of the best schools in the Straights, Penang Free School, where he won the prestigious Queen's Scholarship and, at age 17, enrolled at Emmanuel College, Cambridge, becoming the first ethnic Chinese person to graduate in medicine from Cambridge. His postgraduate studies on bacteriology were at Liverpool School of Tropical Medicine, followed by further research on malaria and tetanus at the Pasteur Institute in Paris. Dr. Wu returned to the Straights in 1903. It proved a difficult time for him as the best medical positions were reserved for British nationals, even though he was already eminently better qualified than most or even all of them. He researched beriberi disease at the Institute for Medical Research in Kuala Lumpur before entering private practice in 1904. Dr. Wu was also a vigorous campaigner against the opium trade, especially its damage to ethnic Chinese labourers. He founded The Anti-Opium Society in 1906, which had a 3000 strong delegation in Ipoh. He also entered into his first marriage and had three sons, although his wife and two of the sons tragically died after he moved to China in 1907. His anti-opium activities angered local businessmen and the local colonial government, which substantially benefited from this narcotics trade. Ironically, he was found guilty on trumped-up charges of opium possession and fined. He did carry a small quantity of opium at his surgery for the treatment of patients. Disillusioned by this incident, he accepted a post as Vice-Director of the Imperial Army Medical College in Tianjin, China, in the same year. However, Dr. Wu clearly distinguished the behaviour of the British colonial authorities and the British government in London, who provided him with his education, and he later contributed £3000 to the British founded China Branch of the Royal Asiatic Society in Shanghai in 1857.

In October 1910, an outbreak of plague was discovered by Russian doctors in the Russo-Sino border town of Manzhouli (Манжули) in what is now China's Inner Mongolia. The newly established Qing Imperial Foreign Office, shunning offers of Japanese expert help because of suspicions and tensions, asked him to go there and investigate. The source turned out to be a species of rodent called the Tarbagan marmot (*Marmota sibirica*). Before 1905, fur hunters from the region had focused on premium mink, sable, and otter pelts. In 1905, Manzhouli was designated a trading centre, and in 1908 a customs post was established. This opening up brought a flood of inexperienced hunters who could have been contaminated either by the pelts or using the marmots as a food source; the latter still continued today in parts of rural China. In winter, the new hunters were packed into poorly ventilated blockhouses allowing the rapid spread of the disease. Just as today's spread of COVID-19 by air travel, the plague moved rapidly along the railways, and by November 8, 1910, Harbin had a death toll of 5,272 people, and bodies were piling up in the streets as the frozen ground made it impossible to dig graves. One case was even discovered in Shanghai 2000 miles away, and a lockdown of the city was discussed but not implemented, but the north-eastern port of Dalian was shut down. There was a risk that ports such as Dalian with both cruise and commercial shipping could easily have spread the disease to the west.

When Dr. Wu arrived in Harbin, he realized he needed to move quickly. This proved challenging because his Mandarin was appalling (he spoke Cantonese), and not least because of the impending Chinese New Year in January. Mass migration by railway was already a part of Chinese life by this time. He had to break through two significant taboos of the time. The first was to carry out a post-mortem to find the nature of the disease, something at the time considered mutilation of the dead. His autopsy on a young Japanese woman married to a Chinese man, perhaps chosen because of these supernatural Chinese taboos, revealed pneumonic plague rather than the alternative bubonic. Worse, it was the most virulent type with a 100% mortality rate. This is critical because the source of the infection in pneumonic plaque is the lungs, with all the implications of spread by coughing and sneezing through vaporised droplets.

Dr. Wu encouraged people to wear cotton and gauze face masks and even specified suitable designs and dimensions. Contemporary photographs of the time show they were readily adopted. One detractor, a recently arrived French doctor in Harbin, Dr. Girard Mesny, who had experience in India of bubonic plague spread by flea bites, refused to accept Dr. Wu's diagnosis as the inexperience of a Chinaman and visited a hospital without a face mask. He died of the disease, a certain death, in January 1911.

The second step, taken by Dr. Wu, related to quarantine and lock-down. The Chinese government sent volunteer doctors, 1,200 soldiers, and 600 police were also mobilized to prevent terrified residents fleeing Harbin, especially by rail. Russia loaned 120 railway freight cars that doubled up as quarantine centres until a new hospital could be built as the old one had to be burned. The system was brutal. On arrival, those suspected of having the disease, or showed symptoms, were put into freight cars for observation. If no symptoms showed after five to 10 days, they were released with a wristband secured by an immovable lead seal, presumably for identification but also to avoid theft as this would have been a valuable item. However, if any freight cars showed a positive diagnosis, all in that car were left to die because of the 100% fatality of the disease.

Dr. Wu then had to tackle a second taboo related to the inhabitants' desire to bury their dead after the spring thaw. Cremation was another taboo in Chinese life of that time, but the piled-up dead bodies were a source of contamination. Eventually, Dr. Wu, after much pleading, got permission for the forced cremations. On January 31, 1911, a mass cremation of more than 3,000 bodies was carried out, including some that had been exhumed, and the last case was recorded on March 1. The plague had cost around 60,000 lives lost, devastating but a fraction of what might have been including a potential global pandemic.

After Harbin, Dr. Wu's reputation was cemented internationally, and in April 1911, he chaired an International Plague Conference in Mukden (now Shenyang). The World Health Organization wasn't founded until 1948, although the League of Nations did adopt some earlier measures. The conference was remarkable for countries putting aside their hostility of the era and focusing on science. The overseas delegates came from the US, Great Britain, France, Italy, Mexico, the Netherlands, Germany,

Austria-Hungary, Russia, and Japan. There were no politicians present, just scientists. As well as confirming the likely initial vector, the marmot, there was a detailed discussion on asymptomatic and super spreaders, a key element of COVID-19. The work of the conference, and particularly on the wearing of masks, proved valuable in the 1918 global flu pandemic. Dubbed "the world's most famous plague fighter", Dr. Wu grappled and defeated the China malaria epidemic in 1919 and a recurrence of the plague in 1921. He also established the national protocols for the Chinese National Quarantine Service.

In his last few years in China before returning to Malaya in 1937, after his home in Shanghai had been destroyed in a Japanese bombing raid, two other events affected his life. In 1931, he was arrested on suspicion of being a Japanese spy in then Manchuria. In 1935 he was nominated for the Nobel Prize for Physiology or Medicine but was beaten by the Nazi German Hans Spemann for his work on embryonic development. Spemann gave a Nazi salute at his acceptance speech. Spemann was a brilliant scientist and would surely have been fearful of the repercussions to him and his family without this gesture, and there is no evidence he was sympathetic to the Nazi cause.

On returning to Ipoh in Malaya, Dr. Wu remarried and had four further children. He opened a private clinic but provided free medical treatment to the poor. It wasn't his last brush with the Japanese forces either. In 1943, he was abducted and held ransom by the Japanese in Malaya. The ransom was paid, but the Japanese accused him of aiding the Communist Chinese-backed resistance movement. When the Japanese discovered who he was, no doubt including his honorary doctorate from the Japanese Imperial University of Tokyo from 1926 (as well as Peking University, Hong Kong University, and a Masters Degree in Public Health from Johns Hopkins University (awarded in 1924), and for medically assisting a Japanese officer, harassment ceased.

Dr. Wu was also a writer with over 90 published papers and was also a co-author of the 1932 Magnus Opus, *History of Chinese Medicine*, and he was also an avid art collector. He gave many of his books and artworks to public institutions, including 20,000 books to Nanyang University, now part of the University of Singapore, and six of his best paintings are in the Art Museum of the University of Malaysia. Although western trained, he also believed in the value of TCM. He returned to his alma mater in Cambridge in 1956.

He died, age 80, in 1960 in his hometown of Penang. Appropriately there are statues to honour this great man in Harbin Medical University and a road and society dedicated to his name in Penang.

Dr. Wu had laid out most of the basic tenets and epidemiology of pandemics. Yet, in relation to COVID-19, we chose to ignore his century-old advice, with horrific consequences.

Bernhard Arp Sindberg

Bernhard Arp Sindberg was a hero from the Nanjing Massacre of 1937-38. He is one of several such as Robert Jacquinot de Beasagne (Priest – in Shanghai and the founder of safety zones in China, Minnie Vautrin (Educator), Robert Wilson (Surgeon), John Magee (Priest), Georg Rosen (Diplomat), and John Rabe (Businessman), all who chose not to flee and help their fellow human beings. I chose Sindberg from this group, who are all extraordinarily brave, for three reasons. Firstly, Sindberg was Danish, and I have a strong association with that country. My mother grew up in Denmark and went there at age twelve to live first with her much older sister and her husband in Copenhagen shortly after World War II. She later lived with a childless couple, the husband a distinguished sea captain (Captain Andersen). I have tried to locate this family, but Andersen is about as common as Smith in

English. But just maybe, someone will read this story and respond? Mum became bilingual. She didn't permanently return to live in the UK until age eighteen. On her first night in Copenhagen, she was offered a plate of bacon and egg and then offered a second helping. She burst into tears. Wartime rationing had meant one fresh egg per week and 113 grams (4 ounces) of bacon. Bacon wasn't taken off rationing until 1954 in the UK. She loved the Danish people with their big hearts, was an avid supporter of Copenhagen FC and in Denmark had a beautiful and loving upbringing, very different from her previous appalling life in England. To this day, I always say: "GodJul" at Christmas, eat stollen, pickled herring, sup my favourite fruit soup (frugtsuppe), and gorge on roast duck to a Danish recipe. The second reason is that although Sindberg maybe didn't save as many lives as some of the others mentioned, he was also the least likely to take the actions he did. He was a factory foreman/guard and not a priest, doctor, senior businessperson, or government official. The final reason is that Sindberg has often been described as an "adventurer", a description, good and bad, that has been applied to me. He first ran away as a two-year-old and was eventually found. I didn't run away until I was a seven-year-old and was quickly found, in tears, at the end of a nearby road. His story didn't come to light until the diaries of the brave German businessman, John Rabe, working for Siemens, whose diaries were published in 1997. Rabe was the elected chairman of the international committee that created the Nanjing Safe Zone that probably saved 250,000 lives.

The second time Sindberg ran away after his premature efforts as a two-year-old was in his early teens, and this time he managed to cycle halfway across Denmark. At age 17, he finally made his break and spent three years in the US before returning home and then joined the Foreign Legion. After ten months of service in Morocco, he again ran away and managed to stow away on a ship.

Sindberg arrived in China in 1934 and managed to get fired from his first two jobs for his foul temper, probably because of a heavy drinking habit, something that afflicted him all his life. According to his family, he only ever discussed Nanjing when inebriated, and it's easy to understand why. Japan went to war with China in June 1937, nearly two years before the start of World War II. His first job was behind reception at the Cathay Hotel in Shanghai and the second was for a Danish-owned milk producer. He then got a job in China's then Nationalist capital, in Nanjing, demonstrating weapons made by the Danish armament company Nielsen and Winther. After that, he is known to have taken a job as a driver for an English war correspondent who the Japanese killed in November 1937. Finally, he finished up at Jiangnan Cement Factory, which was using the latest Danish and German machinery, protecting the equipment as a watchman/guard for the Danish engineering company, F.L Smidth.

Nanjing capitulated to the invading Japanese Imperial Army on December 13, 1937, in what is called the Chinese People's War of Resistance against Japanese Aggression. It is very respectful to get this name right. The Nanjing Massacre has several names associated with it, including The Rape of Nanking. The massacre is remembered for two reasons: the terrible loss of life and the shocking barbarism of the invaders. There is still some disagreement in terms of loss of life, not uncommon in the fog of war. One of the many commemorative walls at the Nanjing Massacre Memorial Hall reads:

遇难者 300,000 遭难者（300,000 victims）

The Memorial Hall is on the site of one of the Japanese execution grounds with its mass graves. This was a senseless and brutal massacre and touches every Chinese heart to this day. The Japanese soldiers literally went berserk (a Scandinavian and Danish word). Atrocities included widespread looting and rape, using live Chinese soldiers in a race between two officers to see who could kill the most first, and also using them for live bayonet practice. Torture and arson were commonplace.

Sindberg and a German colleague, Karl Gunther, were the only two foreigners at the factory, and they watched the horrors unfold. In December, they decided to build a camp and makeshift hospital in the factory compound. They put up a sign on the front gate, "Danish-German Joint Venture – Jiangnan Cement Factory", painted a large Danish flag on the roof, and put up around the perimeter Danish and German (Nazi) flags. It was enough to deter any Japanese soldiers from entering and the Japanese at the time respected both countries. Inside, the sheds were soon overflowing with fleeing civilians and injured Chinese soldiers. Sindberg's efforts lasted three months and are estimated to have saved 20,000 lives. Eventually, the Japanese, who hated him, managed to get him dismissed, and he returned to Shanghai. Sindberg was later to say, "Only God knows how those poor people suffered".

Sindberg also played another role, a dangerous and brave one. As he moved around the city, he took photographs of the atrocities and submitted these to the International Committee for the Nanjing Safety Zone and talked to the news media and other organizations in Geneva about the massacre. He later confided to his family that he was threatened many times by the Japanese. John Magee also took the same risks using a 16mm cine camera, and the movies are housed in the memorial hall. After returning to the US, Magee became curate at St John's Episcopal Church in Washington DC, the same building where President Trump held up his bible in 2020, while protestors were being tear-gassed nearby.

In 1938, Sindberg finally returned to Europe and was picked up by his father in Italy and went to Geneva and was awarded honours by a Chinese delegation. He eventually emigrated to the US and became a captain in the merchant fleet, another dangerous assignment. He also received a letter from President Harry S. Trueman thanking him for his bravery.

In 2014, Queen Margrethe II of Denmark visited the Nanjing Memorial Museum. Visibly moved, she was carrying a bunch of yellow roses and later planted one. In China, yellow is the colour of courage. The Danish plant breeding company, Rosa Eskelund, had created this rose and named it "Nanjing Forever – The Sindberg Rose". Sindberg's family have also been to China on several occasions to receive honours as well. Above all, Sindberg treasured a silk banner sent by the people of Nanjing after he had left, labelled "The Good Samaritan". The banner was given to the Memorial Hall in 2006. There is also a statue of him in Aarhus, Denmark, at the Marselisbourg Memorial Park, also unveiled by his Queen.

I'll leave the final words to a well-known personality who expressed thanks to the foreign friends, singling out John Rabe, Bernhard Arp Sindberg, and John Magee.

"Without his help, we would not have had any chance to survive. We hope that the goodness in people like Sindberg will live on......The Chinese people will never forget their humanitarian spirit and brave and righteous acts",

President Xi Jinping

Yuan Longping.

For my fourth hero, I was conflicted. It was between Xia Peisu (夏培肃), and Yuan Longping (袁隆平) and my love of agriculture finally won over. It's the occupation that has sustained me all my working life. These are the first heroes in my two books whose life and success are explicitly connected to the People's Republic of China. That's not surprising. The PRC is still a relatively new country.

Xia (1923-2014) was a close choice because this pleasant lady worked in a male-dominated world, not just in China at that time, of computer science, and she was also a brilliant organiser. She was the designer and chief engineer of the PRC's first digital general-purpose computer, the 107, introduced in 1960. This was one year after the China-Russia split in 1959. After that, the PRC was on its own, and Xia was instrumental in developing the institutions and training to allow the PRC to continue developing computers. The final part of her education was at the University of Edinburgh, starting in 1947 before returning in 1951 with her husband Yang Liming, a well-known physicist, to a very different China than she had left. In 1972, a delegation of US computer scientists was astonished to find a vibrant Chinese computer infrastructure, in large part due to Xia.

If Xia isn't particularly famous in China, Yuan Longping certainly is. He even carried the summer Olympic Torch in 2008 for part of the journey for the Beijing Summer Olympics. Every child in China is taught about the work of "The Father of Hybrid Rice". Sadly, as I was finishing this book, he passed away age 91, on March 20, 2021. having only retired three years earlier. It was fitting that the Nobel Peace Prize for 2020 went to UN World Food Programme. I am sure Yuan was delighted, even had his thumbprint on it, as he has given his life to this cause. In 2004, he was awarded the World Food Prize with the American, Monty Jones, who was simultaneously working on rice in Africa.

Born in 1930 in Beijing, as a young man, Yuan would have seen the great suffering of the people from war. Like many of his generation, he was moved by his family several times, fleeing the Japanese invaders, including Hunan, Chongqing, Hankou, and Nanjing. He would also have observed the effects of the 1959 to 1961 China Great Famine, as it is often referred to in western sources. The first catastrophic event in a long sequence was the flooding of the Yellow River, which caused devastating crop loss on 40 million hectares (100 million acres). This was followed by three years of extreme heat, droughts, more flooding, typhoons, plant disease, and insect infestations. Nobody knows how many people died, but a figure of 30 million lives is sometimes quoted. Yuan would also have observed the catastrophic collapse in food supply caused by mismanagement of agriculture during this part of the Great Leap Forward. While the Chinese people were starving, the country in 1959 and 1960 exported seven million tonnes of grain for propaganda purposes. Yuan would also have been aware of Mao's 1958 "Four Pests" campaign to eliminate mosquitoes, rodents, flies, and particularly sparrows. The sparrows were prevented from landing by people banging pots and pans and died in exhaustion to the point the species nearly became extinct. Sparrows are voracious consumers of insect predators, and their elimination caused a spike in damaging insect pests. China is still coming to terms with this calamitous time, and for many years it was not discussed. That changed in 2012 when Chinese media erupted in an outpouring of anger and grief prompted by several intellectuals questioning the scale of the casualties, which they later apologized for. The outpouring was not censored. The Southern People Weekly, a partial mouthpiece of the Communist Party with some independent flair, then published an 18-page feature article with shocking photographs and commented:

"Sometimes history is divided into two parts: history itself and the 'admitted history'.... For the new generation, the history of the Great Famine is like a tale.... if we don't save it, it will surely be lost".

Yuan graduated in agronomy from Southwest University in Chongqing in 1953 and then took a teaching post at Hunan Agriculture University.

His interest was in rice. Geneticists of the time were able to cross two pollinating plants with different characteristics, and the progeny called hybrids were more vigorous and yielded more. The view was that crops, like rice, that self-pollinated could not have this possibility of multiplying (called heterosis). Yuan was also inhibited by the fact that at that time in China, Soviet genetic theories were sometimes considered superior to western ones, mainly from work by Michurin and later Lysenko. Lysenko, a particularly sinister character and as Director of the Institute of Genetics at the USSR Academy of Scientists, was responsible for the persecution and even execution of Soviet scientists who disagreed with his view of genetics. The alternative theories propounded by Mendel (1822-1884) and later Morgan (1866-1945) offered an attractive alternative to Yuan. Along with some scientists in the west, Yuan believed that heterosis was possible in self-pollinating crops and put himself at some considerable risk to acquire foreign learned papers. He experimented with sweet potato plants first, and that convinced him Michurin was on the wrong track. He then secretly worked on successfully duplicating Mendel and Morgan's work on seedless watermelon.

In the end, and after nine years of quiet research and extraordinary dedication, Yuan figured out for himself how to produce hybrid rice at sufficient scale to be planted widespread and published his findings in 1964. The key to his success was to find a wild male sterile rice that could be pollinated from other varieties. By 1976, Yuan, now Research Professor at the Hunan Academy of Agricultural Sciences was able to offer his hybrid rice seed, called Nan-you Number 2, for full commercial use after also working on how to produce it in quantity. Yields were immediately 20% higher than conventional varieties, and subsequent improvements created a threefold increase. This was a major contribution to Chinese food security as well as allowing farmers to diversify their cropping. The method also worked on other crops such as sorghum. In 1979, his methods were so successful that they were introduced in the US, the first transfer of intellectual property in the history of the PRC. In 2007, Yuan was named a foreign associate of the prestigious US National Academy of Sciences and the first non-American member from Chinese agriculture.

The impact of Yuan's work was felt across the world and particularly in Asia. His team was able to help many impoverished countries step towards food security, such as in India, Myanmar, and Bangladesh.

In 2014, Yuan, not always so politically correct, came out in favour of Genetically Modified Organisms (GMO) even though China currently does not allow farming of such, except for some rare exclusions, and in fibre production, mostly cotton. It does consume vast quantities of imported GMO food such as maize (corn) and soybean. It's only my personal belief, but like Yuan, I think this technology will become widespread in China, perhaps when there is an indigenous and competitive programme not requiring massive royalty payments to western companies and consumer reticence battered by multiple food scandals can be overcome. Yuan's mission in life was about feeding the world. GMO rice is also at the forefront of another non-yield improvement in the treatment of childhood blindness. According to the WHO, up to 500,000 children, each year in the rice-eating developing world suffer from a vitamin-A deficiency. Many more children are blinded, and the effects on foetal development in pregnant women is also a serious issue. This can be partly resolved by introducing "golden rice", which uses GMO to improve the quantity of vitamin-A in this staple food.

In another part of my life, I write articles on Sustainable Intensive Agriculture (SIA) for a sizeable British company. SIA is about feeding the ever-expanding global population without damaging the environment by excessive emission of greenhouse gases. It means not using excessive inputs such as nitrogen fertilizer produced from fossil fuels, not gobbling up additional land for agriculture, and especially by not destroying rain forests. Yuan Longping has demonstrated that by using science to increase yields (even without GMO) and not unnecessarily increasing inputs, it is possible to resolve the conflicting needs of food security and global warming. This research was not his main thrust, but it is another reason why I included him in my list of heroes and why he may be judged even more important in the future.

Chapter 12: The Rich in China

China's rich people's list, the equivalent of the Forbes list, is called the Hurun report, named after Chairman Rupert Hoogerworf. His name in Mandarin is 胡润 – hu2run4, and he was born in Luxembourg and educated in the UK at Eton and Durham University.

The 2019 Hurun list ranked by wealth order, the following billionaires and their associated companies: Jack Ma Yun and family (Alibaba) (£28 bn), Pony Ma Huateng (TenCent) (£26 bn), Xu Jiayin (Evergrande) (£21 bn). It's still a long way behind the global richest with Jeff Bezos (Amazon) at £100 billion, and Jack Ma Yun only makes it to number 21. One of the biggest surprises in the list is that of the top ten Chinese billionaires, three are under 40 years old and another two under 50. To make the list at all requires a minimum wealth of £207 million, a total of 1819 individuals. Although the list is heavy on manufacturing, real estate, and IT, amongst the mentioned are also some fascinating members, and there is a hint of the "wild west" in some of the figures. Huawei founder, Ren Zhengfei, 75, could only make 126th and Hurun reports: "Pig farmer Qin Yinglin, 54, and wife Qian Ying, 53, of Muyuan broke into the Top 20 after their wealth tripled to £14 billion on the back of selling 5.8 million pigs in a market where pork price increased due to an outbreak of swine flu". 17 members of the list were reported as in trouble with the law, 16 under investigation, and one in prison. It's also conceivable that there is a lot of hidden wealth. In China, not everyone wants to be rich and famous; some just want to be rich and avert the ever-vigilant state's gaze. Being ultra-wealthy is still a relatively new phenomenon in China. By 2006, China only had 31 dollar billionaires, and it's only recently that the transfer of wealth through inheritance has started to appear.

"The bird that flies at the front of the flock is the one that gets shot".

Old Chinese Proverb

Being super-rich in China does have its risks. Opening your mouth too loud and over ostentatious displays of wealth can quickly bring you to the attention of the regulators. Jack Ma found this out when the authorities cancelled his planned IPO placement for Ant Financial, an affiliate of Alibaba, for $34.5 billion on the Hong Kong and Shanghai stock exchanges on November 5, 2020. Talking about mainstream state-owned banks, as opposed to Ant Financial's more innovative banking services, Ma commented:

"Today's banks still have a pawnshop mentality.... we cannot regulate the future with yesterday's means".

That was extremely unwise, and it's not the only company in the government crosshairs. As in the US, there are concerns about monopolies and duopolies and the power of their personal data holding and manipulation. In China, it's TenCent, Alibaba, and Baidu. In the US, it's Facebook, Google, and Amazon, and others.

The Chinese ultra-wealthy do get a lot of stick from the home audience, and some of it is amusing and deserved. Weibo has a popular web area called "Flaunt Wealth Fake Fall" (炫富假摔– xuna4fu4jia3sh-uai1) based on the Russian invented "Falling Stars Challenge". Typically a beautiful young woman dressed in only the best designer shoes and clothes will "accidentally" fall out of a high-end sports car or the steps to a private jet or helicopter, and then spill the contents of her purse onto the pavement. Popular items are Balmain sunglasses, Falcon Supernova phones, top-of-the-range makeup and perfumes, solid silver or gold Baretta pistols, Seitz cameras, and BVLGARI jewellery, but part of the fun is to come up with new, expensive and exotic items. Sometimes extras are employed such as a street cleaner sweeping up the "worthless" rubbish and putting it into a nearby bin. There have been a few cases of minor obstruction of traffic violations, but I suspect the police return to the station guffawing after a more exciting shift than usual.

A new and divisive group has emerged for a China still undergoing rapid economic development: the wealthy young scion. Children who come from money in China, colloquially called fu'erdai, are often associated with many negative stereotypes. Fu'erdai literally translates to "rich second generation" and are generally either guan'erdai, meaning "government official second generation;" xing'erdai, meaning "super-star second generation; or hong'erdai, children whose families have strong roots in the Communist Party and can "eat from both plates".

Probably the worse backlash against hong'erdai occurred in 2010, when 22-year-old Li Qimin, drunk and speeding in his expensive sports car, hit a college girl and killed her. When apprehended, he shouted, "My father is Li Gang!" referring to a well-known local official. The phrase quickly went viral, and to this day represents hong'erdai arrogance".

Another recent case that brought little sympathy is from the actress, Zhen Shuang. Her notoriety started when it turned out she was accused by her ex-partner and well-known producer, Zhang Heng, of abandoning him in the US along with their two surrogate children and not prepared to do the paperwork to allow the three of them to return to China. Zhen had tried to stop the surrogacies and was furious when her demand for late-term abortions at seven months pregnant was turned down. Surrogacy is banned in China and would not have played well. Zhen also got ridiculed for abandoning her pet dog in the US rather than pay a $300 vet's fee. Next came the juicy revelation that Zhen had allegedly broken several tax laws, including a maximum earning per film of RMB

150 million (£17.2 m). She allegedly earned something between this price and RMB 180 million (£20.7 m) by having two contracts ("ying and yang contracts"), putting her number four on the 2020 female actress earners list (Angelina Jolie was top). This is the second female actress to get into difficulties over this. The first was Fan Bing Bing, but she at least pleaded contrition. Little wonder that this nasty piece of work, Zhen, has had many of her international and lucrative international and Chinese advertising contracts cancelled, her fan club has deserted her, and that's before she has to face the tax authorities. Such is the backlash that currently if you order a Meituan home food delivery in the name of Zheng Shuang, you will be advised you will not receive the delivery.

So, once you have a private plane and yacht, have a few Lamborghinis in the shed, a holiday home in Gstaad, sucked Galerie Lafayette dry, re-patriated every Ming Dynasty vase that comes on the market, lost a small fortune in Las Vegas, made substantial philanthropic contributions, also reported in Hurun, and always have the Chinese edition of Vogue on your coffee table, which is suitable if you want to practice weightlifting, what do you do next?

A few ideas do come to mind. What about pigeon racing or equestrianism?

In China, pigeon racing is not like in Europe, with weekend aficiona-dos letting loose their racing birds and then having bragging rights in the pub with a winner. In 2019, the top global long-distance Belgium bred racing and homing pigeon, called Armando, was snaffled up by a Chinese buyer for £1 million ($1.4 million). That's chump change for the Chinese wealthy and their bragging rights and the high stakes gambling oppor-tunities. History does not record how Armando got to China, whether he used the VIP lounge, was served a special cocktail of healthy cracked wheat snacks, which airline he was transported on, or whether he tried to fly, homesick, back to Belgium on his first release. If he can cope with his new home, the opportunities to breed profitably are enormous. Unfortunately, with so much money swilling around in bets and prize money, there is a danger of fraud and no more than the 2018 Shannqiu-Shanghai racing scandal. The prize money was a mere RMB 1 million (£115,000), but this was a prestigious event. On race day, the pigeons set off for Shanghai except for the four trained fraudulent but capable pigeons who flew back to the coop in Shaniqiu and were promptly caged and put onto the bullet train to Shanghai. Unfortunately, the bullet train to Shanghai is so fast that the birds arrived too early because pigeons cannot fly at 260 km per hour (160 mph). The fraudsters confessed and avoided jail time.

I have a soft spot for the game of polo, and horse racing. For several years, I lived in the beautiful English village of Avening, a short drive to the polo field at the Beaufort Club, or a slightly longer one to Cirencester Park, both with their strong royal associations. In particular, the Beaufort was so relaxed that the aristocracy, the old- moneyed, the voyeurs, and the fashionistas all happily rubbed shoulders with a couple of bobbies (policemen) present in case someone drank too much to advise them not to drive home Sir. This was about skill and sweat with lithe Argentineans taking on pugnacious Brits. For observers, the Pimm's No1 cup cocktails, always with mint sprigs of course, under the tented stands were cooling refreshments. It never occurred to me when I came to live in China that there would be any interest in this sport. In the UK, I'm sure the paparazzi were lurking in trees somewhere nearby, especially as this was a salacious era in English royal history, but I never saw them. Similarly, I was fascinated by horse racing as several of my largest clients in UK agriculture owned racing stables and stud farms. The joy of being in a box over the finishing line at Goodwood Race Corse after a glorious lunch and a professional tipster to make sure we went home satiated and wealthier is one of my happiest memories.

Polo has multiplied in popularity in recent years amongst the well-healed in China, but it's not a new phenomenon. Although generally credited to have started in Central Asia, the discovery of the tomb of a noblewoman, Cui Shi, who died in 878 AD, and was buried with her beloved polo-playing animals, demonstrates this. They were in fact donkeys as horses were only used by men, or women dressed as men, as perhaps they were considered too dangerous. I suppose the closest to a western type club is the Beijing Sunny Time Polo Club (est. 2005), some 65 kilometres (40 miles) from downtown Beijing, with its elegant European furniture, mountain and river scenery and moderate membership costs. It is the closest to a western model as this is still a lot about the grunt, sweat, and skill of the game. For those in the Shanghai area, Nine Dragons Hill Club in Zhejiang is also well-reviewed, not least for its sponsorship of the prestigious Ambassador's Cup.

Since 2010, there has only been one club worth being a member of for the flaunting billionaire, irrespective of wanting to play the game or just to rub shoulders with similar types. Tianjin Goldin Metropolitan Polo Club (and hotel) has been placed by Tatler Magazine (Hong Kong edition) as in the same class as Coworth Park, Berkshire, UK,

La Aguada Ruta, Argentina, and Umaid Bhawan, Rajasthan, India. High praise indeed, though membership is a little pricey compared to the other three at RMB 1.05 million (£118,000) per year, although if you purchase one of the adjoining apartments or a villa, the latter with top prices of RMB 555 million (£64 million), the annual fee is waived and included is a free private tennis court. In the hotel and playing area, there are 14 restaurants and cafés to choose from, many featuring famous Asian and international chefs, and a cigar bar. The hotel makes no effort to disguise its snobbish clientele:

"With the hotel's proximity to the Metropolitan Polo Club's well-heeled coterie of movers and shakers, wherever you are seated, you are sure to be amongst distinguished company, moreover never far from one of China's most extensive private wine collections".

The commentary also extends to the general surroundings:

"Imagine a world of utmost exclusivity at China's new nexus, where the people that matter meet. The Metropolitan Polo Club is located at one of Tianjin's most desirable new addresses, set amidst a 222-acre private estate of rolling lawns, manicured gardens and sparkling fountains and within easy reach of Beijing and Shanghai. Here, at China's largest and most prestigious polo club, the new nobility gathers. The thunder of hooves and the crisp crack of mallets create a heady atmosphere for serious moving and shaking. Play with the power elite. Network with those in the know".

Although typically polo ponies are not owned, buying them from the carefully chosen international stud lines and keeping them in one of the 300 stables is possible. It's a challenging game to play, but fortunately, the training facilities and coaches are of the highest standard, and even those wealthy members who don't have a lot of time to practice, probably most of them, can take advantage of the fact it is a sport with handicaps. China's first international star, the businessman Liu Shilai, a high-ranked amateur, took advantage of the handicapping system when he formed the Tang Polo Team that won the 2020 Thai Open and was awarded the 2020 January World Polo Player of the Month. The other three players were well-known Argentinean professionals.

Several prestigious events include the annual international Snow Polo World Cup event, which requires an annual RMB 12 million (£1.4 million) expenditure on artificial snow. It does snow in Tianjin in winter, but it is obviously the wrong type of snow. Other ad hoc events are frequently held, such as England vs. the Commonwealth and the Metropolitan Intervarsity Polo Tournament (Oxford, Cambridge, Harvard, and Yale).

That other great gobbler of equestrian money, horse racing, has faced a difficult path in China. Although horse racing has been active in China since around 1850 with a substantial facility of the Shanghai Race Club (1863 to 1954, but effectively 1947), its history since 1949 has often been associated with negative attitudes to British colonial Hong Kong, to colonial influence in general, and government rules on gambling, which for horses is only allowed in Hong Kong and Macao. The biggest issue, though, is gambling, and it's not just gambling per se but the real threat of it being manipulated by triads and "black hands" (think mafia). A good example is the 2000 closure of the Guangzhou racecourse with the CEO, Huang Qihuan, sentenced to 19 years in prison for corruption. Several attempts have been made to pressurize Beijing into relenting, often by pre-emptive measures such as building state-of-the-art racecourses and stables with no planned races or a very thin schedule. Some have come close, but all have failed so far at the final hurdle. In 2002, the Beijing Jockey Club at the Tongzhou racecourse in Beijing opened to great fanfare. Wealthy Hong Kong businessman, VP Cheng, is believed to have invested at least £70 million in the project, which also had 2000 horses stabled there. There was no legal gambling and just a tote, but by 2004, the club was shut down, and tragically many of the horses were euthanized. The latest potential failure could easily be the Hong Kong Jockey Club's (HKJC – est. 1884) $HK 3.7 billion (£34 million) investment in the Conghua Racecourse opened in 2018 and located in mainland China but close to the Hong Kong Special Administration Region (HKSAR). It has a world-class racecourse, state-of-the-art training, and care facilities, and currently has 13 trainers and 70 horses. Although the HJKC has deep pockets from its Happy Valley and Sha Tin courses and the legal monopoly for betting on horse racing in Hong Kong, having a facility larger and more advanced facility than Sha Tin makes some sense.

Surely the demonstration race days are more intended to sway public opinion and politicians on the mainland to adopt racing with betting in the future? This may be misguided because, at the time of writing, relations between Beijing and the HKSAR are strained, and even if regularised gambling on horses and casinos ever come to the mainland, there is plenty of circumstantial evidence that the Chinese government would choose to develop tropical Hainan Island for this purpose.

So, with money burning holes in the pockets of the wealthiest Chinese, how are they supposed to get into the horse racing game? The answer comes in the form of the China Horse Club, founded in 2013. With approximately 200 members, this secretive club has moved in seven years to be one of the premier breeders and owners worldwide. Founded by Malaysian Teo Ah Khing, it has become Asia's exclusive thoroughbred racing club. The club thrives on shared investment in breeding and the associated prize money. To date, its most notable success has been as one of the owners, others including WinStar Farm, of the US 2018 Triple Crown Winner, named Justify. The club is dripping with respectability and employs John Warren on its International Advisory Council as a bloodstock advisor, a position he also holds for Queen Elizabeth II. In 2016, Prince Harry worked with Teo Ah Khing on a project in St. Lucia. You won't find the Chinese owners celebrating in the winner's enclosure at Churchill Downs racecourse. They are a reclusive and secretive bunch.

One final possibility for the wealthy is art, and no better example is in the purchase of a painting by Sanyu. His Chinese name is Chang Yu (常玉), and he is sometimes dubbed "China's Matisse". Born in Nanchong, Sichuan Province in 1901, he travelled to Paris in 1921 and after a brief stay in Berlin in 1923, enrolled in the Académie de la Grande Chaumière. In 1928, he married a French National, Marcelle, whom he had met at the Académie, although they lived together for several years beforehand, something unthinkable in China at the time. Equally, the excitement for a young man to paint and draw nudes would not have been unfamiliar to him in China. As with many painters, Sanyu fell on hard times. He eventually switched from pen and ink to oil painting and found a patron, the American Stein Family, who was also patrons of Picasso. The Steins hung Sanyu's paintings next to those of Matisse, hence Sanyu's nickname. Sanyu died in Paris in 1966 when he accidentally forgot to turn off the gas after a late-night dinner party. Today, this is precisely the type of art (and story) the Chinese want to buy, and at Christie's Contemporary Art Evening Sale in 2019, Sanyu's Five Nudes sold for £26 million, and I am betting that was to a Chinese buyer. That may well prove to be a bargain. The record price for a Matisse was £28, but that was in 2009.

Part 3: Life Under COVID-19

Chapter 13: Wuhan

What a contrast Chinese New Year 2020 turned out to be. My year, the Year of the Rat, started inauspiciously, with the outbreak of a novel virus, in Wuhan, China, and eventually was named COVID-19. It was initially thought to have begun at the Hunan Seafood Market, which also sold many types of edible live wild animals or bushmeat (野味— ye3wei4). It did not, however, sell bats, which have been suggested as a transmitting species. The market was closed on January 1, 2020. These "wet markets" are found all over Asia. Our local one in Suzhou is where we choose to buy our food and none-more so than in the outbreak of a pandemic virus. It doesn't sell exotic animals, but it does sell live poultry that is slaughtered to order. With sometimes lighter foot traffic than a supermarket, with potentially virus-infected checkouts, never mid re-labelled products to make them in date, these markets offer a viable, fresher, and cheaper alternative. An inconvenient truth is this devastating virus could have emerged in many parts of Asia and Africa, although in this case, it was likely China.

I'm sometimes accused of being too respectful to my hosts. Let me very clear, in the early stages of COVID-19 (SARS-CoV-2), the Chinese government, by their own admission, at least at a regional level, botched it badly. The original SARS (SARS-CoV-1) was the 2002/2003 epidemic that killed 8,422 people worldwide. The Chinese government covered up that problem by underreporting cases to the WHO, including their inspectors, and quashing any media comments. It's a bad, dangerous, and continuing habit in China and is the worst face of a country that, in many other ways, has found its way to live and cooperate in the world order.

I had assumed that after SARS, the Chinese government had developed a more comprehensive system of early detection and strategies to cope with any future pandemic. If it did, sadly, it was not effective, and the initial response was shambolic, not helped by the fact that it was assumed the COVID-19 virus would behave in a similar way to SARS. Some of the mistakes were bureaucratic as well. Also, going first in the world in a situation like this exposes a country in the starkest terms. Many of the problems were later encountered by the west: lack of PPE, inconsistent reporting, inaccurate or unavailable tests, failing IT systems, and underfunded regional public health. At least the west had a warning. If the reader is taking any satisfaction from China's initial failings, beware! Later I have ferocious criticism of the west and, in particular, the United States of America.

The first symptoms of COVID-19 appeared sometime in early December 2019. At the time, Wuhan and two large cities in the nearby area was suffering from a major flu epidemic, at least twenty times worse than the previous year, and hospitals and medical staff were already overstretched. In the last few days of December, doctors on WeChat in Wuhan discussed what appeared to them as something similar to SARS, and tests up to mid-January 2020 were based on almost useless older SARS tests. Even after a COVID-19 nucleic acid test became available, at that time, the results were wildly inaccurate and were taking more than 20 days for a result. So clinicians ordered repeat tests and thereby inadvertently created another chain reaction problem. The demand for tests overwhelmed the system, and doctors, therefore, had to resort to other conventional methods of diagnosis such as CT scans and X-rays. In reported figures, three categories were created: confirmed cases, clinically diagnosed cases, and suspected cases, all with a significant time lag. Time lag has been a feature of this pandemic in many countries and has hampered efforts globally. This caused confusion and obscured the severity of the problem to scientists and especially lay readers like me.

With reporting all over the place, this would have allowed local senior managers to obscure the problem or at least selectively release findings to central government and the general public, and some of this concealment indeed did occur. More seriously, it left an essential management tool, accurate and immediate data, unavailable. In some situations, case and death statistics were even over-reported and were later corrected downwards, such was the confusion. Only in mid-February were confirmed and clinically diagnosed cases added together. It just might have been different if the defunded US experts with experience of data management and presentation who had already long gone home were in situ (see later). I don't think anything I have written will come as a surprise to the Chinese population at large, and most of it has been openly discussed by the Chinese government. I can't say if there were more deaths than reported, but as in many countries, it's certainly a possibility.

China needs to increase both its regional-national interface in the future and provide staff and cadres with better crisis management skills and better public communication and public relations skills. And it needs to fix its failed IT system and find out why something China is excellent at failed so badly. In my opinion, China should never have allowed itself to respond to the lowest levels of vitriol, mostly emanating from the US government and western social media with accusations of deliberate bioterrorism by throwing similar mud back accusing the virus of coming from the US. It was a terrible start to what became a global catastrophe. It's one thing dealing with a pandemic when you know what it is, but in the early days, China was disorganized, its population frightened, creating scars that will take a long time to heal.

A further disconnect between Beijing and the provinces came in March, with reports of black Africans in Guangdong Province being picked on. There's a lot of bad history here. For several years there have been racial problems in Guangzhou, including civil disturbances or race riots depending on your definition of scope and size, both in 2009 and 2012. I discussed in detail in *Lure of the Red Dragon* that the Public Security Bureau there had been itching to identify Africans who have overstayed their visa requirements, and COVID-19 gave them the excuse they had been sought. I believe that at least some of these more recent ugly events are related. Some actions appeared to be from the private sector, such as immediate forced eviction from rental properties and re-fusal to accept them in hotels, leaving perhaps 100 or so Africans left to sleep on the streets. However, some were provincial and local govern-ment measures, including "random" selection of COVID-19 members of "high-risk groups" for testing and paperwork checks for this group, even for those who had not left China before the outbreak. On April 1, there were also reports and horrific pictures of multiple lacerations from a Nigerian who allegedly beat up a nurse, including biting her face when she tried to stop him from leaving quarantine and complying with taking a test. Six days later, the Guangzhou Health Commission announced that four out of five Nigerians who regularly visited Emma Food Restaurant on Kuanguan Street had tested positive along with the Chinese owner and her daughter. While effective in finding a few new positive tests, this random dragnet was like pouring petrol and fanning flames at the same time. Then a photograph went worldwide from Guangzhou. It was a sign on a McDonald's:

"We've been informed that from now on black people are not allowed to enter the restaurant".

The reaction in the press from most African countries was, unsurpris-ingly, ballistic, as well as anger at the government to government level and from the African Union. In one provincial act, the work China had undone in Africa more than fifty years of work, including the help on COVID-19 to come for African countries, and in so many ways, all became diluted. The complaints from several African countries at government to government level were vociferous, including from the African Union, none of whom would have wished to upset mutually beneficial and cordial relations with China. Beijing did step in quickly with reassurances and (on behalf of Guangdong authorities) "were working promptly to improve their working method", and the issue subsided, but this was a serious and embarrassing failure.

Nothing I have discussed is restricted information. Even the possible number of extra cremations above and beyond the declared deaths was openly discussed, including in Caixin Magazine (something like The Economist in China).

I don't take the view that China needs to suffer a payback, "nuked", or be sued and other emotive and threatening terms for the crisis that evolved any more than the US should be fingered and punished for the 1918 global flu pandemic often attributed to having started in Kansas and New York (which probably killed at least 50 million). Nor do I believe, as later claimed by US trade adviser Peter Navarro, that China deliberately sent its citizens around the world in "gleaming aircraft" to "seed" COVID-19.

There may be future consequences for China, and many other countries, after this disastrous global event. One possible future occurrence could be a diversification of medical supply chains away from over-reliance on a few countries that include China. That is not yet clear because the cost, for example, of the western world producing most of its own medicines and ingredients may well ramp up costs so massively in counties whose health care systems are sometimes exorbitant, exclusive, and inefficient. That pain might be too great. If this were carried out, the most significant pain would not be on China but on India who makes many of the generic drugs but with raw materials made in China.

Coming back to China, it became clear from publicly available minutes of Politburo meetings on January 3 and February 7 that the central government had started to take much-needed control. On January 9, the WHO announced a new and unknown type of coronavirus, and in its *"Disease Outbreak News: Update"* on January 12 reported no person-to-person spread could be confirmed. That negating statement should have set off global alarm bells. By January 15, the Chinese Health Commission also said the person-to-person transmission was a possibility. That should have set off every alarm bell in the global building and is a critical date. In Wuhan, TV media also showed a mass banquet of more than 10,000 on January 19 with no one wearing masks. These people were unwittingly killing each other, and I don't believe anyone truly understood the severity of the situation.

Could the WHO have moved quicker? It's a reasonable question. Is it possible the virus accidentally (not deliberately produced) escaped from a laboratory? From current scientific evidence and not politically motivated intelligence reports, the evidence suggests it is possible, but extremely unlikely.

One of the darkest moments started on December 30, 2019, when a 34-year-old Wuhan doctor, Li Wenliang (李文亮), started a discussion in his WeChat group that he saw something he first believed was a reoccurrence of SARS or a variant. However, he had, in fact, correctly identified the symptoms of the new coronavirus. Dr. Li, and eight others, was quickly censured by the Wuhan police for rumour-mongering and signed statements they would desist. Dr. Li had already checked into a hotel to avoid infecting his family, which was the same day he was hospitalized. In something I never believed could have happened, on February 4, 2020, China's Supreme Court declared, "It might have been a fortunate thing if the public had believed the 'rumours' then and started to wear masks and carry out sanitisation measures, and avoid the wild animal market" (from Caixin magazine). Dr. Li died in the early hours of February 7, leaving a pregnant wife and one child. He and his contemporaries were later pronounced martyrs, an extremely rare declaration in China and, to my knowledge, the first-ever for people who didn't conform. Whistles were blown, the metaphor understood in China, outside the hospital by a crowd, and the expressions of sympathy were intense and heart-rending. What also followed was a massive outpouring of virtually uncensored public anger, particularly against the local Wuhan government.

The frightening confirmation came on January 20, when the China National Health Authority confirmed transmission after two medical staff became infected in Guangdong Province. The world respected Chinese scientist and President of the Chinese Medical Association, Zhong Nanshan, went on TV and confirmed human-to-human trans-mission. January 20 was the same day President Xi went on television to confirm the gravity of the situation in a broadcast speech and admitting to shortcomings in the Chinese emergency response systems. I could hardly believe it: this type of admission is rarely heard of in China. Xi also threatened to punish officials if they did not take responsibility or follow instructions, as well as a clampdown on illegal and criminal ac-tivities. He provided several examples, such as on counterfeit drugs and sanitary materials, and looting. The need to maintain social order and stability was mentioned several times. This was getting more and more serious by the day, possibly even fearful. It was the Communist Party taking a long hard look at itself and in public: a rare event in the open indeed. It was also the same day that both the US and South Korea got their first cases, but how different the responses of these two countries. By May, once China had more control over the virus, there were more admissions of failings from Li Bin, Director of the National Health Commission, who said that investigation was needed of "the weak links in how we address (a) major epidemic and the public and the public health system".

In one egregious photograph that I will never forget, there was a line of public officials wearing the best quality and safest N95 respirators meeting front-line doctors wearing flimsy surgical masks.

Another consideration was that with reasonably free reporting, the public could see the chaos on their TVs and social media: price gouging on face masks, face masks being sold already used, medical staff wearing rubbish bags as hazmat suits, paper cups used as masks, nurses crying and overwhelmed, and empty shelves in shops, cremations without funerals for the deceased, sports stadiums full of hospital beds, etc. The national anger and frustration didn't quickly go away before it finally turned to grief.

At this point, China was failing, and I didn't need western media to tell me this was a great challenge to the nation.

Three days later, on January 23, in a staggering decision, Wuhan was closed off and then other nearby cities, all for 76 days; incredible given the size of the problem and based on flimsy statistics. At that point, official figures stated more than 500 infections and 17 dead. Even if these figures were multiple times higher, it hardly seems like a catastrophe? Compare that to the medieval Black Death, also believed to have started in China, which wiped out an estimated 20-40% of the population in Europe. In the US, in 2017-18, the worst year for many years, 461,099 people died from flu-related illnesses with a population only a quarter of the size of China. This decision was a complete turning point both because of the foresight to recognize the severity of the situation. A second consideration, surely, would have been the impending mass exodus and potential spread from the Chinese New Year. After all the mistakes, this turned out to be one of China's finest hours and probably could have only been achieved in China. It saved, reasonably, tens of millions of lives. It also caused terrible hardship, not least for those in Wuhan from elsewhere and trapped in the city, some of whom had to find shelter in tunnels in freezing conditions and find food out of dustbins. It was also tough for food delivery drivers to get supplies into the city and undergo 14-day quarantine on their return.

The inevitable purge came, and on February 5. Xinhua, the state-run press agency, in a revealing article listed many of the offences of 337 sacked officials. They included dereliction of duty, misappropriation of relief funds, mismanagement of statistics, failing to provide proper health screening, slow progress of testing, and lack of testing personnel. The sackings included the Party bosses at both city and provincial levels, the Deputy Director of the Chinese Red Cross in Wuhan, and the Deputy Head of the Wuhan Municipal Bureau of Statistics. The sacking of the statisticians was particularly troubling as it would appear to have been a tacit admission that in the early days, critical reporting was not being carried out correctly. It didn't take long for the newly found freedom of expression to dissipate, and by February 11, dissenters and "rumour-mongers" were being locked out of their WeChat accounts, but criticism didn't dissipate immediately. On March 6, Vice Premier Sun Chunlan, was filmed on national television and Weibo, being heckled in Wuhan with shouts of "fake, fake!" from quarantined residents who thought their emergency food deliveries were for the cameras and not an accurate reflection of daily life.

To put the Chinese actions into perspective, Wuhan has a population of 11 million, and with the other prefectural cities, the total lockdown was 57 million. In the UK, that would be the equivalent of locking down London (7.2 million) and almost the entire population of the UK (which is eventually what happened). In the US, it was the equivalent of locking down the 70 largest cities. On top of this, other individual Chinese cities started imposing restrictions such as the number of householders allowed out in a time period, with the most Draconian, two districts in the city of Zhumadian in Henan (not Hunan at the epicentre), allowing one person per household outside every five days. Reports of roadblocks/checkpoints across the country started appearing. Yet, there was seemingly little or no civil disobedience. Still, there were some distressing pictures of citizens having to be dragged into isolation by medical officials, and I would think with police support as required (it's hard to tell the cops from the nurses in full hazmat suits).

The Chinese New Year period arrived, and the national government then wisely extended the one-week holiday by a further week with schools not to open until at least mid-February. This deadline was extended many times. There were no smiles from the parents or children, just a deepening understanding of the grim reality, which also, in many cases, meant no work and no pay. In Wuhan, two new prefabricated isolation hospitals were built: Huoshenshan (火神山医院) and Leishenshan (雷神山医院) both to be managed by the military. The former 1000 bed hospital was constructed in 11 days, and the latter 1600 bed hospital in 12 days. The buildings may have been prefabricated, but the equipment inside was state of the art. It's a staggering achievement, a little offset by the fact that the much-needed beds were slow to come up to full commission. In addition, 40,000 doctors and nurses were sent to Wuhan. A key strategy was that families were split up if a positive test was discovered, and they were sent to reception centres rather than share the same home, not something to be tolerated in the west, and it might be the last time they would see their beloved alive.

My home city, Suzhou, was never put under total lockdown. Although few non-essential stores and restaurants remained open for months and as you will see later, many other safety measures were implemented. People were frightened to go out, and self-discipline and fear were enough.

The US did begin fever scanning arrivals from Wuhan at three major US airports nearly a week ahead of Europe, so someone was vigilant in the US CDC, and yet this is hardly ever mentioned. Unfortunately, the virus was almost certainly in the country by then. According to the Washington Post, Trump was told of the virus on January 18, on a phone call with Health and Human Services Secretary Alex Azar and described this reporting as "very inaccurate", although not elaborating on which parts of a multi-faceted story. On January 29, Peter Navarro, Trump's trade adviser, wrote a memo to the President explaining that the virus could become "a full-blown pandemic", which could cost trillions of dollars in economic damage and risk the health of millions of Americans. It was one of several other memos at the time to the President on the same subject. Trump, later, on April 7, said in a press conference that he hadn't read the Navarro message until "a day or two" prior to this conference. He was more concerned with an issue related to flavoured vaping products. January 29 was also the same day as President Trump had a phone call with President Xi, who specifically warned him of transmission through the air. Navarro's memo also advised an immediate travel ban on travel from China which was, to Trump's credit, adopted. In an interview with Bob Woodward, Trump later claimed that he understood the virus was dangerous and didn't want to cause panic. I get that bit. China also may well have taken a few days to get organized to avoid panic. The problem is that Trump then did nothing much and lied to Americans for months while China very publicly went on the offensive against the virus. That was the day I realized Trump would never get re-elected and the day the number of cases in the US was touching 400,000 cases with nearly 13,000 deaths. Americans are realistic about politicians and their economy with the truth, but the lies and incompetence of the president were becoming untenable.

At home, the crisis crept upon us. I got a regular winter cough and cold. In some cities such as Hangzhou, sales of cough and flu remedies were banned to stop people from covering up their sickness. I don't think that could ever happen at UK Boots or American CVS Pharmacy.

Yan Yan had to fill out several pages of documents to get me cough syrup.

Mama had come to visit a week or so before Chinese New Year along with her cat, and as events unfolded, it became clear that she was going to be safer with us. There was no way if we sent her to her home that she would conform and wear a face mask even with drones above with loudhailers telling her to put a mask on or get indoors. She's too much of a free spirit. Once she had watched all her favourite romantic Korean movies, with Chinese subtitles, on satellite TV, she became bored. Equally, her oversized cat that came along for the ride started bullying our little sensitive one, and fur would fly several times a day. The "boss" cat even managed to break my treasured Head Gardener British National Trust fine china tea mug. Bastard, that's akin to treason, and I was incandescent. In our apartment complex, first came the men in blue and white hazmat suits spraying disinfectant with abandon, including on much of the outside flora and fauna, which unsurprisingly died. Next, all but the main gate to our apartment complex was sealed off, and you couldn't get back in without passing a handheld fever scan test. That was a little unnerving. If you failed, were there men in little white coats lurking around the corner ready to take you away? I had to stop cycling for fear of the fever scanners making a mistake as I raise a sweat, but Yan Yan kept exercising because her gym coach arranged virtual sessions on her phone. Who knows what the neighbours below thought as the floorboards bounced up and down, but these were unusual times. Deliveries of foodstuffs and take away food (if available), and sundries all had to be collected from the main gate. Outside, the streets were deserted. Public venues such as for sports and museums were shut down. Because movie theatres were also in this category, there was no audience for the traditional annual New Year blockbuster, called "An Embarrassing Mother" (how appropriate – in my case, mother in law), and the film company provided it free for online viewing to raise spirits.

By this stage, several expat friends, and especially those with children, had left for their home countries, and many had also been evacuated from Wuhan by their governments, although I am not sure some of them realized they would not only have to pay for their flights but also for the ambulances and quarantine lodgings at the other end. I don't blame my friends: they had to look after their needs, and the requirements of their children called little blossoms in Chinese (小朵朵 – xiao3duo3duo3). This, in most cases, turned out to be a poor decision, especially for those going to Italy and Spain. It wasn't an option for us, although I had bought three flights to Thailand as it had a visa on arrival for Chinese and other foreign citizens. It soon became clear that the logistics and the hostility of the usually welcoming Thai people caused us to cancel that plan.

A letter was circulated from Jiangsu Provincial Foreign Affairs Office (Suzhou is in Jiangsu Province) in near-perfect English explaining the seriousness of the situation and providing an English language phone helpline. It was so well produced that it was only after the third reading, I found some small clues that it had been written by someone Chinese. I was impressed.

Then one day, all the select floor buttons on the lifts/elevators were sealed over with plastic wrap and a pad with cocktail sticks in a paper cup with disinfectant placed underneath. The smell made me gag. The cocktail sticks were to be used for selecting the desired floor button, without fingers, before being discarded in the paper cup. It proved challenging wearing steamed-up glasses from warm breath from the face mask and wearing plastic gloves. Some types of food were starting to run out, so I sent Yan Yan and Mama out in the car to the big Auchan supermarket with instructions to buy staples. The local wet market was closed. Expecting them to return with rice and noodles, they returned with an enormous basket of fruit, vegetables, potatoes (which count as a vegetable and not a starch in China), and one bag of pigs' feet. My fault for not being clear. We were trapped in a cage, albeit a gilded one. The one good thing was that the young lady with the piano upstairs, who had been struggling for weeks on a particularly difficult piece of Bach, became very accomplished due to many hours of available practice.

On March 6 and again on March 7, I went on TV. I'd been contacted by our local television station, with a circulation of over 10 million people, paltry compared to the national stations (CCTV), to see if I would be willing to be part of a short documentary about a man called Ling Feng, who I had been acquainted with for a couple of years. I was asked because I spoke passable Chinese. A second station followed it up, I think, riding on the coattails of the first the following day and miffed they hadn't found the story first. It was a charming story. Ling was one of the security guards at our apartments and took it upon himself to try and learn English phrases in his downtime using translator software on his phone to protect all his flock and especially foreigners. In the documentary, he is seen learning and talking to me in English and Chinese with a great deal of compassion and pride.

Community spirit and watchfulness, such as insisting masks be worn, undoubtedly helped people protect themselves from each other. There was still a debate on the benefits of masks globally, but not so in China and most of Asia. China had taken it upon itself to use community members to watch out for each other. Of some concern, though, were some national reports of local neighbourhood committees (居委会 – ju1wei3hui4) being over-zealous with the national government having to issue dire warnings against this through its mouthpiece, People's Daily. This was unnerving to me as I know my Chinese history. In Maoist times, community and even family members were encouraged to spy on each other and unleashed petty tittle-tattling with the state's retribution on the alleged offenders. This lowest level of CCP administration, the petit fonctionnaires, were tasked with surveying people under quarantine, including ensuring masks were worn outside, posting "person under quarantine" notices on doors, and later installing electronic sensors to make sure people remained in place. We received phone calls to check temperatures three times a day, especially as time went along, they monitored returning foreigners who were potentially bringing imported cases from other countries. The bulk of these imported cases, however, were fleeing Chinese nationals from Europe and beyond. The Juweihui do have another important and admirable role in China. Suppose you can't get to the hospital or need to collect medicines or are impoverished or incapacitated. In that case, you go to the local CPC neighbourhood Juweihui office who are versed in the five guarantees of providing food, clothing, housing, medical care, and burial. Their job, not volunteers, is to help you, and for some, it's a desirable and much-admired vocation. If you are too old to go shopping, need a home haircut, a hot meal cooked, etc., they will help you for free.

One day, not near to home, I'm afraid I snapped with one of the Juweihui. I was getting essential provisions and had stopped in an outside corner to take off and adjust my mask with a substantial distance to anyone nearby. The official was inspecting the ID of a motorcyclist to see if he was from out of town. This is ludicrous because people with a local accent don't drive hundreds of miles from another jurisdiction and would run out of electricity anyway. He immediately jumped on me and told me to mask up, which was correct. When I shouted back why several locals were breaking the rules and why me, he told me it was because I was a foreigner. We were both wrong, my anger and his ignorance. This pandemic had, on occasion, brought out the worst in people, including me.

As time went along, the daily rumours and jibes from the west about bat soup became increasingly vicious and irritating. It wasn't so much the western social media comments as you expect those, but the overt racism of some of the world's leaders was shocking. Trump, a well-documented racist, was bad enough but wasn't even in the big league. That goes to the government of Brazil, with attacks on its largest global trading partner, China. It came first with President Bolsonaro's son, a federal employee, firing off a series of racist tweets and then Education Minister Abraham Weintraub, tweeting offensive, racist comments and mimicking a Chinese accent in Portuguese. I just hoped China would act in a way that great religions council and other ethical teachings, such as turn the left cheek when hit on the right or help the wrongdoer to become a moral person. The first is Jesus, and the second is Confucius. In the end, Brazil needed China for injections. I almost stopped talking to Yan Yan about some aspects of COVID-19 after increasing reports of verbal and physical attacks in the west on Chinese and people of Asian descent. I had become a censor. Think about that.

On March 19, the day reported deaths in Italy overtook China; it was time to step out for non-essentials and mask up. I had broken my spectacles and needed an optician. The mall had fever scanning attendees just to park the car and an inspection of an ID card to prove I was a resident followed by a second line of defence, officials in hazmat suits scanning QR barcodes. To gain access to the mall required a one-time registration and challenging for foreigners (easier for Chinese), including address, nationality, passport, work permit number, and photographs. The purpose was to provide a QR code of green (safe), orange (dodgy), and red (big problem and need quarantining) and was linked to GPS so that all social contacts, current and historical, could be traced if necessary. From this day on, the government knew my location at all times. From a public health viewpoint, it was superb. The same day, China introduced severe penalties of up to three years imprisonment with hard labour for deliberately concealing an infection.

Such was the fear of China re-importing the virus from other countries that I was being contacted politely several times per day by local government and neighbourhood committees. Had I been out anywhere? When was my last entry date into China (information the government already had)? Friends returning from other countries were either sent to medium quality but acceptable hotels or were sent home for 14 days for self-quarantining, but this eventually changed to hotels only at their own expense.

My city, Suzhou, took a more benevolent view and procured rooms at full-board and a reasonable rate and then added on a subsidy of 400 RMB (£46) to leave a cost of 200 RMB (£23) for the incarcerated per day to pay. There was a choice of five delicious menus and food three times per day, plus soft drinks delivered to the door every day. As one foreign couple posted on social media, tongue in cheek, "we never had a honeymoon when we got married, so we'll take it now". Not bad, but it didn't match the all-expenses-paid quarantine by Singapore at the ultra-luxurious Shangri-La Rasa Resort and Spa on Sentosa Island. It was a much-needed light moment in a dark time. It was also the time to get a haircut for the first time in months. By this stage, I didn't care if it was Vicki, Coco, Kevin, or Tony, as Chinese hairdressers typically name themselves, that cut my hair, and I found a local one that quickly and nervously cut and washed my hair, and I briefly dispensed with a mask. In the end, such was the fear of a second imported wave that, on March 29, all foreigners even with existing visas or resident permits were banned from entry. Flights were restricted to one per country per-week with only one entry point for a foreign airline, although modest daily numbers of returning citizens were being identified as positive and quarantined. China hadn't been so isolated since the 1970s. It was the first time we realized we might not be able to go to my daughter's wedding in the UK in August, something that didn't happen and was delayed indefinitely.

Next, for many reasons, including probably some guilt, projection of soft power, philanthropy, enormous and flexible production capacity, and a genuine willingness to help, China went on the offensive. It's also important to note that in the early days of COVID-19, China received a great deal of support and help from many countries as its time of need came first. This, and rarely discussed, included from the US. Yes, there were unscrupulous Chinese manufacturers, traders, and exporters who tried to make a quick buck, and because of their actions, the Chinese government had to clamp down, which delayed much-needed shipments. There were too many acts of generosity to mention, but two stood out to me. The first was the retail giant Suning, owner of the football team Inter Milan, who, on March 12 and using its advanced supply chain, shipped 300,000 desperately needed major items of PPE to Italy. The second was Jack Ma, former CEO of Alibaba, sending 500,000 testing kits and 1 million face masks to several countries. One of the reasons he was able to do this is that within a matter of weeks, the giant private Chinese car company BYD, which includes Warren Buffet as one of its investors, had managed to retool automobile production into face mask and disinfectant factories quickly; no small feat of engineering. China also started to send not just equipment but doctors and nurses.

The virus blindsided Europe, with terrible damage, particularly in Italy, Spain, and the UK, and there was an initial wooden effort by the EU, of which the UK was not a part by this stage. It proved much more difficult to control the spread in democracies than in authoritarian China. It's one case where authoritarianism has some distinct advantages. While a crisis was brewing, Europeans were still eating in favourite restaurants, going to parties, going to the pub, and found the concept of social distancing confusing. The UK, Holland, and Sweden were particularly lax in following an unproven theory of herd immunity, which had to be withdrawn. Europe became the second part of the global pandemic, the US the third, and the rest of the world the fourth. Each had more warning than the previous, but it is how they reacted and the resources and wealth they had available that would initially determine the outcome. Most of the countries of Europe failed, although there were some notable exceptions, such as Germany with its efficiency, robust health system, and a Chancellor, Andrea Merkel, who has a relevant scientific background. The British proved particularly belligerent about any rules or intervention. In one survey (YouGov) conducted at the end of April, only 25% of people wore face masks in public in the UK compared to 83.4% in Italy and 63.8% in Spain. It cost many lives.

Chapter 14: The Governors

When I became an American citizen in an immigrant's ceremony in Philadelphia in 2007, it was a proud moment. I still keep a copy of the constitution and an embossed letter from the White House (signed as a copy: George W. Bush) in a special place. I learned that ordinary Americans were some of the most generous people on the planet and, as this story unfolded, would at least theoretically "step up to the plate", as Americans say, in a time of national crisis such as COVID-19. When I moved to my new home in Pennsylvania from Texas, neighbours brought me welcoming cupcakes, and even the local mayor, who later became a national Congressman on an anti-immigrant platform, bought me a drink and told me, jokingly and in slightly poor taste, he wouldn't have to watch me so closely anymore. At Friday night pool, the men would have a few beers (the women were paying cards by choice elsewhere) and "bust each other's balls" about our diverse general and political views. Parties and happy days!

I saw many acts of generosity and knew that the ordinary "Joe" and his factory and bosses would respond generously in a time of crisis and often did in extraordinary numbers. I wasn't blind to some of the needs of the US before COVID-19 because on my first temporary job, I saw deprivation in the wealthiest country in the world. In my first work week working on a railroad project in Texas, I encountered a ramshackle wooden hut where a low-income family sat outside with their undernourished, poorly clothed children playing dangerously near the right of way. The hut was for sale for $1000. Later in New York, I found out 30% of the children in the Bronx didn't have enough to eat. The concept of the American dream can sometimes be jarring, but that's the way it is, and there are many examples of those who have hauled themselves up to achieve great things.

I knew enough, however, that COVID-19 was only going to bring terrible misery to the most disadvantaged in the US even though I had left several years earlier for China. What I couldn't have imagined is that one man, albeit elected, would turn out to be a narcissistic, racist, and dangerous huckster that could destroy so quickly much of civilized American life.

There are some things Americans just know intuitively. They know that they have some of the best doctors and surgeons globally, and many also know the medical system is bureaucratic, expensive, and not available to all. Many also know or have observed emergency rooms in hospitals that get overcrowded, from the need for immediate attention and because it's the only place the 27 or so million uninsured can get treatment from doctors. They are sometimes obliged to give treatment by law but are more likely to provide compassionate care by working pro bono. Eleven million undocumented immigrants in a pandemic mostly wouldn't dare go near a hospital, and it was going to be a certainty that underprivileged and, statistically more frequently unhealthy blacks and Latinos, were going to suffer disproportionately. Americans also know that it's all too easy to catch a cold or flu in winter, as I did with a cold most years probably from travelling on the New York subway, and that COVID-19 could possibly behave similarly. With many Americans not getting paid sick leave, the incentive to keep on working is ever-present. If medical systems were going to struggle with COVID-19, the US was in terrible shape for this type of event. What made matters exponentially worse was an incompetent president with no scientific knowledge and unwillingness to listen to experts.

Confused Americans allowed a severe event to become more challenging to manage because of political polarisation on issues such as lockdowns and mask-wearing.

"There's no question the United States missed the opportunity to get ahead of the novel coronavirus".

Bill Gates, April 1, 2020, who happens to know a lot about disease because of his charitable work.

"GO INTO THE STREETS FOLKS. Visit bars, restaurants, shopping malls, CHURCHES and demand that your schools re-open. NOW! If government doesn't stop this foolishness…STAY IN THE STREETS. END GOVERNMENT CONTROL OVER OUR LIVES. IF NOT NOW, WHEN? THIS IS AN EXPLOITATION OF A CRISIS".

Ex-Sherriff David Clarke, Milwaukee (also floated as a candidate for a Trump post in the Department of Homeland Security). March 15, 2020.

Take your pick, but there are plenty of Americans who would have agreed with Sherriff Clarke.

As I saw from afar the tragedy in the US unfold, I wanted to scream at the daily incompetence of the federal government and some state governments. In particular, Donald Trump and the tribalism he and his cronies created became maddening. The US sadly missed a chance to avert the crisis early on. After SARS, the US CDC had built up partnerships with their Chinese counterparts, which at its high point had 10 Americans and 40 local staff working in situ with the Chinese CDC team and concentrating on infectious diseases. Trump slashed these types of programmes so that by the start of COVID-19, this workforce in China had been cut to two people. If you were a Trump supporter, you just swallowed the lies that this was Obama who made these cuts. There is enough blame to go around at the federal level, but I personally believe our leader, the President, should be held to a higher level of accountability and where deserved, praised, not just in the case of COVID-19, but always. In this case, he failed miserably.

The federal and state interactions (White House to Governor particularly) proved to be a weak point and unsuitable for this type of crisis. That wasn't just the case in the US. The Spanish have powerful autonomous regions that resisted many COVID-19 federal proposals until Prime Minster Sanchez managed to wrest control. As described earlier, China also struggled in the early stages with national and provincial interactions.

On April 13, President Trump even tried to rip up that constitution I keep in a safe place by declaring he would decide when states could open up, something that was not within his power and fortunately prevented by this extraordinarily farsighted document of the founding fathers who knew how to devise checks and balances. It is why there will never be a King Donald.

I have a lifelong background in mathematical modelling and my university dissertation, rather eerily now, was on a branch of mathematics called catastrophe theory and related statistics. I didn't even need this to see what was about to unfold in the US. The US has some of the finest thinkers, analysts, institutes of learning, and scientists, in the world, and it's not surprising that the Chinese covet a place at an American university. Despite the tribalism Trump was whipping up, there were brave and responsible politicians on both sides who tried to do everything to combat the ravages of COVID-19. Out of this quagmire appeared some wise politicians who could cut through this tribalism and many thousands of courageous doctors and nurses on the front line with genuine medical experts backing them up and other givers in the true American spirit described.

I want to mention one such politician specifically. It is Michael, "Mike" DeWine, the Republican Governor of Ohio, ably supported by his Health Director, Amy Acton. On any pre-COVID-19 given day, I wouldn't agree with 90% of his politics, except for improved gun control. It doesn't matter that I disagree with him. This calm, intelligent, and organised governor moved into action. On March 3, he cancelled a large public event, the IFBB Arnold Classic, and by March 9, declared a state of emergency after only three COVID-19 cases in the state. On March 12, he was the first governor to announce state-wide school closures. On March 15, he closed all restaurants and bars, provided unemployment insurance for laid-off restaurant workers, and even instituted an alcohol buyback program for bar owners. On March 23, he issued a stay-at-home order. In their mortality statistics, Ohio municipalities also included deaths, presumed or tested, such as at home or in care homes. It was not normal to do this at the time. This is just a short list. It doesn't mean he and his team got everything right, and Ohio had a severe problem controlling COVID-19 in its prisons and a later second wave in rural areas of the state. Similarly worthy of mention are Republican Governors of Massachusetts, Charlie Baker, and of Maryland, Larry Hogan, and Democratic Governors Jay Inslee of Washington State, Gavin Newsom of California, and Phil Scott, of Vermont. But it's DeWine I like the best. His reward was that on August 25, 2020, Ohio State Republican Representative, John Becker, drafted articles of impeachment against his own party's governor, DeWine, primarily on behalf of business, even though Ohio's unemployment rate of 8.9% was well below the national average at 10.2%. At this point, DeWine had a performance rating in the polls of 81%: and that was amongst Democrats. In the second wave of the pandemic, these governors all struggled to keep events under control, but I single them out because I believe they tried everything within their powers to mitigate.

These governors and their teams must have worked day and night to figure it all out and used various blends of lockdowns, restrictions, and testing, while the White House fiddled and fudged with the President claiming a perfect response, and that only after he had decided it wasn't a hoax. He blamed everyone but himself: the press, the CDC, the later US defunded WHO, Mexicans, Democrats such as "crazy" Nancy and "sleepy" Joe, Obama, the governors, the Chinese, impeachment, the weather, the deep state, Antifa, and later the popular and trusted Dr. "idiot" Fauci and "pathetic" Dr. Birx, school administrators (including using defunding threats against them), Pfizer executives, and anyone else who placed themselves above his superior knowledge which included the promotion of hydroxychloroquine, oleandrin, and the possibility of shooting up with household disinfectants. In the case of hydroxychloroquine, a distinguished scientist, Dr. Rick Bright, Director of the Biomedical Advanced Research and Development Authority, was removed from his post. Described by Trump as "a disgruntled employee", his later sombre testament of an autumn second wave was frightening. As a terrible example to the nation, Trump eventually started taking hydroxychloroquine. When he failed to convince anyone in the US that this was dangerous, supplies as aid were shipped to Brazil.

The week of February 24, a new low point was reached. The world just seemed to be turning upside down. The virus was spreading rapidly, especially in Korea, Italy, and Iran, and the U.S. reported its first community spread (i.e., person to person with no connection to China). It was clear living in China that things were not right and that factories, restaurants, and shops weren't opening quickly. As many as possible were working from home. It started to dawn on the west that the integrated global supply chain issues were going to be severe. It wasn't just the potential for a shortage of PPE but potentially essential medicines and accessories in the fight against COVID-19. The medical community in the US was also starting to issue warnings that it may not be possible to contain the virus and prepare for the worse. Then, President Trump did two remarkable things. First, he instructed Dr. Anthony Fauci, Director of the National Institute of Allergy and Infectious Diseases, not to speak to the press without clearance from the White House, also citing the "tremendous success" of this administration's response to COVID-19. Second, he appointed VP Mike Pence as "Coronavirus Czar", a man with no medical experience who had already bungled an HIV outbreak caused by the injection of painkillers by addicts with contaminated needles when he was Governor of Indiana in 2015. Even in April, Pence went to the Mayo Clinic and was seen talking to a COVID-19 patient surrounded by doctors and the patient wearing masks, but not Pence, which also defied hospital rules.

In China, the US presidential flip-flopping was astounding and confusing. On January 7, Trump had praised China for handling the pandemic "very well" and tweeted. "Great discipline is taking place in China, as President Xi strongly leads what will be a very successful operation. We are working closely with China to help!" and on April 1: "So, look, the relationship with China is a good one, and my relationship with him (Xi) is, you know, really good". By March, political expediency had turned this into a "Chinese virus" and by April into new threats of sanctions on China, which would have put further financial pressure on a suffering US populous if carried out. There was also increasingly bellicose rhetoric about COVID-19 originating in the Wuhan Institute of Virology with unsubstantiated evidence and contrary to his intelligence and from others such as Five Eyes and most credible scientists. Trump never did master the basic economics of sanctions and who it would hurt the most.

This bonhomie with China and then reversal became much clearer after the later publication of John Bolton's book, *The Room Where It Happened: A White House Memoir*, which in June, described that Trump had been begging Xi for help in winning the 2020 election and offering up silence on contentious issues in Hong Kong and Xinjiang Province in exchange for increased purchases of American wheat and soybean. It's always advisable to be cautious of a lucrative tell-all story from a disgruntled former employee, but Bolton's account does fit well with the timeline.

The mud was starting to stick: "just flu" and "perfect" response from Trump was wearing thin. Reporting of failed testing kits and inadequate parking lot testing stations, shortages of respirators, swabs, chemical reagents, PPE, and everything else started to circulate. On one horrific day, March 12, the US had carried out 80 tests nationally in a day, whereas China was testing 200,000 per day and Korea 15,000 per day. The Trump defunded relevant parts of the CDC had already stopped reporting the number of tests on its website but estimated 5,000 tests year to date from inception (2,500 really as each test mainly was done twice). This was the same day that Trump announced a ban on all European travellers (except strangely the UK and Ireland), magnifying tensions between the EU and the US and trying to put his usual wedge into things by leaving out one EU member and the post-Brexit UK, both, perhaps coincidentally, with Trump golf courses. The ban included cargoes to the US, this part only to be rescinded this the following day. On March 19, Trump and the well-trusted, long-serving, and liked Dr. Fauci openly contradicted each other on mask availability in the nightly briefing.

The problem with these inconsistencies is they sent a confusing and potentially deadly message, not least to the general public. Partying on spring break in Florida was still going on. As one of several examples, Pastor Tony Spell at the Tabernacle mega church in Louisiana carried on his services for more than 1000 congregants despite restrictions of gatherings of over 50 and socially distancing at the time. Tell me how you are supposed to carry out hands-on healing with social distancing? There were no required masks either. Presumably, Pastor Spell (later arrested for driving a church bus at a protester) had no idea that the epicentre in South Korea of COVID-19 was a church?

Trump apparently held a great store in the stock and financial markets as an approval rating, and indeed before COVID-19 in the US, the Dow set a record of 29,551.42 on February 12. Thereafter, the records kept on coming: the Dow's biggest single-day drop in history (March 9), a record single daily points drop on the Dow ever (March 12), the Dow's biggest single daily percentage drop in history of 12.93%, beating the previous Great Depression record in 1929 (March 16). On March 9, US treasuries went into an inverted yield curve, and a recession had also arrived. By March 25, as most of the country shut down apart from essential services, food stores, and pharmacies, and in most cases, "essential" gun stores. In a rare spirit of unity under this administration, Congress agreed on the first of several rescue packages of nearly two trillion dollars to help increasingly desperate households and businesses. In one of the most extraordinary examples of free advertising in history, the $1200 cheques for qualified individuals had to be delayed so that the President's signature could be added rather than the regular Treasury official as "Economic Impact Payment – President Donald J. Trump". The stock market eventually recovered and went to new highs, but only after Trump had lost the election. Trump was to leave office with the distinguished record of the only president since World War II with fewer jobs than when he came to office.

March 26 was another dark day. New files for unemployment 3.3 million, and this trend continued until unemployment reached 14.8% in April 2020 before eventually making some sort of recovery but still leaving over 500,000 Americans weekly filing for first-time unemployment benefits. Trump was to leave office with the distinguishing record of the only president since World War II with fewer jobs than when he came to office.

As the US stimulus package made its final passage, the US became the most infected nation on earth (Johns Hopkins CCSE Tracker) with

81,836 cases to China's 81,782, and my realisation China was a much safer place. I also guessed that it might be difficult to spend such a large sum of money in such a hurry without there being some of it not finding the intended target and some masquerading or fraud. It's not really a fault, just a difficult situation to manage.

China's approach was radically different. In the 2008-09 crisis, when America sneezed, and the world caught a cold, China ramped up spending to about 12% of GDP. The other way around with China sneezing, spending as a first tranche was only increased by about 4% of GDP with a much larger economy than 2008, and some fiscal loosening. Part of this was because of China's very high debt to GDP ratio of nearly 320%. Also, in 2008, China had more opportunities to build useful and high employment infrastructure projects. As one wag told me, "soon we will have a high-speed train from the bar to our home". Another reason was China's quicker recovery from COVID-19 compared to the great recession and a stronger middle class and consumer base than ten years earlier. Nevertheless, Q1 economic output plunged a gruesome 6.8%, the worst ever recorded, and unemployment reached a record in February of 6.2%, which is around 80 million people, but it is hard to estimate in China because of the number of people who returned to hometown or just eked it out aren't a statistic. Being the first to recover doesn't mean there is an overseas audience to buy your production. At the May delayed national convention, there was no growth target for the year announced. Suddenly we were inundated with big box stores like Gome and Suning, internet giants like jd.com and Alibaba, and cinemas offering huge discounts. Even the normally unmovable China Rail was offering 40% discounts. Local government joined in with our provincial capital, Nanjing, offering lottery tickets for shopping discount vouchers. This is the equivalent of Chicago or Glasgow doing the same. This was a much more direct and readily available approach than sending, albeit much-needed stimulus cheques, to cover rent, pay off credit cards, etc., in the

US and an option not available to China. China does have a nascent and minimal social security and unemployment protection system, and even I am eligible for it. By the end of March in China, over 8 million had received some unemployment benefit or subsidy, including for a ground-breaking 67,000 migrant workers, but with small businesses suffering and most migrant workers not eligible, the pain and suffering were immense. It was going to take years for Wuhan itself to recover as people crawled out of their homes in trepidation and small businesses had gone, never to return. Even in our affluent city, many businesses sadly didn't make it, leading to a great deal of hardship on levels not easily understood in the west. Contrary to images of China's massive state-owned enterprises belching out unwanted steel, small and medium-sized companies make up 60% of the economy and a much higher proportion than the US. There were even relaxations on something China had tried to eliminate from its pristine cities by using city management (城管– cheng2guan3) ag-gressively issuing fines and even resorting to sundry violence. There was a resurgence of street stalls selling cheap food and clothes with empty malls as a backdrop. It was a rich source of entrepreneurial income and this was a way to generate rapid employment. Suddenly there was a backorder issue for Wuling Motors RMB 56,800 (£6500) minivan to get all this stuff to the streets. The impact of this decision was substantial and unknown, but a rough guide would be for a realistic five million new street stalls, countless jobs, and a boost of 2.5% to GDP growth.

I knew China had the resilience to recover and had suffered events much greater than this in its short post-1949 PRC history, and I also knew it would bounce back, but it was going to take time.

Nothing was working for Trump, and he was increasingly becom-ing irrelevant, something that with such an overbearing ego must have been intolerable for him. Nearly every time he opened his mouth, his popularity dropped, and if he kept clear of controversy and hid, his popularity also dropped. His lengthy nightly COVID-19 briefings became more like a political rally. Spats with the press and his medical experts became increasingly fractious, especially when several predicted a second wave in the autumn. Press coverage of the full nightly briefing on some channels was reduced to the Q and A sections. Some reporters stopped showing up, and eventually, this event was cancelled, and soon after, the input from the CDC working group was cut. Without clear leadership, state governors started acting independently, including forming their own groups and globally sourcing their own PPE. The Democratic Governor of Illinois organized secret flights from China, and the Republican Governor of Maryland got help from his wife Yumi, who is a native of South Korea, to broker a deal with that country for testing kits. In Illinois, there were fears that Trump would seize their purchases and possibly redirect them to favourable "red" states.

Following high volatility in the stock market, another economic problem occurred. On April 20, the price of oil dropped to minus $37.63 per barrel as a result of a spat between Saudi Arabia and Russia and threatening countless American jobs. There were just no more onshore tanks, floating offshore barges, tankers, and holes in the ground left to fill with crude oil. China as a country benefited from this and from low prices of soft commodities and stocked up. China is the world's biggest importer of oil, corn, and soybeans, and these purchases assisted in trying to meet its trade agreement Phase 1 deal with the US. Some wealthy Chinese individuals, however, got a cold bath as a Bank of China Oil Crude Fund linked to the US Oil Fund, LP was forced to liquidate, leaving "negative profit" (there is no such word as a loss in China, and this term saves some face at least) of over $1 billion, leaving punters crying foul because they hadn't read the small print.

Next came one of several stunning acts not just in Trump's presidency but in American history. Having previously stated that he would decide when the states would reopen, on April 16, Trump revealed his back to work, Opening Up America Again Plan, which required a 14-day flattening of the curve by state and a ramp-up of testing. He also explained that this was now the governor's responsibility to decide when to open up and not his, thereby passing the buck. Several states immediately took action to open up, including Georgia, South Carolina, and Florida, even though none of them had passed the 14-day essential downward curve requirement, never mind meeting a fraction of the testing requirements. The following day, Trump sent out multiple tweets calling for the "liberation" of three states with Democratic governors. Militias, sometimes armed and some waving Confederate flags and swastikas, and others masquerading as nurses, turned out along with more normal Trump supporters. The previously mentioned Governor Inslee didn't mince his words accusing Trump of "fomenting rebellion" and "spewing dangerous, anti-democratic rhetoric". To me, Trump's actions, except using adults and not students, were straight out of Chairman Mao's 1966 Cultural Revolution playbook! On April 20, Trump was projecting 50 to 60 thousand deaths in total (as he didn't believe in a second wave in the autumn). The higher figure was exceeded eleven days later. Then, on April 28, he again invoked the Defense Production Act, this time ordering meatpacking plants that had become something of a Petri dish for the virus to remain open. With inadequate PPE but promised from the federal stockpile, he was potentially exposing immigrants and minorities who tend to have high employment rates in this industry to a high risk of infection or even death.

On April 3, despite a ravaged 401k pension and reduced savings, it was time to take a break and do what the Chinese call "revenge spending" related to having Chinese New Year 2020 cancelled. Work projects were also thin and backed up with no obvious suggestion when this would be resolved. There's only so much you can do by Zoom. It was Labour Day week, and we booked ridiculously cheap flights to Chengdu in Sichuan

Province and found great hotels at 25% of the regular price. During the train journey to Shanghai and at its second airport (Hongqiao), I didn't see one single foreigner, had eleven fever scans on the trip, and my credentials (safe green QR code) and passport were inspected multiple times. The flight attendant, in particular, was worried that I had somehow escaped the net. On arrival at Chengdu Airport, within ten minutes, the local security agencies called on my phone and wanted to see by WeChat that I had been in China since a November 2019 visit to Cyprus. I don't know if they used the flight manifest, GPS, or someone else, but I was sure if I went for a pee, they could hear the tinkle. I got many strange looks from the wide-eyed general public, and I wanted to smile at them, but it's a wasted gesture from inside a mask. All the officials were polite, but this was thorough, and I thanked each one for taking good care of me and everyone else. The restaurants were open, but masks were compulsory, except when eating and drinking, of course. I felt free and that night sat on the hotel room balcony in night-time searing heat and could see the stars in the sky because of the reduced pollution and realized the world would be a different place after this. My thoughts turned introspective. A week before, I had called an ex-colleague and friend in the UK, where we had worked together for many years in agriculture and trading, and discussed the possible ramifications of potential worsening food insecurity in poorer countries as we had seen this several times in our lives. I'm not very good at praying but had a silent moment to remember the traumatized people and tragic losses worldwide, especially in my former homes, the USA and UK.

Chapter 15: Successes and Failures

"I never believed the best we could do would be the worst in the world".

Dr. Sanjay Gupta, CNN Medical Adviser, neurosurgeon, and journalist.

By May, the world had to consider the possibility of a second and third wave of COVID-19 infections caused either by opening up in different countries or a possible fresh surge in the autumn in the northern hemisphere. Opening up made some sense in Asia and Europe as people couldn't be locked down forever, and it was shredding their economies. It made less sense in the US, where, also with a damaged economy, progress and curtailment of the virus was behind. There was now enough evidence, even with different definitions of mortality, of countries or claimed jurisdictions that had found ways to keep the virus from spreading or had better functioning medical systems in China, South Korea, Japan, Taiwan, Australia, Thailand, Vietnam, Germany, and New Zealand. South Korea was particularly inventive with drive-through mass testing, contact tracing, and eventually development a dual flu and COVID-19 test ready for the winter months. There were also examples of failures: Belgium, Sweden, Peru, the UK, Italy, Spain, Brazil, and Chile, to name just a few. It's hard to be definitive about relative success and failure because of different methods of counting and reporting. Every country and its sub-units had a different way of counting COVID-19 cases and deaths. In some countries, deaths only applied if they were in hospitals and not at home or in elderly care centres with high mortality rates. In other countries, presumed cases were included, and in others, not, and cases could be described as flu. In some instances, asymptomatic cases were included, and in others, not. Finally, if a country wanted to indicate its progress in testing, it was possible to add COVID-19 tests plus antibody tests as a lump sum figure. In the end, it became clear that the only reasonably reliable measure was the number of deaths above the typical pattern, although deaths per capita have some value as a statistic.

I included China in the relative success list because it had got its act together by this point after the initial sputtering. The authorities were thankfully highly vigilant. Although the daily increases in all cases were down to a handful, including asymptomatic cases by this stage, two hotspots were still causing problems. The first was in the Russian border area requiring lockdowns or partial lockdowns of 25 million people. The second was Wuhan, and on May 12, the decision was made to test all 11 million inhabitants within a period of 10 days and just slightly less than the entire US had carried out in total on the same date. This was achieved, and 300 asymptomatic people were discovered.

In the US, at this stage, the key medical players, Fauci, Redfield, Birx, etc., started to disappear from view slowly, and Trump started to comment less on medical matters, having probably wisely stopped his nightly briefings. His focus was now on the economy and picking fights with everyone and anyone. The historical comparisons were breathtaking. More Americans had died of COVID-19 in the previous 12 weeks (to May 22) than died in the Vietnam and Korean wars combined, and nearly twice as many as died of battle wounds during World War I. The death toll had almost matched the number of people killed by the initial blasts of the world's first atomic bombs dropped on Hiroshima and Nagasaki. By May 28, The US reported more than 100,000 dead (the same as Korean War (1950-53), Vietnam War (1961-75), Iraq War (2003-2011), Afghanistan (2001 to present) combined. It would take a total of 600,000-800,000 to reach the military losses of the American Civil War.

Trump focused on the success of a range of stimulus packages and not the headline 14.8% unemployment rate and 20.5 million jobs lost. To him, I am sure, it was a logical diversion from COVID-19 failures.

Inconvenient discussion of COVID-19 could be suppressed. On May 9, the White House buried new CDC guidelines on how to return to work safely but later allowed publication of a much reduced six-page document.

On May 18, the announcement that a test for a vaccine made by Moderna in the US had succeeded in creating antibodies in eight patients was important news. Out of this came Operation Warp Speed. As I intimated before, a president should always be judged to a higher standard. In this case, Trump deserves considerable credit for eventually getting this and other vaccines produced.

Another convenient diversion was to attack China. Trump and Secretary of State Mike Pompeo, who claimed COVID-19 started in a Wuhan laboratory, intensified their attacks. China was indeed working on coronavirus in bats in the Wuhan laboratory. Professor Shi Zhengli had been doing so since 2004 in relation to the previous SARS epidemic. None of the viruses were similar to COVID-19. The war of actions and words was now on (both ways), with Trump threatening to "cut off" relations with China. On the same day at the World Health Assembly, President Xi stated that China would agree to the EU draft resolution for a WHO impartial and global independent inquiry of the coordinated international health response once the virus was contained. This was very different from previous attempts by the US and Australia, who wanted an investigation just into China's part. Senior leaders in the EU were at pains to emphasize international unity and the need for a strong WHO. The US was a no-show at the meeting. Although it didn't block the resolution (inadvisable as supported by 144 of 194 members), it later put out a statement that any new vaccine should not be considered as "global public goods". Then I knew if the US got the vaccine first, it would benefit its citizens and possibly dispense some to other countries or even internally on a political basis. Trump shortly thereafter threatened to leave the WHO. In the dying embers of the Trump regime, the President proved my point and signed a spurious executive order saying that Americans should be globally prioritized for vaccination even though most of the coming available vaccinations were by international joint ventures.

China's response, on May 21, was to announce that it planned to insert clauses into an annexe of Hong Kong law that would ban sedition, secession, and subversion and pave the way for mainland Chinese national security agencies to work in the city. This is the subject of a whole book, one day which I hope to write. In the simplest terms, the west believes China broke an international agreement, which it at least circumvented. China believes that waving light blue and total independence flags and creating anarchy is a threat to its sovereignty. I have never met a mainland Chinese person who does not think Hong Kong is part of China.

Up to this point, the developments could be described as a rather extreme form of politicking. After all, Trump had won his presidency by a substantial margin. He had the elected right to run the country his way. It was popularist and sometimes not pretty, but he certainly did have the right.

What happened next was to destroy the credibility of a country considered the leader of the free world and democracy.

On May 29, Trump was furious at having been censured on Twitter for inciting authorities to shoot rioters, and he then threatened action through executive orders to bring in the armed forces. The following day in a press conference, he went on an all-out attack on China with no mention of the COVID-19 dead in the US or the riots in Minneapolis and other cities after the alleged police strangulation of a black man

(George Floyd) and Trump took no questions. He announced the end of Hong Kong's special status and multiple further measures against China, to be announced later.

Reports start to appear of police intolerance of the press first by arresting a reporting team of colour, working for CNN in Minneapolis, and later in the Washington DC Bunker Incident, police beating up a team from Channel 7 Australia. These weren't isolated cases; there were several hundred similar instances reported. Over just that one weekend, there were 12,000 complaints filed for excessive use of force by the police in Seattle. Later, Jacob Blake was shot in the back seven times in Kenosha, Wisconsin, in front of his three young children. An angry China got in on the propaganda act with Xinhua in a particularly scathing article called "The coming suffocation of the American dream" (referring to Floyd).

Chapter 16: Democracy Under Threat

In August 2019, Trump suggested that Xi should meet personally with some of the Hong Kong protestors stating "there would be a happy and enlightened ending...I have no doubt". That didn't happen, but on May 30, Trump certainly met with his own protesters in Washington DC but only from the end of the barrel of a gun. On June 1, Trump had to be moved to an underground bunker with his family, also in residence, for his safety, although he claimed it was to make an inspection. No doubt miffed, and in one of the most ignominious events in US history, he then arranged for crowds to be forcibly moved back. Peaceful protestors were attacked by police and armed forces using rubber bullets and gas labelled CS riot gas (a type of tear gas and denied by the authorities), and other types of sprays. His purpose was to get a photo opportunity holding a bible at St John's Church, a short walk from the White House. I just shuddered. This was starting to look more like 1989 Romania than 2020 America, although, in Ceausescu's case, the roles were reversed as he was blaming the fascists and miscreants whereas Trump blamed Antifa and thugs. If wiser heads in the military hadn't prevailed, shooting the American public with real bullets was a possibility. One wondered if Trump's helicopter was fired up and ready to go, just as for Ceausescu's initial, and eventually failed, bid for freedom, and that is assuming it didn't collide with the show of force of intimidating and noisy army helicopters already in the sky. From this day on, Trump was surely finished? He had managed to lose almost all of the vote of people of colour, the expendable elderly, the moderate clergy and their flock, the unemployed, the medical profession, women, college graduates, potential swing voters, and later a good chunk of the military for calling fallen soldiers in France losers and suckers (or something similar as the exact words couldn't be corroborated). A rump group of mostly blue-collar men from the rust belt, rednecks, and a bunch of evangelicals would need to be bolstered by other groups to give him a chance in the upcoming election, although they did turn out to support him in record numbers. Cheating looked like a more viable option, and Trump is very good at cheating; in exams, at golf, and allegedly on wives and tax returns.

It was also becoming difficult for some foreigners to be in China, but not because of any overt aggression. Most of the Americans I have met in China, from whatever political persuasion and like their diplomats, believe in public that they should put up a common and supportive front and present the US as a moral beacon and leader on the world stage. Yes, there are grumbles that many US citizens have to pay double income tax above a threshold (in the host country and the US) and other minor gripes, but the overall effort is one of showing the best side of the US at all times. This was becoming almost impossible and embarrassing.

On June 21, Father's Day, also recognized in China, was celebrated. It was the time for Trump to step out and conduct a political rally in Tulsa. OK. Back home in China, we had a new COVID-19 scare in a Beijing market that had afflicted 227 residents. I'm very familiar with the Xinfadi wholesale market in Beijing as I had been carrying out market research there for an overseas client for the last three years. It's one of the worst places for an outbreak because of its sheer size (about 270 football fields) and extensive foot traffic with deliveries from many Chinese regions and other countries. By China's standards, this was a serious and dangerous outbreak and stood in stark juxtaposition to the events in Tulsa.

In truth, most of China, including me, had become a little complacent. After no cases for many weeks and 1180 km (734 miles) by car from Beijing, the masks went on again in Suzhou. I had got used to going to the bars and restaurants unmasked and the day before had a BBQ at home with some friends: no social distancing or masks needed. No new ordinances on masks were required: people knew what to do. This time in Beijing, it didn't require a Wuhan-style response but more specific and targeted lockdowns in the capital. It was a block-by-block lockdown, and information was sent mainly by phone requesting the potentially infected to go to a testing station and get the results within hours. Flights out of the capital were cut in half, and those in wider designated residential zones, not just where COVID-19 had been discovered, couldn't travel without a negative test certificate. In just one person's case, 1300 people had to be traced and checked. Even though the Xinfadi market provides some 70% of the food in Beijing, there was no panic or rushing to the shops to stock up, but I am sure behind the scenes, the market's closure and food distribution logistics must have been a nightmare. Shortly afterwards, Anxin County in Hebei, close to Beijing, had 400,000 people put under lockdown. Strict measures for tough times.

At the same time as this activity came the embarrassingly thinly attended speech by Trump at his Tulsa rally, a city that had already suffered in history from appalling racism. His excuse for the lower than anticipated turnout was "thugs" outside barring access to the event. There was little evidence of them and only one arrest, and a scarcity of delegates and protestors marked the occasion. My Chinese friends were either shocked or bemused. Few masks, COVID-19 described using the racist term "Kung Flu", and event advanced staff testing positive. Perhaps most disturbing of all was Trump stating he had told other senior staff to slow down testing. The logic seemingly being less testing equals fewer reported cases and flying in the face of all known medical opinion, including his expert advisers (Birx, Fauci, et al.). After this and a rally in Phoenix, Arizona, Trump all but disappeared from public view. By early July, as infections spiked predictably and alarmingly in states that had opened up early, such as Texas, Arizona, and Florida (as well as California who hadn't), the majority of people started to wear face masks and were even encouraged to do so by senior Republicans in the House and Senate. It was only nearly six months too late, but I suppose better than nothing. Little wonder then that the July 1, EU list of acceptable travellers from 15 countries did not include a pariah like the US. China was included on the acceptable list, subject to reciprocal arrangements being offered, which didn't occur.

When Trump reappeared on July 2, from an apparently busy period discussing confederate statues, it was to discuss the wonderful state of the economy, which had seen unemployment reduced by 2.4 million and a spike upwards in the stock market. Better not to mention the 50 million jobless claims in 15 weeks and the 11 to 16% unemployment rate depending on how it was counted, give only a cursory mention of COVID-19 and say nothing about race issues. The latter had been dealt with in Trump tweets calling Black Lives Matter (BLM) a "symbol of hate".

I got a COVID-19 test, a requirement to enter a Chinese hospital as I needed a minor surgical examination: the one boys hate. The test was free as for all people. It was marked as 240 RMB (£28) and over stamped gratis in Chinese, no doubt to remind me of the cost and effort that had gone into this and for which I was grateful. In the US, according to the Kaiser Family Foundation, the price of a test, if you could get one, was £14 ($20) to £600 ($850) for a single test plus doctor or clinic visit costs. Medicare reimbursed a maximum of £70 ($100).

Trump continued his grand tour. On July 15, he visited Atlanta and didn't wear a mask, and against city ordinance. The following day, Republican governor Brian Kemp issued documents to sue the Democratic Mayor of Atlanta and her council over Atlanta's law to insist on wearing masks as suggested by the CDC, which happens to be based in Atlanta. No action was taken against other cities with similar laws, such as Savannah and Athens. The eloquent Mayor Bottoms, infected along with her husband and child at the time and in isolation, used a delightful American word (not used in the UK anymore) that she didn't think the Trump visit and the legal case was "happenstance". I am not bound by such diplomatic niceties. This was a vindictive, vicious, conniving, and egregious act. On the same timeline, rumours started to appear that the US government discussed banning all Chinese Communist Party members and their families, a number north of 100 million people. That would include an elite group of Chinese businesspeople, some of whom are admired and have strong connections in the US, such as Jack Ma, and Xu Jiayin, head of Evergrande Group. Apart from being impractical to enforce unless the US owns a list of Communist Party members, it was extraordinarily incendiary and another poke in China's eye. It reminded me of my first visits to the US when the arrival card had the question, "Are you a member of or an affiliate of the Communist Party?" or something similar (I can't remember the exact wording). I gave Yan Yan the emergency phone number for the British Embassy (the British also out of favour for cancelling Huawei contracts and issues in Hong Kong but at least sane) in case of retaliation, and she learned two new words from me: the US government doesn't care a "flying fuck" about its foreign contingent. It's hard to explain to her that I support and like the US and admire many of its principles, but I am just as expendable as those dying daily of COVID-19. That's actually reasonable but try making this argument to your wife.

July brought many new lows to the US. Abject failure in contact tracing became apparent again, particularly in Florida. There were still testing stations running out of tests and shortages of PPE (because of the delayed use of the Defense Production Act). During this period, the US government decided not to procure extra potential doses of one of the leading vaccinations (Pfizer) and tried to "play the market" for alternatives, something the EU was also doing. Trump and Fauci were no longer speaking to each other, with Fauci reduced to newspaper commentary, podcasts, and radio. On July 13, Trump wore a mask and suggested there was no downside to it. Supermarkets such as Kroger, Wal-Mart, and many others started insisting on them while Trump was busy making a promotional ad for Goya beans from within the White House. Crime rates had also begun to soar, but the federal government's response was to try and circumvent local police forces. In Portland, OR, federal authorities, including Homeland Security, in generic camouflage and no name or agency markings, were pulling people off the streets and into plain vans just as in Venezuela, Syria, and Belarus, all in the name of protecting federal property. I suppose these storm troopers did score a civil rights notch above the aforementioned as they didn't, or forgot to, put hoods over the heads of the captured.

By now, in the US, accurate statistical information had become less available, some because of cynical manipulation, but much more because of hospitals filling up, more people dying, this making counting difficult. One suspicious move was the July 15 directive when the Trump administration asked hospitals from July 15 to report COVID-19 data directly to the Department of Health and Human Services (HHS) and not through the CDC, using a private company called TeleTracking Technologies. The COVID Tracking Project (CTP), an independent volunteer organisation, found the data to be "erratic", "spotty and difficult to interpret". TeleTracking refused to comment, citing a confidentiality agreement, and the government also declined to disclose the other five bidders.

On July 20, Trump finally endorsed masks and shortly afterwards started daily press briefings but was not interested in talking about COVID-19. Instead, he was focused on potential mail-in election fraud. However, puzzlingly he suggested this method should be allowed in Florida, with a favourite Trump governor, because of its peerless historical record on election organization, conveniently forgetting 2000 Bush vs. Gore and hanging chads.

The attacks on China were relentless, and on July 23, Trump ordered the immediate closure of the China Consulate in Houston. China responded by shutting the US Consulate in Chengdu. The Chinese Foreign Ministry felt it necessary to issue a warning to its citizens in the US to be "on guard" as a result of "US law enforcement agencies having stepped up arbitrary interrogations, harassment, confiscation of personal belongings and detention targeting Chinese international students in the US". This time it wasn't just China fighting back, though, because, on the same day, another country issued a court ruling that an asylum agreement with the US was unconstitutional because the US violates the rights of refugees as there is a chance the US will imprison the migrants. That country was Canada.

The next assault on China came on August 7, and this saga was widely reported in the Chinese press as it was something of great interest. Trump issued executive orders to ban Tik Tok unless sold to an American company such as Microsoft or Twitter within 45 days and similar for WeChat, both on the grounds of national security. Tik Tok is owned by the Chinese company Byte Dance, which goes under the Dou Yin brand in China. The servers for Tik Tok are in Singapore and the US, and the company, claims they are ring-fenced from any Chinese government access. I like Dou Yin. It kept us all going in China during the darkest days of COVID-19 and other countries. In the US, Tik Tok had by this stage 100 million monthly active users. On Dou Yin, I like to go to the art pages and watch speeded up watercolours and gouache artists creating their own work. Of course, there is a shopping trolley in the left-hand corner, and there I will find all the paints, pencils and paper I will need. That's the Dou Yin model. For Trump, the ban would have made a lot of sense. For him, it achieved multiple objectives in continuing to attack China (he wanted Tik Tok altogether banned immediately until it was pointed out how many votes that would cost), it allowed him to take revenge for being trolled on Tik Tok for his Tulsa rally, and he claimed the US was going to receive substantial tax revenue from the forced sale. He also claimed he was helping US companies such as potentially Microsoft, Twitter, Google, and Facebook, which was beta testing its Instagram Reels in Europe, India, and Brazil. It was certainly interesting to see the US adopting a China-style censorial approach to internet media usage where several apps such as Facebook, Instagram, and YouTube are not available. Beijing's response was, yes, you can force the sale and steal a Chinese company, but we will not let you, by our law, have the source codes, thereby making the purchase of Tik Tok a risky proposition. This was followed up on August 12 by: "China will own the United States if this election is lost by Donald Trump", bizarrely speaking about himself in the third person. "If I don't win the election, China will own the United States. You're going to have to learn to speak Chinese, you want to know the truth".

It was inevitable that sooner or later, I would suffer some personal blowback from the Chinese government, but it came in a most unusual form. From time to time, I transfer money from my US bank account to my Chinese one. Moving cash in reverse, which I have also done, is reasonably straightforward for small amounts, although there are strict exchange controls for large amounts of money. I wanted to move $10,000 from the US to China using the SWIFT system. My bank, one of the largest in China, contacted me and refused to speak English, although I know from previous experience the foreign exchange department is more than competent. I asked Yan Yan to take over the call to avoid any misunderstanding. Initially, they said that there were new rules and my money would have to be returned to the US before relenting and allowing it as a one-off. In the future, they would be unable to handle these transactions.

Although I hold a VIP account and have a high credit limit, they told her that I needed to close my account and take my business elsewhere. I wasn't angry. I knew that these inconveniences for Americans in particular and some other foreigners were going to come, and I was surprised it had taken so long. Eventually, I found a bank that helped me but only because the manager asked the right question:" I don't suppose you have a passport from another country?". Bingo as I do (from the UK). The rule of not allowing transfers only applied to Americans. That's the Chinese way. Beijing doesn't have a flurry of signings with fanfares. They just quietly make life difficult for people who upset them. That might be Australian coal stuck off the coast near Shanghai, extra inspections on products from undesirable countries, or in my case, restricting financial movements. Shortly after this, many foreigners also had their credit cards taken away (all countries). Now, this I get. There were just too many people maxing out their credit on pieces of fine jade and then leaving China knowing they would not or could not return without any intention of ever repaying the money. A piece of the finest jade will fit into a corner of your pocket and will max out the credit card of all but the very wealthy.

The August party congress season arrived. There were a few good speeches: Melania Trump for a passionate rendition recognizing the people's suffering, Mike Pence for oratory (not content), and former President Obama ripping into Trump. It was Republican law and order with minimal mention of COVID-19 and in person, often without masks, versus Democrat inclusiveness and concerns on COVID-19 carried out by conference calls. It didn't move the needle in Trump's favour, and he was still badly trailing in the popular vote and a little less in the Electoral College. China mainly remained quiet during these events, apart from lobbing a couple of missiles into the South China Sea, probably concluding it was better to wait it out for a result. The exception was the continued Chinese media attack on Secretary of State Mike Pompeo, the second most reviled person in China, for illegally (under the Hatch Act) making his speech while on a taxpayer-funded trip from Jerusalem on August 25. The message was simple enough: some American politicians are above their own laws. Although Trump tried a charm offence at the RNC, he returned to his usual self within days.

A parallel theme of the conferences was the decommissioning of automatic postal machines, fraud in absentee ballots, etc. I think some of these arguments may have been lost in China, where voting is less commonplace. I would doubt many senior party members in China would know the cost of a first-class postage stamp and probably haven't used the China Post service for years for personal matters. That the newly inducted US Postmaster General didn't know the price on a postcard would seem amusing or irrelevant to many Chinese.

In the US, employment prospects finally showed signs of improving. By July, the rate had fallen to 10.2%, still stubbornly high, but the US had survived a great shock.

It's difficult to pin down, but sometime around this point, something snapped within Trump, and he started to look more like a demented, dangerous, and racist dictator than POTUS. His interference and messaging became more and more confusing at a time of great need for leadership. Until the election, China moved down the agenda as the focus was more on internal US affairs.

On August 20, while the sometimes gruff-voiced Dr. Fauci was undergoing a general anaesthetic to remove a polyp on his throat, the CDC changed its guidelines for people coming into close contact with a person with a COVID-19 for at least 15 minutes but did not have symptoms, stating they did not necessarily require a test unless recommended (from a range of quoted medical officials). The changes were an order from the top (the White House). It was another way to try and make the testing numbers go down, a consistent theme of the Trump administration as they thought it made them look bad. Next, Trump said that New Zealand had a "massive breakout" of COVID-19 after it reported 11 new cases in two days and after 102 days with no cases at all. He also accused the FDA of deliberately delaying vaccine trials until after the election, with the deep state also being involved. Then on September 3, he re-tweeted theories that only a few people had died from COVID-19 because the death certificates listed underlying causes (not as well as) and demanded Biden gets a drugs test as he must be on "enhancements".

The racist rhetoric also became amplified.

"You have good genes, you know that right? You have good genes. A lot of it is about the genes isn't it, don't you believe? The race-horse theory. You think we're so different? You have good genes in Minnesota".

Donald J. Trump, Bemidji, Minnesota rally, September 18, 2020 (audience almost all white)

For those not familiar, the racehorse theory concerns the belief that some people have a better genetic endowment than others, and by their breeding together, their offspring will be superior. It is deeply rooted in eugenics and was espoused and practised by the Nazis.

"She's telling us how to run our country. How did you do where you came from? How is your country doing?"

Donald J. Trump, discussing Democratic Representative Ilhan Omar, a first-generation immigrant from Somalia, September 24, 2020 (and has on occasion produced anti-Semitic rhetoric).

I was furious as I am sure most first-generation immigrants would be, especially as in "my country", the UK, we were having a terrible time with the ravages of COVID-19. The UK had tried to follow the science and had just got a mobile phone tracking app which wasn't working very well. Worse, I got it; the Representative is originally from Somalia. Perhaps Trump didn't mean people like me because my skin is white?

In Trump's world, he likes to get advice from people who feed him what he wants to hear. Little wonder then the advice he got from former Republican Representative Michele Bachmann resonated. She claimed to be a member of Trump's "faith advisory group" (existence of the group denied by the White House) and, on the Victory Channel, stated that the US government was being taken down by "transgender Black Marxists".

The following day came the mark of a true dictator as Trump several times refused to accept if defeated that he would leave the White House in the customary peaceful transition. Perhaps he was emboldened by the tragic death of Ruth Bader Ginsburg (RBG) and an imminent improved right-wing majority on the Supreme Court. The strategy was becoming more apparent: win on election night and declare victory and then invalidate as many postal ballots as possible, as these were likely to be more from Democrats than Republicans. Possibly enforce it if necessary with the "legal" use of the Insurrection Act and deploy troops to ensure a win. Throw in a couple of sweeteners like reducing immigration to 15,000 per year and debate sending seniors a $200 medical gift card like you get a shopping card from Bass Pro or Wal-Mart. Try and declare a vaccine available before the election, if necessary, by strong-arming the CDC, even if less than 35% would take the vaccine because of no trust in POTUS. If necessary, get the now "stacked" Supreme Court involved. Divide and conquer by any means, whether constitutional or not. He couldn't even bring himself to condemn the uncovered plot to kidnap

Democrat Governor of Michigan, Gretchen Whitmer. I don't blame Trump for trying to take advantage of the RBG situation. It was unethical but not actually illegal, and in politics, that is considered acceptable most of the time. And in another mark of a true dictator, he refused to condemn the kidnap plot.

September 29, and time for the first presidential debate: 9 am September 30, in China. I settled down with a cup of coffee to finally see Biden and Trump face off in what I hoped would be a revealing debate. There was also serious interest and commentary in China. It was a national embarrassment with a respected Fox moderator, Chris Wallace, barely able to keep control and Trump making 73 interruptions. The lowlight was when Trump refused to condemn white supremacist groups and the Proud Boys, telling them in classic black shirt language, "stand back and stand by". Biden didn't debate particularly well, but nobody will remember that in the future, although his line to the president, "Will you shut up, man", may be remembered for longer. The second debate with muted microphones was a significant improvement, and Americans were finally able to hear issues of substance. It didn't do Trump any good, and he remained around 10 points adrift, too much to overcome a somewhat more favourable electoral college.

Then the New York Times revealed some of Trump's tax information. The headline figure was a paltry $750 in federal for two consecutive years, which could be legal as tax avoidance and not fraud, but it wasn't going to play well. $70,000 on hairdressing was the eye-catcher in China as that is a very expensive "Tony" or "Coco", the generic words for a hairdresser. Suddenly, there were more questions about his financial empire built on sand, suggesting that holding meetings and conferences at his own venues was pumping up his empire at the taxpayer's expense. It also raised questions about foreign interference as a hook into Trump by actors such as Putin. Worse was to follow when it was revealed that

Trump had a secret bank account in China and had at least paid his $188,561 taxes there.

The bombshells just kept coming. In the early hours of October 2, Trump tweeted that both he and his wife had tested positive for COVID-19. The likely but not proven spreader was reckoned to be Hope Hicks, but another possibility was a packed event in the Rose Garden of the White House for the Supreme Court nomination of Amy Coney Barrett. Trump had actually travelled to a private fundraiser on October 1 in Bedminster, NJ, knowing that Hicks had already tested positive, an act of astounding recklessness. By the end of the day, Trump was ensconced in Walter Reed Hospital. In China, President Xi sent a get-well message. Perhaps wisely, there was a major clampdown in the Chinese media and social media, especially on some gleeful and derogatory comments. Even while in hospital and recovering, Trump managed to go on a tour of his supporters outside the perimeter and endangered the lives of several of his security detail on this frivolous mission.

In China, October 1 is the double festival of National Day and the Mid-Autumn Festival, also called Golden Week. In the COVID-19 world of 2020, over 600 million trips were made. Yan Yan and I had the chance to go to a wonderful party at a friend's house, no social distancing needed and great fun. Everyone brought wine and something to eat. My contribution was homemade fiery Buffalo wings and blue cheese dressing and celery, gratefully received by the Americans and undoubtedly delicious, but there was better. The host had made boerewors, that delicious South African sausage, and homemade pizza. For most, it was a combination of guilt and pleasure combined. There was a lot of talk about Golden Week because this was the first time Chinese people had returned to mass travel within the country in nearly a year. Would it all start again? Could China pull it off? It was mostly a success, but a new cluster did occur in the northern city of Qingdao with two dockworkers as the source, requiring testing the entire city of nine million people in four days. The alleged problem was with contaminated refrigerated imported frozen food that had started in June and persisted. It was on a wide range of products: chicken, shrimp, squid, beef, and tripe, and from a wide range of countries including some with excellent or reasonable relations with China (Russia, Ecuador, Bolivia, Argentina, Germany, Norway – only recently restored from frosty after Norway gave the Nobel Peace Prize to activist Liu Xiaobo in 2010), and some who do not (Australia, the US, Canada, and India). It was hard to know what to make of this. The occasional spread of the virus had to be coming from somewhere, but where? The odd one out was the October 26, 137 asymptomatic cases in inland Kashgar, which needed 4.75 million tests and spread from a garment worker and discovered by a routine inspection. Frozen food of the types described was removed from shelves in some cities, tested, and returned with a virus checked and free of it label. Some cynics in the West even suggested China was positioning itself to eventually declare that COVID-19 had started in a different country.

By mid – October, the US economy had made a stuttering but admirable recovery, with unemployment at 7.8% and 11.4 million jobs replaced of the 22 million lost in March and April and without any new economic stimulus. Even this wasn't helping Trump's ratings, and an increasingly desperate POTUS by this stage was demanding of his (not the) Attorney General that charges should be brought against leading current and former Democrats and had started to threaten imprisonment to anyone who disagreed with him. There were still shortages of critical COVID-19 medicines too. Alarmingly, all civil servants, as a right enshrined since 1883, were to be reclassified from competitive service to expected service. In the furore, this mainly was lost, but it means that independent civil servants must now answer not to the country but to POTUS with all the perils that entailed.

On that very day Biden was stumping in my home county (October 24 – Luzerne County, PA), and I had been to a magnificent Beethoven concert given by our accomplished city orchestra, I came home and checked my email. I finally received a definitive answer on my wish to vote. I had an agreement that I was an eligible and a registered voter from weeks before, and I had even been sent a ballot to fill in, but it was only for military personnel. The last missive from the PA Bureau of Election Security and Technology finally beat me.

"If postal mail is not an option for you to return your ballot, you can try one of the following:

- Reach out to the US Embassy to see if there is something they can do to assist
- Reach out to APO or Military to see if they can help send material back
- Utilize a private carrier, like DHL to assist."

I realized I was living in a parallel universe. Regular international mail even before COVID-19 was unreliable, and the US Embassy only has a "dangle line", and it's impossible to speak to someone unless you are about to die, and as best I know, in China, there is no US military presence. DHL is expensive, and I obviously couldn't vote in person. I don't believe it was a scurrilous attempt to benefit one or other candidate but a total lack of understanding of the world beyond the US. Voting, to me, is an important matter, ingrained as a right and even an obligation.

Trump's final roll of the dice before the election was disgusting. On October 28, he made inquires to the Department of Justice (and the Attorney General, William Barr) as to why more people in the CIA and FBI aren't being investigated, charged, and put in jail. Later, Bill Barr resigned or fell on his sword and didn't see the mayhem out to the last. There was still time for one final insult. On October 31, Trump made the appalling claim that US doctors were inflating COVID-19 numbers as "they get more money if someone dies from COVID".

On November 5, late at night, Trump declared himself the winner as planned. He knew he couldn't survive the blizzard of postal votes weighted heavily Democrat. In the end, he lost by a landslide, and it should have been more, except the Biden team had a misstep in Florida and misunderstood the different types of Latino voters in different parts of the country.

Finally, on November 8, it was all over. Trump had lost Pennsylvania, and his fate was sealed, although he was still inclined and definitely allowed by the constitution to litigate, and was prepared to stand on a podium in the White House claiming corruption and malfeasance. The election was a huge success for American democracy, with nearly 160 million voting and people who had never paid much attention before choosing to vote. Voting records were broken, including for Trump. It didn't matter about frivolous lawsuits; the people had spoken. Even an extra vote on the Supreme Court wasn't going to fix this for the outgoing President.

The Trump era was a sad and massive loss for the US and its standing in the world. I will try and explain why.

Many Chinese people watched this election, but if you don't live in a democracy, it's a little hard to understand the nuances, especially when a sitting president claims in two separate speeches from the White House that he had won before the votes were counted. With a bit of patience, it was possible to explain why the overall number of voters don't win, although Biden would have won by more on this basis. You have to wonder what all the Chinese netizens who had their moment of relatively free speech after Wuhan thought of democracy now. Trump was fast resorting to his usual thug tactics of threatening lawsuits, but he failed to understand that there is a big difference between cudgelling creditors and taking "we the people" to law. There were going to be inevitable shenanigans, many of them underhand and profoundly undemocratic, but Trump had lost. He was, of course, going to try and burn the barn down on his way out of the door leaving many Americans sick, scared, and sometimes hungry just in time for Christmas, and his ire then focused on any Republican who disagreed with him. He was eating his own babies.

The more complex questions from Chinese friends and damaging to the US international standing (and not exactly discouraged by the Chinese and other media), and questions I can't answer, include why if claimed the process is so corrupt (as asserted by Trump), aren't there international observers as in many countries? Will black people and dissenters be safer from being killed and beaten now? Why, if he, as the loser, refuses to leave, doesn't the army come and take him away? Will people try and save themselves and wear masks now? So now why can't you immediately tackle the COVID-19 problems (a president sits for 75 more days)? It's shameful even to try and answer some of this.

China and its autocracy versus the US and democracy is not really the issue. It's about investing in medicine and succour for all the people and about caring. It's about the collective good, even if sacrifices have to be made. China eventually responded for the collective good, as well as, of course, preserving the regime. The US? I can't even begin to frame an answer.

President Biden inherited a nation divided but at least to the rest of the world, looks and sounds like a statesman. He doesn't carry a bullying megaphone, and before he embarks on international reconciliation, he will have to try and bring a divided nation together. Biden won't be soft on China and has a cross-party mandate not to be, but there is some chance to communicate and negotiate.

On December 5, I decided to close this chapter. The UK had just approved its citizens getting the Pfizer vaccines it had wisely procured as the first western country to do so. According to Johns Hopkins University, global deaths stood at 1,515,530 million and the US at 278,417, with the rate of cases and fatalities accelerating at a precipitous rate and Trump ranting and raving and playing golf leaving the US international reputation in tatters and having to start again to become the leader of the free world. And somehow, it's going to need love, care, understanding, and affection from all sides. It won't be easy, but it's a laudable aim. Please do it – I beg you.

Postscript. Although I finished this chapter on December 5, on January 2, Trump, on a phone call that became public, tried to strong-arm the Republican Secretary of State for Georgia to "find" votes. On January 6, in a clear act of presidential sedition, insurrectionists stormed the Capitol Building and domestic terrorists in Nazi and Confederate regalia, directly encouraged by Trump. This prompted former President George W. Bush (yes, that one who signed my citizenship) to say "this is how election results are disputed in a Banana Republic". Trump was impeached for a second time and was acquitted, leaving the rest of the world wondering what democracy is.

Part 4: A Post COVID-19 Future

Chapter 17: The Tipping Point

One of the questions I ask urban-dwelling Chinese friends is, "what about the countryside as a possible place to live?" This often occurs after a conversation about my previous life in rural America. My modern house, bought new, in Pennsylvania was on a half-acre of land, opposite the golf course ninth hole and clubhouse with restaurant and bar. The house had a lounge, a drawing-room, a study, a large island kitchen, four bedrooms, the master with two walk-in closets, two and a half bathrooms, a basement room with a pool table, a wrap-around front porch, and two garages with electric doors. Work was a fifteen-minute drive to the nearest town, which also had all the needed shops and amenities. It was definitely rural and beautiful, and over an early morning coffee, I sat on the front porch, where deer and sometimes black bears would wander across the front garden. There were a few downsides: the brutally cold winters, the constant need to shovel snow, and the dangerously icy roads. When I moved to China in 2015, I sold it for $182,000 (£114,000), and even at that price tag, it took six months to sell. That wouldn't even buy (leasehold only) the bedroom in an apartment in Beijing. This affordable price might be baffling to westerners and some other Asian and South American nations. To the urban Chinese, it's incomprehensible, not just because of the price but also because few places like this exist in China. Those that come close are the preserve of multi-millionaires and are either close to or within city boundaries. Rural China is based on farmland centred on a village. Local village leaders, party members all, allocate the land, primarily based on traditional occupancy rights. You can't just show up, buy an individual plot of land and build a lovely house, although property developers are always looking for new land.

When I ask my urban friends and colleagues whether they would ever consider living in the Chinese countryside, the looks are bemused, horrified, and mostly negative. The bemused are those who moved to the cities and return to home town or village in the countryside for festivals. They often remember the poverty and the back-breaking work in the fields of previous generations of the family. The horrified are those who have always lived in the cities or have lost ties with their rural origins. Their opinion of the countryside is a place full of ill-educated farmers in filthy houses with no basic amenities such as a modern toilet, adequate electricity, no gas and the need to cook or keep warm with firewood, little or no hot and running water, inadequate medical care and a host of other inconveniences. They don't have a clue what the different crops in the field look like or how the fish they eat are caught, or even sometimes that the basis of their favourite ice cream is milk that comes from a cow. In this way, they are similar to many of their urban counterparts in other countries. Their knowledge of rural poverty is based on a few documentaries on television. One exception is a Chinese friend, Heidi, who, with a pressured job in international logistics and a demanding home life coping with a two-year-old daughter, with her colleagues, gives up her holidays to climb up mountain tracks and deliver much-needed bags of food and clothes in Yunnan Province. The children were in tears as they had a proper warm coat for the first time in their lives and wouldn't be cold in winter. It's why I don't mind meeting Heidi sometimes for an early morning coffee to help her improve her English.

The energy to help alleviate rural poverty appears to be across all age ranges. Generation Y and Z have different names in China, and the dates are not quite the same. They are called the "Post 90s Generation" (born 1990 to 1999), so the oldest members of this group at the time of writing is 31 years old. Those born earlier are called the "Post 80s Generation" (born 1980 to 1989). The Post 90s receive a lot of bad press in China, and some of it is justified, such as breaking away from family traditions to look after the elderly, unhealthy lifestyles, failing to have enough children, and extreme materialism. The other side of the equation, less discussed, is they are under massive pressure in both their social and work lives, and I was easily able to find examples of generous Post 90s behaviour.

Something is changing in China, and it's happening quickly. There are many reasons for this, and some, but not all, are led by government policy. Huge disparities in wealth between rural and urban areas are not in keeping with modern Chinese socialist thinking and are potentially inharmonious or even divisive. Rural poverty alleviation is the government's number one priority, with its elimination finally announced in November 2020. After spending RMB 17.5 billion (£2 billion) per year in the previous five years, a further RMB 130 billion (£15 billion) was needed to meet the end of 2020 goal. There were roughly 17 million people still in dire financial need before this target was met. Poverty, as defined by the government, is an annual income of less than RMB 2800 (£320) per year, still perilously close to the edge. To get a feeling of what this type of poverty looks like, it means things like no warm coat in winter, children with one meal a day and the inability to concentrate at school because of under nutrition, no doctors, walking to school on muddy tracks, not roads. It's a brutal existence.

It's a very different lifestyle to the first farmers I got to talk to when I initially came to China as a visitor. I was in a relatively prosperous rural area of Zhejiang Province. One middle-aged farmer was proud to show me around as we talked about what farming looked like in the Mid-West of the US, something that fascinated him. The farm was beautiful and typical of this village and found along country lanes lined with poplar trees. Behind the three-storied farmhouse were carefully planted shade trees and a pond with plump fish fed on maize stubble and growing for the pot. The pond was also ornamental, with mauve and pink flowering lilies in one corner. There was a pigsty and a boisterous farm dog who seemed interested in the smells emanating from this foreign imposter. His wife, and elderly parents, produced tea and bowls of snails, home-grown apricots, and peanuts, all delicious and served on a terraced area with little wooden stools on a low-lying table with cascading pot plants all around. The family had a worn Toyota car, a television, a refrigerator, and pleasant indoor furniture, items accumulated not just from farming income but supplemented from a small rural trading business. It had much in common with an agreeable rural French Provençal farm. It taught me an important lesson because the well-documented urban/rural inequality also has an element of rural/rural disparities. Haves and have not's if you like.

Central government dispatched three-quarters of a million officials to the countryside to try and help in this final push against poverty. This effort was then supported by an even larger local government cadre who went to each rural householder to identify needs and solutions and use some of the current annual spending on this initiative, plus another £4 billion donated from state-owned enterprises. Any remaining money will be used for infrastructure improvements, particularly roads and internet access, the former so that enterprising farmers can sell their produce to a broader market or attract tourists, and the latter so they can get that produce out and tourists in. The latest push also involved something a lot more controversial and caused apoplexy on social media. It was the plan to send Youth Wing members of the Communist Party on 10 million volunteering missions to impoverished rural areas over a three-year period. To many, it harked back to a previous era in the form of Chairman Mao's 1960's and 1970's "Down to the Countryside" campaign, when about 17 million of China's privileged urban high schoolers were sent packing to all corners of China to educate themselves on rural life. Many lost a chance to go to university and are known as 知識青年 – zhi1shi4qing1nian2, literally "know-how youth", also referred to as "the lost generation".

It was very clear from numerous Chinese media outlets that failure was not an option. The government wields a giant stick. The threat of being fired and losing a well-paid and one of the most desirable jobs in China, a civil servant, with excellent benefits and a state pension was intimidating enough for the officials. For the Youth Wing "volunteers", not participating would impair them for a move up the ladder. Running in parallel to this has been an explosion in personal charitable deeds and philanthropy, which fits with older Confucian philosophy and has been less common until recently in Communist China. It's unclear what has caused this, but in my opinion, part of it is akin to that genius of understanding the Chinese, Pearl S. Buck's, observation that: "The test of a civilization is in the way it cares for its helpless members". It's that and a new consciousness of what China should be and more disposable income to help. Other factors at play are probably a growing trust in Chinese charities, which previously, with plenty of evidence, were considered both corrupt and inefficient, a change in the charitable tax and registration laws in 2016, and the ease of donating to an ever-increasing number of web-based charities. Whatever the reasons, Chinese charities have increased in numbers 500% in the last ten years. There has also been a growth of high net worth and well-known individuals becoming philanthropic. China has one-fifth of the world's billionaires.

Alongside this activity in the countryside has become the beginning of a tipping point in the larger urban areas. The Post 80s and Post 90s generations are starting to question the actual value of city life. The punishing work schedule, 9-9-6 (9 am to 9 pm, six days a week) eschewed by Jack Ma, and owning a car that can't be driven anywhere because of traffic jams, having to have multiple generations in one apartment to afford a purchase, insufficient time or resources to have a second child, all take a toll on urbanites. Suddenly, living in the countryside looks interesting. For sure, countryside to them doesn't mean a farm halfway up a mountain with no electricity or plumbing and back-breaking manual labour. The dream is more of a small town with modern amenities, skilled work opportunities with fast internet connections in the burgeoning services sector, and space to breathe and have a reasonable work-life balance. It might still mean living in a high-rise apartment but with everything on a smaller scale. For a few, it also opens the opportunity for retirement to some of the more beautiful parts of China, such as Hainan Island or Yunnan Province. Add in migrant workers who want to return to their hometown because of fewer city work opportunities as the economy cools, and often neglected urban poverty from a group with no chance of ever finding a spouse. Also, the differential between rural and urban wages has narrowed as urban wages stagnated and rural wages went up because of labour shortages. The effect looks like the start of reverse migration, if not yet an exodus, with the government at all levels is encouraging it.

One striking example of this is the lingerie revolution in China. It's a rural, not an urban story. The town is called Dongwangji in Jiangsu Province. It used to be a sleepy place surrounded by rice and wheat. It is now one of the intended 1000 towns and cities planned by the Ministry of Housing and Urban Development, focusing on developing specific industries. The local government provides the framework and suitable conditions, but the enterprises are private. This is now the centre of the Chinese lingerie industry. There were challenges to overcome, not least because local, mostly female potential employees didn't want to produce such tawdry and overtly sexy garments, especially those with a role-playing element. Bras and panties, well knickers really, were traditionally used to cover things up, so underwear, with, in some cases, virtually no material, was shocking. Once this reticence had been overcome, the Dongwangji lingerie industry expanded to 600 manufactories employing 20,000 people and representing 60% of all Chinese production. The initial market was concentrated on exporting, but now the home market is booming as the younger generation of Chinese females have far fewer inhibitions and really want these goods. They don't even blush and giggle anymore when they go to Victoria's Secret.

This doesn't mean China has abandoned urbanization because running parallel is the concept of cluster cities. This is not a new concept globally, although other cluster cities such as Tokyo Bay and San Francisco Bay have developed in a less planned way. China is much better able to control where its population lives through the hukou (戶口 – hu4kou3) system of household registration, which records, amongst other things, a place of permanent residence. The idea behind cluster cities is to make urban planning and infrastructure more manageable compared to ever-growing single cities like Beijing and Shanghai and for each cluster to concentrate on its own economic and competitive strengths. Many of the clusters will encompass already established free trade zones that offer a more liberal economic environment. It is intended for there to be 13 of these clusters, and they are huge. For example, the Pearl River Area, which includes Hong Kong, Macau, Guangzhou, and Shenzhen, will have a population of over 120 million.

Although less discussed, to my mind, there is another benefit of this nationally organized effort, namely to reducing "land grabs". As China boomed economically in the last two decades, all too often stories emerged of local government appropriating land by both frequent coercion and sometimes incentives. An immediate mark up on the land of thirtyfold or so is a powerful incentive to do so with plenty of developers ready in the wings. By far the largest number of mass (street) protests in China relate to this issue, perhaps 150,000 to 200,000 per year, the rest made up of a tapestry of, for example, workers protesting and going on strike having not been paid by companies, frequently inefficient state-owned ones. Technically this right to protest is guaranteed under the PRC constitution, but there are many pitfalls. Anyway, China can't afford to continue to give up agricultural land at this pace.

With the lines becoming more blurred between urban and rural areas and poverty waning, the Chinese government will face a new problem: the middle-income trap. Some of this entrepreneurial activity may well assist with this. Introduced as a concept by the World Bank in 2006, the middle-income trap seeks to explain how many countries have become stuck in a GNP per capita range of $1000 to $12,000 (as of 2011). This is considered a result of becoming uncompetitive, particularly in exports, due to wage inflation and other deleterious effects. Only 15 countries have escaped the middle-income trap since 1960, most notably Japan. I have to believe Chinese economists and planners look at this very carefully, not least because of an implied contract between the government and the people to continue improving living standards in return for a certain amount of subservience. The usual escape route from the trap is to go high-tech and often has a sizeable advanced education component, things that China has high on its list of priorities. Some also believe the Belt and Road initiative is part of this strategy. Beyond this, and not in China's immediate purview, is the higher income countries where middle-class wealth in real terms stagnates and is sometimes called the middle-class squeeze. This is a problem that has particularly afflicted the US, but it comes in many forms. In Europe, several countries have inadequate funds for their pensioners unless they take dramatic action: the UK, Spain, France, Germany, Austria, and even Switzerland are such examples. It's something China needs to watch out for in the future because of its low birth-rate.

Chapter 18: Driving Me Crazy

There are two parts to this chapter. The first, related to the Chinese driving test, is all true. The second part about Artificial Intelligence in vehicles and electric vehicles (EV's) is part fact and part fiction.

One of the worst mistakes I have made since I came to live in China and a costly one in time and money was not converting my foreign license to a Chinese one before it expired. Please, don't ever make this mistake, because the consequences, the punishment, are severe. Assuming you avoid this error, drivers will have to pass Level 1, a series of tests on the Highway Code brought up on a computer, and a cursory medical examination. It's available in several languages, including in English. The pass mark is 90%, and although some of the questions are poorly translated, you can rote learn the answers. You can pass with some study and diligence unless you take it in Japanese when the translation is apparently so inadequate that it becomes a significant challenge. For the valid foreign license holders, that's the end of the requirements.

For the rest, new learner drivers from any country and forgetful idiots like me, you must pass parts 2 and 3 in Chinese. I enrolled at the Big Fat Tiger Driving School, and the misery commenced. It hadn't made life any easier that I had been accidentally registered for a manual gear test rather than for an automatic. I hadn't driven one for at least twenty-five years when I lived in the UK, as Americas don't like stick shift cars. Part 2 is on a driving school track, with a series of exercises. Teaching instructions are in Chinese as there is no need for anything else as almost every foreigner has avoided this step. Learning is done in one car with three or four pupils taking turns. It means spending half a day each time, waiting for your turn, and is very time-consuming. Some schools do offer a fast-track VIP service. Most of the skills tests revolve around not touching solid yellow lines or parking in exactly the correct and strict way. A few inches deviation if you haven't stopped exactly at the proper distance from the curb on the exercise to stop on a hill and then release the handbrake will result in failure. The biggest problems are reversing into a parking bay from two directions and parallel parking, both very tight. This all has to be done using only the mirrors. I could see amongst my young team that some of the learners might never be able to do this. When you have wasted many hours, you are taken to the examination track to look around, and our team spent many hours walking around in the baking sun with the coach pointing out all the details and pitfalls using the school's car which we followed on foot. You do get one try-out of the circuit each. Finally, on test day, you spend hours waiting for your name to be called. The first time much to my annoyance, I failed. I hopped into the actual test vehicle and waited for a policeman or someone to join me. Then a man pressed a button and said, "your test has started; off you go". No one had told me that I would be on my own and that sensors and radar would monitor the entire test. Worse, although I never touched a yellow line, the coach had not made clear to me, or I had not understood, that the parking must be done in one continuous smooth motion whereas I had stopped at one point to line up correctly just as I had done at the school without being admonished. The sensors picked this up, and that was an immediate failure. Two weeks later, I went back, and it was a breeze.

Part 3, for a foreigner, is an extremely tough ask. Yan Yan had assumed that I would be allowed a translator, and when she discovered that was not possible, she begged me to give up. This is the public road test. The first part is in training when you get in the car with your team, and it is your turn to drive. First, you go through the formalities, have your photograph taken and matched, etc. Then you begin the lights test. You are asked to switch on the lights and then respond to the correct light setting from a series of randomly selected questions coming out of a voice box. In rapid Chinese, it might say "approaching a sharp bend with a pedestrian bridge", and you have a few seconds to flash your lights. If you are Chinese, this may not be too difficult, but if you are a foreigner, it's very hard, especially with your team chattering and making phone calls in the background. The second part is to drive around a public road circuit conducting a series of exercises, turns, acceleration, gear changes, U-turns, etc. These are real roads with real traffic committing every possible violation. The voice box will tell you what each scenario is, such as "factory crossroad ahead", where you need to brake and look around. Any speeding or failure to use indicators is an immediate failure. In some domains, you will apparently also given instructions on how to palm off a gratuity to the police examiner who will be sitting next to you without being observed on camera or by a senior officer. I'm not sure the examiner can help you much as there are also sensors on the car so that if you ride your clutch, you will fail, but I suppose the examiner might offer help in some cases. All of the manoeuvres I found very easy, and after a few sessions, I was ready. Then there was a team trip to the examination centre to learn one of four possible routes. Another day lost.

Finally, test day came, and on arrival, I was called into the office as I didn't have a government ID, just a passport. In the background, a senior policeman, an Inspector, looked at me with astonishment and concern but got one of his staff to enter me into the computer, and I asked if he had ever had a foreigner do this test. He told me very few, which in Chinese, with an appropriate shrug, is the equivalent of maybe zero. Then I sat down in the waiting room for an hour or so. On the electronic waiting board was each name and an ID card number except my name (马福民 – Ma Fu Min) with a blank by it. I kept hearing people asking why this name had no number attached, and "who is Ma Fu Min? He must be different?" Slowly it dawned on the assembled it must be me and the staring and pointing made an already nervous candidate feel worse.

When I was finally called, the Inspector was outside talking to the police examiner and pointing at me. I will never know what was said, but my guess was something like: "we've got a right one here, a grey-haired foreigner, who only speaks some Chinese – just make sure he doesn't kill anyone and try and be accommodating within the rules". Fearful, I failed the first lights test because the volume control on the box was turned up to maximum and distorted the voice. Not a problem if you are Chinese, but for me a disaster in the making. The examiner told me to calm down as I was shaking and asked me to do it again, as you are allowed a second try, and somehow, I must have passed. The rest went well enough, although I may have detected a discreet cough a couple of times. As the examiner drove me back to the centre he told me I had passed, we laughed, and I wanted to hug him. We were met by the Inspector who congratulated me and told me I was the oldest foreigner ever in Jiangsu Province (population 80 million) to have passed this test. He was grinning. Yan Yan took me out to a German restaurant for lunch, and I downed enough strong lager until the shaking stopped. I did not drive home, of course.

Part 4 is mostly available in English, with some Chinese, and is a peculiar hybrid of etiquette, situations with flash videos, and safety, done on a computer. It's incredibly useful, and I learned many new things. It's only moderately difficult, but some of the questions are multiple-choice. The pass mark is 90%. Here is an example:

"At 3: 40 a.m. one day, Mr. Sun drove a large bus with 54 passengers (capacity 55 people). At the spot of 229 kilometres mark by 300 meters on Suiyue Expressway, the bus had a rear-end collision with a heavy semi-trailer driven by Mr. Li when passengers were getting off from the bus. As a result of the accident, 26 people were killed and 29 injured. According to the investigation afterwards, Mr. Li had been driving the bus since he left the place of departure at 6 pm the day before without any rest. What are the main illegal acts of the two drivers?"

A. Mr. Sun illegally parked
B. Mr. Sun carried more passengers than permitted
C. Mr. Li exceeded the speed limit
D. Mr. Li kept driving when tired

(AD)

Suddenly the ordeal was all over. I scored 96% and went for another long wait to get my Chinese driving license, earned the hard way.

I'm fascinated by modern transportation and none more so than electric vehicles (EV's). EV's and developing and associated Artificial Intelligence (AI) are exciting and wonderful new things. They are now things and not just drawing board ideas. I should declare, I own stock in this sector, including in the Chinese electric carmaker NIO, a potential rival to TESLA, a company I have shunned to my cost. NIO won the inaugural 2014-15 FIA Formula E championship (as NEXTEV) and now has two precision-built SUV EV's and one imminent sedan EV, all pitched at a price similar to the top German models. I also hold stock in the US company, NVIDIA, which will hopefully be prominent in the chips to make these machines function, in UBER (bought well below the IPO offer price) and an Exchange Traded Fund (ETF) for lithium-ion batteries. I've also held Apple stock for years, although it is not clear how much success Apple will have in this sector, although they might one day buy TESLA. So long as they keep selling iPhones and other new gizmos, I'll be alright. These are not widow and orphan stocks, and picking the winners is difficult. For example, lithium batteries for cars could quickly be superseded by the massively improved energy density of Redox flow batteries which in theory could take an EV more than 1000 miles (1600 km) on one charge. What if the cars don't need batteries at all, but they take their electrical charge from the road like a real-life Scalextric track? This technology has already been developed on a small scale in Holland and Sweden. What happens if we can get rid of batteries altogether one day and use Graphene super capacitors? Buyer beware.

China has multiple compelling reasons to be involved in this sector. It is heavily dependent on imported oil and still has awful pollution, some of which is caused by conventional vehicles. However, a more significant issue is the burning of fossil fuels. It is also a signatory to the 2016 Paris Climate Accord, which should put a curb on greenhouse gas (GHG) emissions. France has declared it will phase out diesel and petrol cars by 2040 with no new sales after 2030, and the UK by 2050 with further measures to follow. Some of this is a long way in the future, and much can be done immediately. London, for example, has expanded its ultra-low emission zones with a hefty daily fee for entering that area. China wants 20% electric, hybrid, or hydrogen by 2025 and has already legislated to make this occur. Top of the class for progress in this area goes to Norway who plans to ban all petrol and diesel cars by 2025 and is on target. It will also be the first country outside China where another Chinese EV will be sold: the XPENG. However, perhaps surprisingly (think pristine fiords and brightly painted wood houses), Norway, by European standards, does not have a good record on GHG emissions because of its exportable fossil fuel sector. The other problem for countries like China is a matter of scalability and overall wealth per capita. China has a population over 2500 times that of Norway, over 100 cities bigger than Oslo, and its biggest cities are over 20 times larger.

China's method is ferocious. It forces companies into producing a reasonable percentage of EV's with fines if they can't earn enough carbon credits standards or emission standards, only achievable by having EV's.

There is another less altruistic reason for China's interest in this sector outside of the environmental issues. China has shown itself adept in both transportation technology and AI. It missed out globally on conventional automobile sales or purchased a stake in other companies such as Volvo, MG, and Peugeot-Citroen. Even the company that makes the famous London black cab is part Chinese-owned. EV's level the playing field but also creates challenges of consumer acceptability. Chinese companies featured prominently at the 2019 Detroit Auto Show, with the GAC Entranze EV crossover catching the eye. At the New York equivalent show, the Chinese EV Qiantu K50 sports car also made a good impression with its 0-60 mph in less than 4.2 seconds.

I had a dream about the near future, well, a nightmare actually.

I was on my way to look and perhaps try out the new Model W Driverless Electric Car from Gao Fei Motors, which David Beckham has heavily promoted. I had seen the Model W on the advertising boards in my apartment lift. If it's good enough for David, it's good enough for me, but I did wonder in passing if he will ever get all his royalty payments. Still, at least he won't get a six-month license suspension as he did in the UK for using his mobile phone when driving, as everyone does this in China. Branding, style, and design have improved a bit since the ever-popular Trumpchi model by GAC Group and the unashamed Range Rover copy, Land Wind X7, from Jiangling, at a third of the price of the Range Rover Evoque.

The Model W looks sleek. As always in China, all the car and related showrooms are in a neat and glossy line in one part of town: a collective huddle of glass-windowed concrete structures adorned with pink blow-up arches and balloons. I pulled up at the showroom sandwiched between the Porsche dealer and the popular Melon Car Rental Company (瓜子– gua1zi), smiling to myself that Melon is an anagram of "Lemon".

I've dressed well: blue and white striped shirt, yellow tie (the power colour of the emperors and rarely worn by the Chinese), and light Italian wool suit. I don't want to look like a poor foreigner and want to give the impression I will be going to the Porsche dealer nearby for some more conventional juice as the next part of my shopping trip. A young, well-dressed salesman, Mr. Wu, jumps up to greet me before the electric doors to the establishment even open. He beckoned me to a polished hardwood table, summons tea, and presents me with his card: always presented with two hands with the name facing the recipient. His language is near flawless private school English, perhaps from Eton House College or Wall Street English. Mr. Wu is a serious young man, so I decided not to tell him about the latest research from the Annals of Tourism which assesses that sex in driverless cars will become commonplace and deliver a different kind of thrill to breaking the speed limit and that one-way tinted glass windows will become de rigeur.

I asked Mr. Wu a little about the Model W. How was it developed? Is it safe? Is it legal? He explains that the Model W was first developed at the company's test track in Shenzhen and inspected by a global safety consortium. It was millions of hours of work, and the vehicle is completely safe and is programmed with all the rules from the Highway Code. The car has a vast array of sensors using radar, cameras, ultrasonic and more. He explained that the Model W even negotiated with ease the world's most complex spaghetti junction in Chongqing, something nearly impossible for average Chinese drivers. As one writer on Weibo put it, "if you miss a ramp, you will arrive in (the city of Chongqing) one day later". Chongqing is known by the Chinese as a rogue traffic city and also installed twenty working traffic lights as a decoration on a single pole at a junction. It's the only place in the world you can run multiple red lights all at one go.

It's nearly 11 am, and Mr. Wu suggested a test drive to my office, which is a couple of miles away. We got into the car with its green number plates (showing it is electric in China), Mr. Wu in the "driver's" seat, and me riding shotgun. On scanning his retina, the car fires up and starts to talk in Chinese. Mr. Wu explains that the retina identification will automatically give the appropriate "driver's" language, but this technology of race identification is a "little bit secret". He manually switches the settings to the English Language. We were told to buckle up and reminded that as I am a smoker, this is strictly prohibited and that the tea we have brought with us in cardboard cups from the showroom might be hot and to be careful. Both the retina and anti-smoking technology already exist in China. Leaving China by plane, all bags going to the cargo hold are scanned, and the equipment can detect matches or lighters, leading to a delay and a visit to the Inspection Room.

The road outside is a standard four-lane divided road with a separate lane in each direction for non-motorized vehicles, sometimes in the west called a "bicycle lane". As we leave the lot to enter the main road, the sensors on the car pick up an electric scooter in this lane coming in the opposite direction of flow to the traffic, and our vehicle dutifully stops, as does the scooter driver expecting to be hit which is common enough. Electric scooters count as non-motorized vehicles in China and can use the "bicycle lane". I am impressed. The car sensors both know the rules and what to do when they are broken.

We turned right and joined the oncoming traffic. Unfortunately, a pedestrian was waving down an available taxi. The taxi weaved across our path to grab the passenger and abruptly stopped, causing our car to make an emergency stop and the car behind us to do the same. While the taxi driver speeded away, the man in the following vehicle got out and hit Mr. Wu's window with his fists until he opens it. A five-minute shouting match ensues with several references to each person's mothers' private parts. When this is over, we continue, and I am grateful that the AI is in control as Mr. Wu was visibly shaken. As we approached the first set of traffic lights, a dog leaped into the road. This is unusual in China as stray dogs have, over time, become genetically modified to cross at junctions on the pedestrian green "walk" sign. Maybe this one has a death wish or rabies. We screeched to a stop again rather than either running over it or weaving around it, the more normal manoeuvres.

After 275 metres (300 yards), the first traffic lights approached. Ours was red, and the Model W executes a perfect and gentle stop. An old lady was moving between the cars selling flowers, and when the lights turned green, she was still in the middle of the road. The Model W refuses to move, and the lights went red again with furious honking from cars behind. At the next green light, we moved forward, but a fast-food delivery driver on a scooter and not in the non-motorized lane ran the red light as he was late for a delivery. The early lunch delivery was maybe due at 11.30 am, and both he and the restaurant would have to give a discount to the recipient if he was late. Another bone-jarring emergency stop. Mr. Wu was ecstatic as he pointed out how safe this car is.

The next obstacle is one not found in the west. On the main road, a father was giving cover behind his two kids in a child's electric car in front (this is true and got an RMB200 (£23) fine). As we progressed down the road, a line of cars, drivers frustrated by the jams, were coming down the wrong side of the dividing do not cross yellow line, a pretty regular sight in China. The Model W did not make the more normal manoeuvre which is to push the same direction traffic towards the edge of the road to try and create an extra lane. More furious honking from both directions.

The next set of traffic lights was interesting. The traffic signs indicate no right turn and no left turn, i.e., straight only, but this was blocked by a barrier (I have actually seen this). The Model W voice is temporarily silent, no doubt fizzing with terabytes of calculations, and then announces, "driver, please take control of the vehicle" in perfect Eton House English.

We then joined the lunchtime traffic jam and couldn't move. A manual "U" turn meant the one-mile journey had taken one and a half hours. Perhaps the single file Scalextric model is the best for China?

Active AI testing is going on, mainly on California public roads, with Chinese companies logging the largest number of collective miles there. The company Waymo (Google) has easily been the leader and whose 98 test cars logged 1.2 million kilometres (1.2 million miles) in 2018 with only 18 collisions. Shanghai, Shenzhen, and Chongqing are all currently soliciting companies to carry out tests on Chinese public roads, and both TenCent and Alibaba AI cars have seemingly already been testing at, unsurprisingly after my dream, secret locations. Beijing now has a small area with driverless taxis. Let the mayhem commence.

Chapter 19: X-Ray Specs

As a precursor, I should explain that some, but not all, of this chapter, may not be of direct relevance to foreigners visiting China as a tourist. I still hope this is a valuable background as it explains if you are in this category, many things you will observe. For someone coming to work in China, it becomes very relevant so as to understand the business background and the thoughts of Chinese business people and their government.

Several developments are occurring in China that could have profound implications for the country's future. Since 1947, China has had more than its share of sociological experiments such as the Great Leap Forward and the Cultural Revolution. The new revolution I have dubbed the Artificial Intelligence (AI) Revolution. It's fascinating, shocking, avant-garde, controversial, dystopian, potentially beneficial, and potentially damaging. To be fair, the Chinese government is still getting its ducks in a row as to how this AI Revolution will develop and how it will explain it to 1.4 billion people.

There are five pieces of technology currently being developed in China that will have long-term ramifications for its citizens: Facial Recognition (FR), 5G networking, social credits, blockchain, and monitoring/welfare.

Let's start with FR, AI, and related cameras. A few weeks ago, I was travelling through the district of Wujiang (吴江), a part of Suzhou. It had just gone dark, and at a busy intersection with traffic lights, I suddenly let out a sharp expletive. Above the traffic lights was an LED notice board listing the registration numbers of the cars where the driver had not buckled up their seat belt. How the hell does that work in the dark? I later discovered that the city of Shenzhen has already been recording jaywalkers through cameras and FR and are now developing a texting system to warn or fine the miscreant. In central Yangzhou, there is an electronic "wall of shame" with images and details of jaywalkers. As one friend told me, "I wish they did that for the dickheads riding the wrong way in bike lanes", but I suspect that will come along with China's recently introduced law (finally) for compulsory wearing of a helmet on an E-bike.

Life has moved on from the American X-ray spectacles of the 1950s to the 1970s, which promised, "See the bones in your hand, see through clothes!" As a boy, I was fascinated by this cheap possibility. I wasn't interested in the bones, but the prospect of seeing through clothes was youthfully stimulating. Unfortunately, they were an optical illusion and a disappointment. The Chinese FR variant being rolled out nationwide is called Sharp Eyes, also called Dazzling Snow (雪亮 – xue3liang4). The Sharp Eyes name possibly comes from a Mao-era slogan: "The people have sharp eyes and clear minds". Today in China, you will see police officers wearing a special type of sunglasses with an attached camera/processor, and these do work. They are used for FR and something familiar to mobile phone users who use FR instead of a password. Next to the person under scrutiny are text bubbles showing items such as name, age, home, and of course, if wanted by the police.

It's one of two areas where China (and several other countries) is already using advanced technology to monitor citizens. This is a big global market of £5 billion with three cross-matched elements: hardware, software, and one for integrated systems. The Chinese are market leaders in hardware, with companies such as Chinese companies Hikvision, Dahua, Huawei, ZTE, SenseTime, Qihoo360, and Megvii doing battle with leading competitors such as Japan's NEC and Israel's AnyVision. But suddenly, companies more associated with software, such as the American companies Cisco and Palantir Technologies, and integrated AI systems such as the American Accenture and Hewlett-Packard, want a slice of the action, for example, as interested parties in an Indian tender discussed later. The development of this market is made more complicated by globally integrated supply chains such as the Chinese companies relying on some advanced American chips.

China has a current advantage in overall sales because of its colossal home market and may well be ahead technologically. In the global market, there is enough new business for all. One reason for this is explained by Daniel Castro, VP of IT and Innovation Foundation in Washington DC, who has identified that the systems work best on their own (or similar) ethnicities. In China, this is not something a visitor or foreign worker needs to think about much. Your facial biometrics and fingerprints are already in the system from your visa application and passport, and from your regular annual work permit renewal, which also requires submission of new photographs. Your most likely encounter with this technology is if you want to open a WeChat or similar account or a needed update is due, and these days a picture of your passport is required for this. This technology is powerful. In 2018, a man named Ao attending a Jacky Cheung pop concert in Nanchang was identified in a crowd of 60,000 and arrested for "economic crimes". I doubt they were major fraud or bank robbery because the opportunity to publicize the actual crime would have been too great. Unfortunately, it has proved impossible for me to discover what economic crimes he committed, which in China could range from bilking your grandmother out of her last 500 RMB (£57) hidden in her mattress to cheating at the Mah-jong table. In December 2017, the BBC's John Sudworth was given access to a police station using FR in Guiyang. From the comprehensive database of the entire city, plus Sudworth's mug shot as a suspect, the police could track him down in seven minutes, with no cheating by using GPS and mobile phone referencing. Now suppose Sudworth, who I doubt has ever had more than a speeding ticket, had just stabbed someone with a knife, a big issue in the UK, and was considering a further attack. Suddenly seven minutes seems like an eternity. Perspective is everything.

In another recent case, a woman called Lao Rong Zhi, as reported by Xinjiang Police Online, was wanted in a murder case committed with her boyfriend from 1996-99 with seven deaths related to money theft to support their extravagant lifestyle. Since that time, she had been on the run and was finally identified by this type of FR technology. Her boyfriend was executed for this crime in 1999. The later DNA tests only supported the facial evidence on Ms. Lao, and this case taught me something important; namely, you don't have to have a modern photo to catch a crook. Perhaps Ms. Lao should have used some of her ill-gotten gains to get a face job done in Korea?

In 2018, When Mr. Zhang (not his real name) of Anxi Village in Sichuan Province set light to his fly-tipping garbage in a public space, he got a nasty shock when a loudspeaker blared out his name and address and told him to put out the fire immediately. He had been caught red-handed on one of the surveillance cameras in the village. The local Party Secretary was so delighted, one got the impression he would invest in robo-rottweilers as an additional backup measure.

FR is also sometimes used to see if a student is paying attention in class as it is more reliable than body language. When combined with electronic "sniffers" to see if students are cheating by using data from disallowed machines in exams, it's a good idea to pay attention and not break the rules.

On this scale, I don't think Chinese citizens will have much sympathy for the likes of Mr. Ao, Ms. Lao, and Mr. Zhang. The Chinese people like their modest crime rates and are used to being in multiple databases and producing their ID cards on-demand. In the past, it was all too easy to skip town after a crime. Many Chinese people also know or suspect that their ID number and the treasure trove of information linked to it are available for sale, something highly undesirable. Furthermore, China is not even the most camera surveyed society in the world. According to Robyn Dixon of the LA Times, in 2018, that honour goes to the UK. After all, there are many helpful applications for FR technology: boarding a plane or train, on the production of a smile for buying a KFC, already possible in parts of Beijing. In the KFC case, there is a trade-off because the stored data on meal preferences and other characteristics such as age will be used for marketing exercises. Presumably, if you are an octogenarian, it will suggest congee (rice gruel), soft savoury doughnuts, and soybean milk, perhaps in case you are missing a peg or two. Maybe if you are 20-year-old, it will recommend a giant chicken sandwich and a coke. Even at home, it's very convenient to get into our apartment block, which has FR, photograph uploaded on a simple app, rather than standing outside looking for keys in the cold. It is undoubtedly a deterrent for intruders.

I recognize that FR and associated AI are controversial and enough to cause civil liberty proponents' apoplexy, not least because it can identify adverse political and ethnic groups and other supposed undesirables. I understand that this whole area is fraught with problems and grey areas. Not even grey but beige, purple, violet, and ultramarine. Is it really a good use of resources for impoverished countries such as Kyrgyzstan, Rwanda, Zambia, and Zimbabwe, all of whom have purchased this technology? Is it appropriate to identify individuals this way who have insulted the monarchy or government, with potentially imprisonment waiting for the guilty, in countries such as Holland, Singapore, Norway, and Thailand? Is it reasonable to use FR to monitor press and demonstrators in countries that constitutionally guarantee media freedom to comment, such as Russia (Article 29 (5)) or of assembly, association, procession, and demonstration in China (Article 35)? I can't speak for the opaque Russian system, but in China, such protests are never anti-government at a national level whatever the constitution says and the mainland Chinese know that would be a step too far. Hong Kong is a different matter and its current protests are patently anti-government, which is why the protestors, and especially those throwing petrol bombs and shooting arrows, try and wear face masks and rip down street mounted cameras to prevent any FR even though their government denies it uses it.

The truth is, good or bad, FR is here to stay, and yes, it will be misused. Countries are racing to adopt this technology. India is currently at the pre-tender/expression of interest phase for developing a national FR database. Existing test systems have successfully identified criminals in rural areas and missing, abducted, and trafficked persons, especially women and children, and rescuing them from brothels, sweatshops, and childcare institutions. It has also run successful FR programs in airports to reduce waiting times. The FR element could even be cross-matched against the Indian biometric data system called Aadhaar. According to Better India, a 2018 pilot scheme in Delhi using FR managed to reunite 2930 missing children with their families in five days. That's just in one city.

China, another country with serious abduction problems despite severe penalties, including death in incidents such as trafficking, has already had success with its 宝贝回家 (bao3bei4hui2jia1 – baby come home – baobeihuijia.com) scheme. It was founded in 2007 by Bao Yan Zhang, whose son went missing after going out to play with his grandfather. Fortunately, her son was found, but it proved the inspiration for something much bigger. This NGO initially, with some success, tried to match up estranged family members using tedious photo and subsequent DNA matches. With the introduction and help from the tech giant Baidu and their knowledge of FR and databases, the success rate has rocketed.

At the time of writing, the website reports 3,188 reunited families and 344,861 postings. Anyone can become a volunteer by taking a photograph of a suspected abducted child and using a simple app. which is then matched in the missing persons' database. One solved case in May 2020 occurred when as a two-year-old child, Mao Yin, had been abducted 32 years earlier and was matched by FR and later DNA verification based on a tip-off. Mao had been brought up by a childless couple in Sichuan Province and was finally united with his parents in Xi'an.

Facial recognition technology by this method has already identified around 700 missing children. The stories are enough to make anyone weep, from the desperate sadness of the unmatched to the soaring elation of the matched. Because the baobeihuijia website is only in Chinese, there is a short English informational movie to be found at:

https://clios.com/awards/winner/branded-entertainment/baobeihuijia/a-thread-of-hope-24622

Even France, that bastion of libertarianism, is rolling out its Alicem programme, which will allow citizens access to a wide range of services by FR alone with promises of almost immediate destruction of the user's details.

Let's continue with my low-tech analysis of 5G network technology development. 5G will eventually increase wireless capability by up to 100-fold. It opens a whole new world. AI cars won't crash from lack of data speed, surgeons could perform operations from remote, massive amounts of data can be quickly manipulated, and it has multiple uses for industrial applications centred eventually more on cloud-based systems. China wanted to and became one of the countries at the forefront of this technology. It fits into the core competencies where the country wants 70% of high-tech core materials as part of the Made in China

2025 plan, a £1 trillion programme. It takes years of sustained investment and commitment. Yang Chaobin, 5G Product Line President at Huawei speaking at the 2017 Barcelona Mobile World Congress, put up an eye-catching PowerPoint slide as to the significance of 5G: by 2035, £8.8 trillion contribution to global output, 22 million jobs created, £143 billion annual investment, 0.2% contributor to annual growth of global GDP (IHS credited for the data). That's a market worth fighting for.

"I want 5G, and even 6G, technology in the United States as soon as possible. It is far more powerful, faster, and smarter than the current standard. American companies must step up their efforts, or get left behind. There is no reason that we should be lagging behind......"

Donald J. Trump (@realDonaldTrump, February 21, 2019)

Eight months later, China launched the world's first 6G satellite from the Taiyuan launch site.

Trump can wish, want, cajole, sanction the Chinese, and tweet, but there are plenty of reasons why the US is "behind the eight ball", as Americans like to say, and this problem is not Trump's fault. According to the well-respected Dell'Oro Group Report (Stefan Pongratz, March 4, 2019), for 2018, the leading players in the telecom equipment market by size were: Huawei (China), Nokia (Finland), Ericsson (Sweden), Cisco (US), ZTE (China), Ciena (US), and Samsung (South Korea). Combined, these seven companies accounted for about 80 % of the worldwide service provider equipment market revenue, with Huawei comfortably dominating with a 29% market share. Nokia followed Huawei on 17% and Ericsson on 13%. The two Chinese companies have a combined share of 37% compared to the two American companies at 10%. So even if the US succeeded in freezing out the Chinese, the primary net beneficiaries wouldn't be American companies.

The problems in the US started in the earlier years of the last century with the break-up of AT&T in 1982, which also saw the forced slicing up the iconic and highly technically proficient Bell Laboratories. By 2015, Nokia had acquired one offshoot (Alcatel-Lucent). Motorola, the other natural choice to develop new technologies, lost its way and didn't have the economies of scale necessary to support expensive R and D. In 2010, it sold out its wireless arm to Nokia Siemens and the remainder (Motorola Mobility), which eventually finishing up in Lenovo's portfolio. Bell is a tragic story of one of the most outstanding innovation companies ever, littered with Nobel Prizes in many science fields. The consequences, which the regulators probably couldn't have foreseen, were disastrous.

It certainly helps to have a planned economy like China, no four-year election cycle, few private stockholders to satisfy in this sector, but even if China's ambitions through Huawei and ZTE are blunted by superior US technology and export restrictions in microchips, China and the Scandinavians have got an almost unassailable edge. When it comes to 5G, there also signs that Samsung is trying to make a move with 58% of registered patents in this technology coming from this company.

An example of the investment needed is the now open (December 2019) Beijing, Yanqing, and Zhangjiakou railway line which will be used for hosting events during the upcoming Winter Olympics in 2022. According to China Railway (CR) Website, the driverless train (there is a nanny driver that shouldn't be needed) can whizz along the 174 kilometre (108 mile) route at speeds up to 350 km/hr (217 mph) and took four years to build, and that is in a country that produces things very quickly. That's exactly ten times the maximum speed on the original line finished in 1909. It is all supported by 5G technology. All the carriages have 5G signals, intelligent lighting, seats with touch screen panels, wireless charging points, and 2,718 sensors to collect real-time data and detect abnormalities. This will all be supported by FR technology to eliminate paper tickets and have robots to help passengers with directions and other needs. The train also stops at Badaling Great Wall Station (八达岭长城站), a key entry point to the wall. CR also explains that there are 41,000 m2 (25,500 feet) of platforms and tracks buried 102 metres (64 feet) beneath the wall, making it the deepest and largest underground station in the world. Suddenly, all those tourist coaches chugging away outside Beijing hotels trying to warm up the interior on a cold winter's morning and waiting for bleary-eyed passengers are starting to look redundant. A word of warning, though: not all the trains on this route are of the new type, so best to check to maximize the experience.

With a few notable exceptions, such as the Elon Musk conceptual Hyperloop, The US has long given up on long-distance railways, but the base stations and investment required to support a 5G network are also massive. Yang Chaobin is also on the record as saying the following:

"To handle 5G networks, a city needs to have more than 100 base stations", says Yang, referring to a structure that sends and receives radio signals to form a cellular network. "If you ask me which country will have thousands of base stations first, it'll be China".

If I had to devise a strategy to overcome this problem concerning China, I would have pretty much chosen the obstructive methods the US companies and their government have chosen, though with trepidation at the magnitude of the global competition and the understanding that obstruction can eventually be circumvented. By any measure I have seen, the west can't compete on price or price/quality tenders with Huawei and ZTE, and the west doesn't have large state subsidies available. The US, however, does have gazillions of legal lobbying dollars. These can be used to argue in Washington that allowing China dominance in 5G is against the national interest, that deployment is a security risk not just to the US but the whole western world, and strangulation of the competition of needed advanced US microchips through sanctions will at least slow down Chinese dominance. The US government has also been both threatening and proactive in dissuading foreign governments, especially in Europe, from using "unsafe" Huawei technology. Lobbyists can also argue that American systems are ethically superior and aren't designed for espionage and encourage western partners, by cooperation or coercion, to adopt a similar stance.

It's not enough. Sanctions on much-needed advanced microchips are a threat which is why the Chinese government howled when in May 2020, the US Commerce Department announced foreign chip makers must obtain a US license to ship to Huawei (and others such as HiSilicon). That put Taiwan Semiconductor Manufacturing (TSM) and Huawei's biggest supplier between a rock and a hard place. Even this strategy isn't forever because it will only accelerate the Made in China 2025 plan. In May 2020, the Chinese government invested £1.6 billion into Semiconductor Manufacturing International in Shanghai, which makes advanced wafer chips, and in April 2020, Yangze Memory (YMTC) announced in relation to its 1.33Tb QLC 3D NAND flash memory chip:

"We are confident that this product will be able to meet a broad range of market needs and provide even greater value to our customers. This QLC product will first be applied to consumer-grade solid-state drives and will eventually be extended into enterprise-class servers and data centres in order to meet the diverse data storage needs of the 5G and AI era".

Grace Gong, VP, Marketing and Sales, YMTC.

The accusations of spying and national security by the US are a convenient diversion.

I've worked for a major Swiss corporation for nearly a decade. I think many would recognize the ability of the Swiss to protect themselves against unwanted intrusion and know how to keep secrets. They are also excellent gatekeepers. There's hardly a week goes by without a computer security upgrade at the office. And yet, in March 2019, Sunrise, the second-largest carrier after Swisscom, used Huawei as its supplier for its 5G network. There's no way the Swiss are letting this stuff near their country if they weren't very sure that it's safe or they can't control it.

In its basic form, all networks are a type of spying equipment, so the real question is, do you choose to be spied on by American, Chinese, Japanese, Israeli (or others) equipment? This point was also raised by Peter Altmaier, the German Economic Minister, on the popular Anne Will talk show, describing the dangers of Huawei transmitting data to the Chinese government as no different from what the "unreliable" and an "untrustworthy" US has already done. The US ambassador to Germany, Richard Grenell, in a sharp rebuff, called the comments an "insult" and then stated:

"There is no moral equivalency between China and the United States and anyone suggesting it ignores history – and is bound to repeat it".

Um, well, that does rather conveniently ignore the furore over the alleged US tapping of Chancellor Merkel's and other German politicians' phones in 2013-15. It also ignores the 2013-16 alleged US tapping of three consecutive French presidents and the 2011 onwards systematic tapping of the Brazilian President and other key members of the government. And that's just among friendly nations. In reverse, Germany is also seemingly not squeaky clean here and has its advanced espionage systems of this type. It also ignores the bulk US National Security Agency (NSA) collection of phone call records/metadata in perpetuity that was forced upon Verizon in 2013, the NSA Prism programme for targeted monitoring of email communications, and the massive storage facility at Bluffdale, Utah, where the information is stored. Spying is a dirty business, and countering aggressive business moves by taking the moral high ground is a useful but a dangerous sales ploy in the competitive world of global trade. Better not to get caught.

The solution for the US is to seriously invest in these types of new technologies to try and remain ahead, and there are signs under President Biden that this is now deemed urgent. The world will not pay a substantial premium for supposedly ethically better products, but it will for innovative ones.

The third development is a peculiarly Chinese solution and is controversial and radical. It is called "social credits". Most Chinese citizens do not have a credit score, although such a system does exist for the better heeled. In most cases, there is no way to assess individual creditworthiness, although there are a few simple precautions in place. If you jump on a train and attempt to evade payment deliberately, you will go on a blacklist which will inhibit future travel, and you are warned of this on the train intercom in both Chinese and English.

So, the thinking goes something like this. Let's develop an all-encompassing system for every citizen that considers creditworthiness and offers incentives and disincentives related to social behaviour and combine them. Who wouldn't want to have such model citizens? If you rent a bike and you dump it in the road rather than returning it to a station or collecting area, that could incur negative social credit points or positive ones for the correct procedure. If you don't go and visit your perhaps needy parents regularly, a serious neglect in the Chinese psyche, why wouldn't your social credit score be diminished? What about the ever-present toilet paper thief because I can almost guarantee you that 99% percent of Chinese women carry tissues in their handbags (and a considerable number of men in their pockets too) because of this? In China, outside of fancy malls and hotels, there is never any paper. Owners or cleaners of the toilets gave up many years ago trying to provide something considered essential in the west. In a perfect Chinese world, the perp would be identified on an in-situ wide-angle camera in the loo and then face a loss of social credit points for such a heinous crime. A good compromise might be to only concentrate on the face, and which when recognized as a non-perp, dispense a reward of a few sheets of paper. The FR system will also know if you are an over-regular visitor. This system actually exists. There is a tourist attraction in Beijing that already uses it. I won't tell you where it is as it might become a weird additional item on this attraction's visit.

This system of social credits is due to be rolled out by the government in 2020/2021. It is currently under beta testing by several of the large online payment companies such as Alibaba's Alipay and Ten Cent's WeChat Pay. These companies already offer credit schemes for the few through Sesame Credit and Ant Financial, respectively. They both provide chat capabilities for social media usage, Alipay Friends and WeChat, respectively. Although there are other companies involved in beta testing, these are the industry giants. They have also been experimenting with social credits for some considerable time and long before the government asked them to become beta testers. TenCent Credit, for example, mentions on its introduction page that the users (online) friend's relationships, described as the "circle of friends", are used as references for assessing a credit score. The algorithms are secret, so it is not clear if this is a major part of a creditworthiness assessment or the weight it holds in the overall calculation. The TenCent admitted criterion for credit evaluation are: social index, security index, wealth index, performance index and consumption index, whatever that means. This leads after a submission of ID data to a credit score of 300 to 850, not dissimilar to the US credit scoring system. Borrowing from TenCent Credit is entirely opt-in, and you are free to go to other available creditors, banks, loan sharks, your family, or others you may so choose. To me, this is worrying. What happens if this type of modelling becomes part of a government opt-in scheme or even compulsory? Will people have to go through their friend's list and de-friend any people who might not quite cut it as socially desirable?

The companies carrying out beta testing do admit they are using spending and shopping behaviour as part of the calculation on social creditworthiness. I would imagine they have many similarities for their algorithms with those used in the west by marketing companies to segment and target their audiences through spending and shopping behaviour as part of the calculation.

The vast deviation from the west is when this information could be used for social credits. Mrs. Wang, age 24, a young mother, this known by purchases of infant formula and other baby products, always pays her utility bills on time and has a gym membership which she pays in advance to take advantage of a discount for this. And young mothers are supposed to be responsible citizens, right? Her social credit score may well be high. Mr. Shen, age 23, is a sloth. He purchases large quantities of beer and cigarettes and rarely buys fresh food at the store, reflected by his preference for delivered take-away food. He purchases obscene amounts of online games and gaming tokens and has a membership in a local snooker club. He regularly pays his gas and electric bills late. Mr. Shen probably wouldn't fare too well in a social credit system, and his social credit traffic light QR Code, also used for disease tracking, now could also monitor his social contacts, looking for signs of social malaise. He would be permanently on code red in this scenario.

So, what Chinese citizens make of this? So far, the reactions I have found have been mixed. The Chinese are a long-suffering nation of victims to fakes and frauds. If they could avoid a vendor with a poor social credit score, it would help them as supplementary information in their purchasing decisions or even selection of a partner, and this would be welcomed. Not surprising then, that singles on one of the top dating sites, BaiHe (百合网), are already flaunting their scores as making them more desirable. The old days of a suitor asking for money and promising diamond rings or a first date suggesting a fine dining restaurant to earn a commission from it may be gone forever.

The Chinese government, as often, has set itself a monster agenda if it wants to roll out a social credit system. To be fair, it is only at the time of writing a beta test. There is a huge difference between losing a few points for a minor infraction caught on camera and being turned down for a job based on a poor social credit score. If it is to be successful, it will require a degree of transparency. What can I do to improve my social credit score, or who do I pay to fix this? What if there is a false report on me, and how do I address it? In the west, there are credit reconstruction agencies. Will there be agencies to restore people to become a worthy citizen, and will this be allowed? What is the ratio between being a good financial risk and a poor social citizen? It's mind-boggling. But experience also tells me that the Chinese government won't design a system that alienates the majority of its citizens.

It's new, it's blockchain, exciting, and it came to my hometown as one of the first! Suzhou and Shenzhen were chosen as the first cities to test China's new digital currency, the digital RMB, along with some leading businesses, including MacDonald's, Starbucks, and Subway. The initial delivery of tokens was by lottery, and Yan Yan was ecstatic when she won 400 RMB (£46) of them.

Hang on, though, aren't digital currencies supposed to be attractive because they are out of the watchful eye of the mainstream banking system and regulators, and didn't the Chinese government put considerable effort clamping down on the use of bitcoin and others to hedge against fluctuations in the RMB or to circumvent exchange controls? Isn't that the same government that in 2018 banned Initial Coin Offerings (ICO) to stop money being raised for a variety of dubious investment opportunities and is planning to curb bitcoin miners? And why would a digital RMB be useful to consumers when they are already using Alipay and WeChat daily? What changed, and why is China suddenly in a tearing hurry to launch its new fiat digital coinage, both internally and to the world?

It appears there were two catalysts. The first is that digital currencies are associated with blockchain and that technology has a host of uses, such as managing supply chains, contracts, and settlements, and China very much wants to be involved in such an important new technology. The second appears to be the development of Libra, the cryptocurrency being developed by Facebook, and other similar ventures. It was a proud day for China when on October 1, 2016, the RMB became a global reserve currency at the International Monetary Fund (IMF) as part of the Special Drawing Rights (SDR) system, and placed third in percentage terms after the US Dollar and the Euro (US Dollar 41.73%, Euro 30.93%, RMB 10.92%, Yen 8.33% and British Pound 8.09%. The proposal for Libra is to be financially backed by a basket of currencies and US treasuries in the following ratio: US Dollar 50%, Euro 18%, Yen 14%, British Pound 11%, and Singapore Dollar 7%. Now the penny has dropped. The dollar has become overweight, and the RMB has been reduced to zero, which is a big slap in the face for China but also for the Euro zone, both of which have been upset about Libra after their downgrade. It's another example of the US versus the rest of the world. It wouldn't surprise me in the future to see China only offer loans to other countries in digital RMB as a means to counterbalance Libra-type initiatives, and suddenly the US Fed in February 2020 started discussing a digital dollar seriously for fear of being usurped. It won't happen in a hurry in the cautious US.

Consistent with everything else in this chapter, digital currency with its permanent record can be used in positive or negative ways. It can certainly help to stop money laundering, to prevent fraud and bribery, and to track criminals. If fully adopted and with no coinage, it means 100% tax can be collected. But the intrusion on daily life also raises civil liberty issues as to how the transactional data might be used.

I hope the Chinese government comes up with a snappy name to match Libra. Perhaps the Hong, the Chinese name for red? In China, red is lucky, and rising stock prices are marked in red and decliners in green, the opposite way round to the west.

The fifth and final development relates to monitoring/welfare. Recently, our apartment complex installed new rules, supported by a prior sent glossy range of instructional literature. All the garbage cans were removed apart from a two-hour period in the early evening and at all-day collection stations, some distance, at the two main gates. The stations, although a model of recycling attempts, were so complicated that for weeks all the residents had to be taught what went where. There were black bins for food waste (no packaging), green bins for recyclable waste such as glass, plastic water bottles, blue bins for non-recyclables such as chewing gum, sharps, coconut husks, Styrofoam take away boxes, plastic plant pots, and more. Then there is a red area (for dangerous things) with separate spaces for batteries, light bulbs, mercury thermometers, makeup, pressurized containers, and paint. Finally, there was another area for cardboard boxes flattened, of course, and one last one as a clothes bank. Confused? So were we. Many countries have perhaps three splits, but this one is at least nine, depending on definition. My immediate thought was that the elderly Mrs. Hu from Number 56 Block was never going to get the hang of it. Fortunately, for weeks, there were smiling assistants on hand to teach us, and for every successful dumping, there was a reward of a free bar of soap. I am sure Mrs. Hu, who learned the correct procedure, proudly showed off her extensive soap collection to friends and family alike. As so often in China, fortunes change quickly. One entrepreneur had placed a printing and scanning machine with a barcode to upload files right next to the clothing bank. In the space of a few years, China has gone recycling mad, and I just hope elderly Mrs. Hu, if she makes a mistake, doesn't get a barking command for a non-conformance from a sensor or camera mounted surveillance system and a deduction of social credit points.

I was a latecomer to taking care of the environment. I'd got used to dropping at least four full-size trash bags of unsorted trash at the bottom of the driveway for the bi-weekly collection in the rural US. It was easy to accumulate it by going shopping for more food than was needed and drive home, park the car in the garage with the electric doors, which was conveniently adjoined to the kitchen by a door to make carrying the pile indoors easy. There was no parking at a distance and lugging the shopping to an elevator/lift or climbing stairs to the fourth floor in Mama's home. Even when I got to China, my bad habits continued. It was all too easy to drop a wrapper in the street where an army of cleaners and sweepers would almost catch it before it landed. Then something highly embarrassing occurred on a visit to Nanning in Guangxi Province. Nanning is an important southern Chinese City (population 7.25 million), and it's a little bit scruffy. I threw a cigarette end onto the pavement, and a well-dressed young Chinese man walked up to me and, in passable English, asked that I did not mess up his city and please pick up my mess. I replied in French that I didn't understand, and in a million to one chance, he then repeated himself in even better French. I blush to this day thinking of this incident, and it was my first day of a long haul to becoming a responsible global citizen.

On the bigger picture, also a late entry to environmentalism, China, is no longer prepared to be the dustbin of the world. In a radical decision in 2018, codenamed "National Sword", China banned the import of almost all plastics and other waste. That's a reduction from 580,000 tonnes to 21,900 tonnes in one year. The biggest exporters at that time by size were Japan, the US, Germany, and Thailand. This took care of part of the problem, but the waste supplying nations started to export their trash to other accepting nations. This didn't prove so easy because of a lack of processing capability or in the face of outright public hostility, as in the case of Malaysia. In a strange way, China set off a chain of unforeseen events that eventually had the supplying nations examining their own bad habits. There is little doubt, the second decade of this century has brought an uptick in environmentalism: the Thunberg effect if you like, but I am also a little cynical of western CEO's sudden condemnation of single-use plastic bags in supermarkets and the elimination of plastic straws in fast food joints, at a time when they could no longer dump this rubbish in China or elsewhere.

Recycling isn't exactly new to China. From the first time I set foot in the country, a common sight was a little tractor like a motorbike hitched to a trailer piled impossibly high with compressed cardboard or plastic bottles, of which the owner had made a business from collecting selective items. These "specialist" collectors are at the top of the tree and below them is a dark world of exploitation, dirt, and grime. A puff of wind could easily send the driver and five metres of cardboard cascading. It was like a real-life physics experiment. Another group was the oriental equivalent of the rag and bone men like the horse and cart of my childhood in the UK, but now motorized. These more general Chinese collectors would go around urban residential areas in true Steptoe and Son style, paying a few mao (pennies) for useful materials: books, paper, clothes, etc. Below this on the social strata are the pickers, often migrant workers who can make a meagre living from scavenging on municipal landfills.

Even as our apartment complex adopted the new green measures, it was only a few days before collectors were allowed in through the gates for a few minutes. Their prime target was five and 10 litre plastic detergent bottles. And like Steptoe and Son, China has its own rags to riches story. To solve a problem of container freight returning back to China empty, it proved lucrative to fill the containers with waste. Some Chinese know the story of Zhang Yin (张茵), who became a multi-billionaire recycling scrap paper imported from the west and turning it into packaging materials and containerboard, eventually becoming one of the five richest women in China. However, along with useful wastepaper, exploited so brilliantly and legally by Ms. Zhang, came a whole heap of useless and dangerous junk. (not in her business).

As urbanization exploded, a second and illegal channel developed. This was to bypass the municipal landfill and move the waste to a site outside of the metro area and have pickers scratch, scrape, and sort the material out of sight and then dump the useless picked remainder anywhere anyhow.

In 2018, the same year as Operation Sword, I was working in Hebei Province and travelling on Highway G1, east of Beijing, and had to pull off the main highway to a small village to talk to a local agricultural contractor. What I found was shocking to me. The houses, some with former white tiled walls which had become brown and grimy, were cloaked in a pallid yellowish haze of pollution from local cement producers and coal-fired power stations. In the middle of the village was what might have been a former beautiful pond, but the water was treacle black and had every conceivable type of rubbish dumped in it. The worst was the unrinsed and discarded empty agrochemical bottles in this important maize growing area. I couldn't read well the Chinese labels on the bottles, but I could read the chemical formulae, and several were those that were considered carcinogens or flammable in undiluted form. The soil pollution from seepage would be severe enough that these people were quietly destroying themselves. On the edge of the village were yards surrounded by high wire fences and no doubt guards and vicious dogs for illegal, bypassed municipal waste to be scavenged through by locally hired pickers. I'm no shrinking violet when it comes to pollution in Asia. I have seen rivers clogged so badly with rubbish they can't flow, people bathing in foul river water, and people living in houses on stilts above raw sewage. All these counties have a border with China. However, these nations, by any definition, are all immeasurably poorer than China.

China does now seem serious about recycling, and different systems are multiplying fast. The country has some built-in advantages. Waste has always been abhorred. Packaging, and especially for food, has always been seen as wasteful, and the consumer preference is to buy in bulk. The Chinese people mostly think that buying pre-washed, pre-peeled, and pre-cut and packaged vegetables in a supermarket and then taking them home with other purchases in a plastic bag is insane. Consequently, they only produce about half of the waste per capita of their American counterparts. There are ambitious pledges to doubling the lead recycling target, waste to energy programmes with a target of 30% from 10% currently by 2030 (although that has other issues with dioxin emissions). It can't come soon enough as China can ill afford to gobble up more of its precious agricultural land for landfill. Then there is the horrific problem of China's plastic ocean waste which also has improvement targets. It's a start, but it's going to take resolve and a lot of money to tackle this problem.

Chapter 20: Opening Up Again

COVID-19 turned up the heat on Chinese global relations, but that was going to happen anyway. It just accelerated it. According to a 2020 survey by Pew Research, 29 % of Americans think COVID-19 was created in a laboratory or accidentally released and that 70% thought the media coverage on it was "very" or "somewhat" good. Little fake news then it seems. Add onto that some US cross-party support for a wide range of grievances, and the immediate future of US-Chinese relations looks, politely, inharmonious. In an April 2020 survey published in the Washington Post, 98% of Chinese citizens' trust in their government, up slightly from 95% in a 2018 World Values Survey (defined in the latter as having a "great deal" or "quite a lot" of trust in national government). So China can also claim support for its list of grievances. Bluster, sanctions, and gunboat diplomacy aren't going to fix these deeply entrenched differences. This isn't a war like the cold war, where the protagonists, the USSR, and the west took military postures. This is an asymmetric economic war where neither side seems willing to back down.

COVID-19 served to magnify two contradictory systems, western capitalism and a centrally controlled autocratic one managed by the Communist Party. The authoritarian system proved particularly nimble in a time of crisis while the US flailed in the wind.

China has no experience of democracy apart from a fragile pseudo-democracy in a brief period in 1911-1925, which saw the overthrow of the last of two thousand years of emperors under the Qing Dynasty. Democracy was primarily about the defeat of, or co-opting of, competing warlords and had little to do with democracy as understood in the west today with voting and elections. By 1925, the head of the army,

Generalissimo Chiang Kai-shek, was running the equivalent of a military dictatorship and even temporarily allied with the communists against Japan and then, after an inevitable split, was defeated in the civil war making way in 1947 for Chairman Mao. The immense suffering of the Japanese invasion, World War II, and the Civil War only continued the misery of previous centuries. It was time for something different, just as the American Civil War became the catalyst for many social and economic changes and strengthened its democracy. China has no particular interest in democracy, especially if it looks at the most populous one, India. On the other hand, if democratic India ever got itself organized economically, it poses a much more serious threat to China than the US.

Some of these democratic versus autocratic debates appear to come from a term I have grown to dislike: "rules-based international order" and the institutions that support it. At its heart is the UN with other relevant bodies such as the World Trade Organization, the International Health Regulations (IHR)/WHO complex, the Court of International Justice, the Vienna Convention, and the Treaty on the Non-Proliferation of Nuclear Weapons (NPT). The problem is when discussing it is who makes the rules? Indeed, there is an argument that with the declining percentage of the US and Europe in global GDP, other nations should have a larger say in the rule-making process, something China would support as it believes in globalization. The problem becomes even thornier if parties (all of them guilty to different degrees) who have signed rules-based agreements then proceed to rip them up when they become inconvenient or act unilaterally.

As the two great economic superpowers of the twenty-first century, the US and China actually need each other, but that realization will likely be slow to come. It's a challenging problem for two systems that are so radically different. Belligerence isn't going to work for either side. If US foreign policy has failed to allow North Korea by sanctions to become a threatening nuclear weapon owner, what chance of self-destructive trade sanctions against a major power like China working? China also has a problematic relationship with North Korea. Sanctions on China by the US put up costs in the US, didn't raise tax revenue, and has become a self-inflicted wound.

The US and China are also facing some of the same difficulties. Global warming is an obvious one, but another relates to big data. China has gone on a tear to stop large internet retailers and operators from becoming monopolies and using big data to gain an unfair advantage. It recently whacked Alibaba with an RMB 15.7 billion (£1.8 billion) fine for this. In the US, there are also similar concerns about the likes of Twitter and Facebook. It's not the same, though, for content, where in China, the government keeps a tight rein, and in the US, there is a messy system of self-censorship and sometimes outrageous and dangerous content finding its way to websites in the name of free speech.

Both "sides" have advantages. The US spends so much more than any country on military development, and it retains a substantial strategic advantage over every nation. China only has enough nuclear weapons to act as a severe deterrent. The US is also wealthier on any current measurement. Technologically, currently, the US has a significant advantage in areas such as advanced microchips, comprehensive education, most computer technology, medicine, the internet of things, augmented reality, and 3D printing. But China is fast catching up or has even possibly moved ahead in areas such as quantum computing, satellite technology, robotics, and AI. No better example of this catch-up was the 2021 landing of China's rover on Mars, achieved in one mission rather than the three it took the US, and the launch of the first part of its orbiting space station. China's astronauts were barred from the International Space Station. It's another example of one of the things China does well: it organizes its resources efficiently and can act in isolation.

China has also shown a willingness to invest in a gleaming modern infrastructure, especially in times of economic stress. In the US, roads are full of potholes, bridges are crumbling, and airports look antiquated.

I can't help feeling China would have preferred more of Trump with his manageable "predictable unpredictability". The Trump outpourings were mostly bizarre and laughable and critically left the US isolated and friendless. Biden has a broader and coherent plan, including criticism of human rights, something Trump didn't care a fig for.

At least for public consumption, the Biden administration didn't get off to a good start in instilling some meaningful sense of dialogue between the US and China. That may have been intentional, but the intense pushback may have come as a surprise. The first major diplomatic meeting of the Biden era, held in Anchorage on March 18, 2021, was a farce with both sides playing up to their domestic audiences. However, this meeting was different from many I have followed over the years because China pushed back harder than I have ever seen before. Some of the concerns expressed by Delegate Blinken were human rights issues in Xinjiang, Hong Kong, and problems over Taiwan, cyber attacks on the US, and economic coercion of allies and that "each of these actions threaten the rules-based order that maintains global stability". There it is again: the rules-based order. The Chinese response was unusually aggressive and confident, making it clear it sat at this table as an equal to the US and not as some scolded child treated with condescension. It had its own grievances such as trade sanctions based on fatuous national security requirements, interference in internal affairs, and encouraging other nations to attack China, and that the US was not qualified to speak from a position of strength when criticising China hinting at "the friends, what friends?" barb. Delegate Yang also criticised US human rights and described Black Americans as being "slaughtered", which was left out of the final US transcript. I suppose it could have been worse if the US, for example, had made more explicit threats against the Communist Party, or China had questioned, after the recent elections, whether it was really talking to the legitimately elected government of the US. The whole meeting was ungracious and undiplomatic by both. Apparently, the non-public section of the meeting was much more constructive because it damn well needed to be. Matters further deteriorated when on March 27, China signed an agreement with Iran to invest $400 billion over 25 years in that country in exchange for oil. Crucially, the oil was to be purchased not in dollars (petrodollars in the old language) but RMB.

There is a way through for the US if it remains laser-focused on its advantages, and it seems Biden has figured this out. President Biden recognized and described China as a competitor in his first foreign policy speech, and it surely is. It's a much more realistic definition than the previous "adversary" and "foreign currency manipulator". A formidable economic and geopolitical competitor is much more accurate. The US needs to win back its friends, particularly in Europe and NATO, in Asia, and it needs to invest heavily in maintaining technological advantages. That may even require some capitalist pain such as higher taxes, and reduced profits and dividends. And it needs to invest heavily in areas where it has competitive advantages and secure supply chains that aren't so easily disrupted.

China's problems aren't as much about international policies as western commentators assume. The meaning of the word for China, (中国 – zhong1guo2), is "Middle Kingdom" and was associated with voluntary insularity for centuries. Even today, the words have significance and imply solidarity against bullying and malign foreign interference. The 100 years of shame where anyone with a gunboat trampled on China is not easily forgotten. Push too hard against the Middle Kingdom, and reluctance or even outright stubbornness ensues. This explains why demanding as a matter of superiority that China joins the New Start Treaty on nuclear weapon status quo or the Open Skies Treaty without offering anything of substance in return is a bust. It also explains why China is sometimes reticent to assist in taming North Korea as a collapse in that regime would likely bring a possible hostile power to the border of The Middle Kingdom.

This doesn't mean that China isn't interested in burnishing its reputation overseas and giving it "face" because it is. It's potentially another area of contest or an open door to negotiations, depending on your viewpoint. Every time a Chinese academic receives global recognition or agreement can be found in areas such as climate change gives China "face" and provides goodwill, cooperation, and opportunities for agreement with Beijing. In one recent case, a joint China-UK peacekeeping force in Mali in 2021 had a British officer serving under a Chinese superior and reporting they got on extremely well. This is big "face" for China, is productive for both, and is far more helpful than just issuing bald threats. China has shown itself willing to cooperate on the world stage in these types of events. It isn't all altruism. China also needs friends and is a glutton for natural resources, which many of its donor countries have in abundance.

China's focus on international affairs isn't as great as some western commentators think. It has plenty of home issues to keep it preoccupied. One of these is the problem of feeding 22% of the world's population with only 7% of global arable land. Another is coping with a rapidly aging population with the latest census revealing around 12 million babies born in 2020 compared to 18 million in 2016. There are no signs that a three child per family policy is going to be enough to fix this problem. Another is the high level of national debt. These are the issues of the day, but they are internal ones.

On the future of US/China relations, selective engagement might be the best choice for both parties, and I'll leave some words on this subject to Professor Anthony Arend of Georgetown University and co-author (with Mark Langdon) of *"Human Dignity and the Future of Global Institutions"* and comments from a TV interview:

"While China is not an adversary, it is the 'greatest' threat to the US where geopolitics is concerned… We can't defeat China. We have to engage China. We have to criticize where necessary, but we have to try to cooperate where possible".

Either that or live with two parallel systems at economic odds and with free trade and globalization severely hampered: not a desirable outcome.

Appendix 1: Language Updated

This is the part that strikes terror into foreigners as much as French does to the Chinese.

Wang Yanfang (China.org.cn) places Mandarin as the most complicated language ahead of Greek, Arabic, Icelandic, Japanese and Finnish. So, if true, all those studying Russian or Albanian are blessed. Flick through a Chinese dictionary, and you will discover that the number of words reflects the country's history. The violent words for death in battle, movement of armies, surrender are diverse, but modern technological words are less frequent or borrowed from other countries.

China has many languages, and although the glue is written Mandarin Chinese, regional languages are commonplace. My local language and my wife's first language are Wu Chinese from the Shanghai/Suzhou region and are spoken by perhaps 70 million people (nobody knows how many) and is a spoken and a relatively pretty language with sounds like birds singing and bees buzzing. It has very little in common with Mandarin, but I learned a few words, and it gives great pleasure to the recipient when I use them. In the west of China, the language is Uyghur, a Turkic language and looks like this: رىكىنلوراپۇۇئشرىكگترتىزالوُم گۇزوُك (enter the password to log into the server).

The glue, the Mandarin language, allegedly is spoken by over 90% of the population. However, this is a likely overstatement as lack of regular usage means speakers become rusty, forget it, or rely on local language TV and radio stations. Even among Mandarin speakers, this does not mean that people from different regions can easily understand each other as the dialects are very different. It's much more difficult and diverse than, say, a Texan speaking to a New Yorker or a Londoner speaking to a Geordie. Almost all television programs have Mandarin subtitles so that everyone can at least follow, whatever the dialect. At the cinema, western movies are shown in English with Chinese subtitles, and western movies and television series on CD's in English have a button on the zapper marked (字幕 – zi4mu4) to get the Chinese subtitles (although sometimes these will be in the older script still used in Hong Kong, Taiwan, etc.). My wife has found this function particularly useful and is developing a charming BBC English accent from watching endless episodes of Downton Abbey with Chinese subtitles.

I want it on the record that I have no linguistic training and had a few Skype lessons in Mandarin before arriving to live in China. Learned professors who wish to disagree with my analysis can address their complaints elsewhere. The lessons I learned were in the street.

There are tens of thousands of books and thousands of teachers advising on how to read and write Mandarin Chinese, and I have met all too many foreign executives who came to China and hired the finest language tutors and failed. All I can offer is a few simple words of, perhaps unconventional, advice:

Spoken Mandarin Chinese is a tonal language. There are five tones (four and a neutral tone). It is impossible to speak the language without using these correctly. So, for example, (买 – mai3) and (卖 – mai4) (third tone and fourth tone respectively) mean the opposite. The former is to buy, and the latter is to sell. As an ex-commodity trader, this is enough for me to understand the importance of tones and sweat a little. If I want to buy 10,000 tonnes of wheat and instead sell it, I may have a furious boss. If I want to discuss my vision, (眼睛 – yan3jing1) are eyes and (眼镜 – yan3jing4) are eyeglasses/spectacles. There is no escape from these tones, and you will get blank looks if you don't use them correctly. Some Chinese people who are used to foreigners can correct your tonal mistakes, but this is rare and Chinese people are not adept at figuring out your meaning by context, probably because they are instead too busy listening to your tones. If you are absolutely desperate, statistically your best chance is for a combination of something like a two and a half tone followed by a four tone (except in Sichuan where try all four tones). You might get lucky.

Mandarin Chinese has a minimal number of basic sounds. To create an extensive dictionary of words, therefore, there are two methods:

- Use the tones as mentioned

- Use two or more words (symbols) at almost every opportunity for clarity. Because there are so few sounds, the combination of five tones and two symbols to describe something creates an extensive vocabulary.

An example of this would be zhan4 (战) which means a war/a battle/a fight/to fight. So, if you want to say: "the Chinese won the war", it may not be clear whether it was one battle or a series of battles that finished in a war that was won. Using two symbols (战争 – zhan-4zheng1) –zheng1 is one way of saying in a dispute, you have immediately made it clear that the war was won (and not just a battle).

There are also many multiple practical symbol combinations, and these can be delightful as you discover them. Some of my favourites are: (水龙头-shui3long2tou2) – a tap/faucet (water + dragon + head), (草皮 – cao3pi2) – turf (grass + skin), (大小 – da4xiao3) – the size (big + small), (老板 – lao3ban3) – the boss (old + plank), (啤酒 – pi2jiu3) – beer (spleen + juice), (屁股 – pi4gu3) – backside (fart + share), (汉堡 – han4bao3) – hamburger (man + fort) and (小笼包) xiao3long2bao1) – a type of dumpling (little + cage + box).

The Chinese are so determined to have two symbols that they will sometimes in speech add a meaningless one. One example is for "to come/to arrive" (来 lai2) but you will often hear 过来, guo4lai2. The guo4 symbol doesn't really have a meaning but it improves clarity.

- Word order is similar to English. It is a subject-verb-object language (like English and French: tough luck if you are German or Hindi speakers). There are some rules about place and time, but you will still frequently be understood if you muddle these up. If you are a speaker of a Latin language (French, Spanish, etc.), you have a slight advantage because the word "de" for "of" is used often and in a similar way.

- There are very few irregular verbs. You use (要 – yao4) to indicate a future action and (了 – le5) to indicate a past action. What ancient genius thought of this? Not having to learn reams of irregular verbs is a considerable advantage, and it is also why Chinese people find western languages so challenging.

- Handwriting (and reading) simplified Chinese is easy so long as you have the memory of a medium-sized computer. There is a basic order (strokes) for writing, but many of the words use the same pattern, and even the shapes sometimes give a clue to the meaning. For example, if you see the symbol for a bird, (鸟-niao3) in other structures, you can be pretty sure that it relates: 鸭 – ya4, duck, 鸡 – ji1, chicken, 凤头鸊鷉 – feng4tou2pi4ti1, great crested grebe, etc. Similarly, if you see the symbol for fire, (火 – huo3), then composites will relate 炖 – dun4, a stew, 烟 yan1 – smoke, 烛 zhu2, a candle, etc. The last one, 烛 – zhu2, is particularly helpful as it is a composite of 火 huo3, fire and 虫 chong2, an insect, one of a candle's functions (to smoke insects away).

- Writing on a computer is also easy. Once you have the software, you type in the word you want in Pinyin and select the appropriate symbol offered in order of likeliness.

- Carry a translation tool on your phone at all times. The best is probably Baidu Fanyi and will give you both Chinese script and Pinyin at the same time. You will be doing a lot of pointing at this machine.

- You will often see Chinese people writing an imaginary word on the palm of their hand. This is particularly useful for names. If your surname is li4, there are many possibilities, so to clarify, a person might say, I mean the "li" as in "chestnut" and draw the appropriate symbol (栗) on the palm of your hand. You can also use this technique for any word if you can remember what the symbol looks like and can write it on your hand. Even if you have used the wrong tone, your listener will probably have an "ah-ha" moment.

- Measure words are pesky things. There are many that qualify objects. Try and learn as many as you can, but you can mostly get away with yi1ge4 (一个) – one of/a and Chinese people sometimes do this as well if they forget the measure word. Western languages do have measure words, just not so many of them: a bunch of flowers, a dozen eggs, and a ream of paper are all measure words.

- The Chinese language doesn't sound pretty to the western ear, and Chinese opera sounds like a complaining cat. But beneath this is a vibrant and amazing language with a range of expressions that can match any language and beat most. This is backed by culture, history, art, music, and poetry that is spectacular. It is worth learning some of the language and opening up a whole new world.

- Once I was on a flight from New York to Shanghai, and a married couple was working as English teachers returning after a summer holiday. They talked to a young American lady visiting China for the first time and told her not to worry about the tones as people would understand anyway. I wanted to scream "so wrong!" because it was the worst of advice. I hope these people stick to teaching English, and I know they will never speak Chinese.

- One last tip if you want to seem more Chinese, Chinese people count to ten all with one hand and have extra signs for six to ten. It certainly beats taking your shoes and socks off to count to sixteen.

In the end, there is no substitute for hard work. I keep all my words in a spreadsheet and use a football scoring system, three points for a win (tone and words correct), one for a draw (one of word or tone wrong), and zero for a complete flop. I try and learn at least five new words every day and engage Chinese people in conversation at every opportunity. Slowly, it all comes together, I promise you. More recently, I have started to read. I mostly use a mixture of Chinese and foreign websites but always in Chinese. It's also worth a trip to the book store, the children's section of course. For the more advanced, a trip to the book flea markets is a good choice. My wife likes these, and she buys her mostly second-hand books not by their number but by their weight.

Zhou Yuguang was a boffin and a native of my now home province Jiangsu. He lived to be 111 years of age. Unsurprisingly as an intellectual, he was sent to the countryside during the Cultural Revolution for two years to be re-educated, was married for 70 years, and is a genius (and his colleagues' too, as collective effort and accreditation were encouraged). He emerged as a linguist that changed the Chinese language forever. The founding date for Pinyin is 1958. Put simply; it is a method of putting Chinese symbols into Roman letters and vice versa. Pinyin came into its own with the advent of the modern computer. Apart from good old-fashioned handwriting, foreigners are often astonished that when a Chinese speaker sits down to type on a computer or mobile phone, inputs are on a standard "qwerty" keyboard. Pinyin is therefore taught from the first day of school in China.

To understand the power of it, some simple example will suffice:

The Chinese word for water is (水 shui3), so I type in the first letter "s", and I am immediately offered a range of alternatives (most likely first) 水, 谁, 税, 睡, etc. In this example, I don't even need to type in the "h-u-i" letters and can proceed directly to hit enter as it is the first available choice.

I explained earlier that Chinese symbols mostly come in pairs. The Chinese word for ancient times is gu3shi2, but this can have several meanings in Chinese, and the computer will offer me 故事，股事，古诗，古时，鼓室，故世，故实，古诗 and 古尸 based on the most common usage. As the first three meanings are 故事– a story, 股事– shares (stocks), 古诗– ancient poetry, and finally my choice古时– ancient times as the fourth most popular. My decision and hitting enter (or the number 4 key) is accomplished in milliseconds.

The intuitive software is sophisticated and can often manage a whole series of symbols or even a complete sentence. The Chinese word for a public bus is gong gong qi che. You will notice Pinyin does not rely on tones but is based on choice. I can type all of this in one go rather than stopping to select individual symbols and will get very quickly to the correct answer (公共汽车). Also helpful and ever-developing are shortcuts in Pinyin. For the English words", the weather is hot today", in Pinyin, I only need to type "jttqr" and the software offers me the correct 今天天气热– jin tian tian qi re).

It should be becoming clear that Pinyin is speedy indeed and maybe faster than typing in other languages. Still, it's not clear on the overall global winner because it depends on things like technical content and subject matter. So, if the subject is of common interest to a Chinese speaker, speed will be improved because the choice of symbols offered is based on what Chinese people prefer to think and write about.

Pinyin has some beneficial side effects, particularly in helping with illiteracy or for a Chinese person learning a western foreign language. It familiarizes Chinese native speakers early on with the written Roman alphabet (combined with English teaching from the first day at school). If a Chinese person is overseas and observes a road sign to "Manchester" or "Dallas", he/she might be able to make a pretty good guess where the place is as the Pinyin for these cities are man4che4si1te4 and da2la1si1. No other Asian nation has such a developed system, although some have become quite advanced.

Appendix 2: Food Discussed in
The Lure of the Red Dragon

Restaurant Dishes

- Crayfish in Season. All China and especially lake regions.
- Lemon Duck. Guangxi.
- Big Chicken Plate. Xinjiang.
- Eggplant/Aubergine Pot. North East and others.
- Beef Noodles. Shaanxi and Xi'an City.
- Dumplings. Northern China and available everywhere.
- Fillet Steak. Inner Mongolia.
- Oven Roasted Meats. Guangdong and Hong Kong.
- Hot Pot. All of China with many regional variations.
- Chinese Sturgeon. Yangze River..

Street Foods

- Congee. All of China.
- Hawthorn Candy. Western China/all of China.
- Meat on a String/Stick/Kebabs. Western China.
- Pies and Moon Cakes. All of China.
- Spicy Duck's Neck. Wuhan.
- Chinese Hamburger. Shaanxi and widespread.
- Steamed Stuff Buns. All of China.
- Oyster Pancakes: Taiwan and Fujian.
- Silky Eel Noodles. Shanghai.

Home Foods

- Pork and Diced Cabbage with Bamboo Shoots in Salty Sauce.
- Chinese Sausage or Dried Pork with Crispy Garlic Shoots.
- Steamed Lake Fish with Spring Onions, Garlic and Ginger in Soya Sauce.
- Green Bean Sweet Treat.
- Runny Egg Yolks in Chinese Sherry.
- Red Braised Pork.
- Fresh Lake Crab and Vinegar Dipping Sauce.
- Sichuan Hot and Spicy Tofu with Minced Meat.
- Hot and Sour Fish Soup.
- Taro Root and Ham.

About the Author

Mark Oulton is a world traveller and astute observer of international culture. Born in the UK, as a child he was moved around the world because of his father's work in education and overseas development. He spent his formative years in Syria, Kenya, Malawi, and Nepal as well as being educated in the UK from age 12. As an adult, he lived in the UK for many years working for the largest private company in the world and then as a company director in Bristol, UK, working in agriculture and related trading and marketing. He then worked in the US for seven years before finally settling in China in 2015. He speaks French and passable Mandarin Chinese and at least another ten languages badly.

His most recent work as the global market research manager for a leading Swiss corporation took him to every corner of the globe. He also writes about topical issues such as sustainability in agriculture, as well as the plastics and aluminium industry.

When not writing, his hobbies are cooking, painting, cycling, and gardening.

He is married to Hu Yan Yan and lives in Suzhou, China, and has two children, Amy and George, both of whom live and work in London.

Cover Design by: Bing Liu

.

Printed in Great Britain
by Amazon

66158653R00201